COUNTERATTACK

*"In a time of universal deceit,
telling the truth is a revolutionary act."*
George Orwell

COUNTERATTACK

Why Evangelicals Are Losing the Culture War
and How They Can Win

PAUL BROWNBACK

Foundation
Stone
Press

Dedication

To my parents,
Lloyd and Helen
Brownback, who modeled
agape as Christians,
parents, and citizens

Table of Contents

Acknowledgements

This book has been in the making across several decades. During that span of time, I have received help and support from many sources. Salient among those are the following.

My dear wife, Connie, has encouraged me as I regularly devoted parts of weekends and vacations to this project. She has also helped as a valuable sounding board and proofreader. My children, Stephanie and Stephen, have also been a special source of encouragement.

At the outset of this mission, I reached a critical point at which I was seeking to decide whether to proceed. A letter from George and Robyn Butler indicating that they believed the Lord wanted them to support this effort, which came totally without solicitation, encouraged me to move ahead.

Connie's brother, Tedd Didden, volunteered to fund the the cost of initial publication, which has been a huge help and source of encouragement.

We Can Win

You, like most mainstream Americans, are no doubt feeling deep frustration as you watch the Left steal and destroy our country. They impose their evil and destructive agenda on us practically unimpeded, mandating that biological men can use girls' shower rooms and inviting anyone who wishes to cross our borders and demand benefits. Victories at the polls do not produce meaningful change. Though we win an occasional battle, the liberal juggernaut moves inexorably onward, fundamentally changing America from the noble and successful nation we once were into an immoral and dysfunctional society.

Their victory, however, is not inevitable. We can beat the Left and take back our country. The American evangelical church possesses the potential to do that. To achieve this, however, will require the restoration of the church's health and vitality and the implementation of an effective strategy. This book provides both a prescription for revitalizing the church and a realistic, workable strategy for waging a counterattack against the destructive agents of the Left that will result in their defeat.

The Decline of American Greatness

America's precipitous decline has been so serious and obvious that I need not devote much space here to making that case. However, as a starting point I offer the following brief synopsis of our societal sicknesses.

Our economy is in shambles and our job market is failing. Oppressive government regulations and high taxes continue to choke businesses, driving many overseas. The cost of living continues to rise while we earn less. Americans now distrust and even fear the government, which no longer functions as a democratic republic but as an oligarchy trending toward despotism as evidenced

9

by its many actions that oppose the will of the people. Our educational system fails to compete favorably with other advanced nations, and with the advent of Common Core it functions more as a propaganda machine for the Left than an institution of learning.

Our military, despite the commitment of brave men and women who serve, has been weakened through drastic downsizing and imposition of misguided social agendas. Our borders are open and our president encourages illegal immigration. Our inner cities are hotbeds of drugs and criminal activity. Politicians are destroying our healthcare system. Taxes on those working continue to climb while payouts to those not working increase. The middle class is shrinking precipitously. Many cities and states are heading toward bankruptcy. The world's respect for America has reached an all-time low, while the lack of American leadership in the world has resulted in global chaos.

The list of symptoms could go on almost indefinitely, all of which indicate a terminal diagnosis that requires aggressive treatment. Nothing about our present course is sustainable. If we continue on it, the question is not *if* catastrophe will strike but only *when and in what form.*

AMERICA'S FOUNDATIONAL PROBLEM

The problems cataloged above are only symptoms of America's terminal disease. These external problems are generated by internal ones. Here are a few examples. Governmental mismanagement results not from lack of capability but from lack of integrity. In other words, governmental failure reflects an internal moral problem. In a *National Review Online* article entitled "Untruthful and Untrustworthy Government,"[2] Victor Davis Hanson makes the case that although America has sustained some dishonesty from its presidents across the years, in contemporary American government this lack of integrity has worked its way into the very fiber of our bureaucracy, leading to distrust of all aspects of government.

Our internal moral disease also shows itself in sexual promiscuity, the decline of the family, and drug use. In fact, we can trace every external problem cited above and many others confronting our nation to irresponsibility, selfishness, and other internal pathologies.

Therefore, although we maintain hope that the political process might remedy some of America's external problems, a realistic assessment of our situation warns that unless we accurately diagnose and prescribe a cure for our internal disease, any external fix will only be temporary. The external symptoms will return with a vengeance.

Restricting our concerns to external issues is tantamount to a physician relieving the headache without addressing the brain tumor. America witnessed this phenomenon in the long-term effect of the Reagan presidency. While it brought relief for many of America's external problems, our untreated internal disease has left us several short decades later at our current national nadir.

America's Only Ultimate Hope

In this book I make the case that American decline has resulted from embracing a culture beginning in the 1960s that is not only ineffective but counterproductive, containing a core cultural concept that promotes moral decay.

God has called the church to be salt and light in society—to preserve it against moral decay. One would think that a church with such deep roots and vast resources as the evangelical church in America would have sufficient strength to resist the Left's imposition of our current decadent and destructive culture. In fact, it does. A problem exists, however, which prevents the church from effectively fighting the culture war.

The contention of this book is that the evangelical church is failing to provide a remedy for cultural decay and national decline because it has adopted the same core cultural concept that is proving to be so destructive to our secular society.

Consequently, the revitalization of America requires that the evangelical church (1) recognize that its belief system has been infiltrated by secular culture, (2) understand the specific nature of its contamination, and (3) return to a biblical belief system and its application, which will infuse the church with the spiritual vigor essential for fighting the culture war. Once revitalized, the church will be empowered to implement the strategy delineated later in this book.

This restoration of the American evangelical church to spiritual vitality and its employment of an effective strategy comprise the only hope for a lasting reversal of our current decline and the restoration of America's greatness. That said, however, victory is not only possible but virtually assured if the American evangelical church will implement the prescription and strategy described in this book.

The process of restoration must begin by identifying what made America great in the first place. Only then will we know how to make American great again. The more foundational question is: What makes any individual or society great? The chapters ahead address that issue.

SECTION ONE

WHAT MADE AMERICA GREAT?

Chapter 1

Core Characteristic that
Produces Greatness

What makes an individual or society great? What quality made America great—producing both internal integrity and external success? Or we might ask the question in the negative: What quality have we lost that is resulting in our individual and societal decline?

In the 15th century, sailors on long voyages manifested an array of symptoms such as lethargy, spots on their skin, spongy and bleeding gums, tooth loss, jaundice, fever, and finally death. This condition, labeled "scurvy," resulted from a lack of vitamin C (ascorbic acid) found in fresh fruits and vegetables. Eating foods containing vitamin C both prevents and cures scurvy.

Just as the physical body requires vitamin C for survival and health, so human psyches and societies need agape for survival and health.

The Nature of Agape

Types of Love

Defining love can create confusion because the English language is impoverished at this point. Greek has several words that refer to different types of love whereas English is limited to one. Agape refers to intentions and actions beneficial to others. Philia describes affection, emotional love, which can cover a broad range of feelings from friendship to romance. *Eros* denotes sexual love.

Since the English word "love" covers all of these, it is often difficult to identify the type of love a person has in mind when using it. In fact, we can even become confused by our own meaning in speaking about love if we do not consciously scrutinize what we are seeking to communicate.

Americans tend to confuse agape and philia love because we

15

possess such a strong inclination to think of love in emotional terms. People tend to allow their thinking to slip from the intentions and actions of agape toward the feelings-orientation of philia.

Let me clarify the difference between agape and philia. Jesus calls us to display agape toward our enemies. We cannot make ourselves feel warmly toward our enemies, but we can seek to benefit them. Suppose a coworker snubs you and treats you rudely. Try as you might, you cannot conjure up warm feelings (philia) toward this coworker. You learn that she is about to get fired because she lacks an understanding of a certain aspect of her job that you know well and could teach her. Despite your negative feelings (lack of philia), you offer to help her get up to speed in that area, a decision motivated by your intention to display agape that results in an act of agape.

God calls us to maintain this intention to benefit others and the lifestyle it produces. Doing so breeds success in the life of an individual and in a society.

Agape in Scripture

Agape is the primary word for love employed in the New Testament, the one Jesus used in identifying the First and Second Commandments, love of God and neighbor. It is the term He used in issuing the New Commandment that calls His disciples to love one another. When I use the term love in this book, I will be referring to agape unless I indicate otherwise.

Jesus described agape in the story of the Good Samaritan, a foreigner who helped a man beaten up by robbers and left for dead. This Samaritan expressed agape by binding up the wounds of this victim, loading him on his donkey, taking him to an inn, caring for him, and promising the innkeeper to cover any added expenses.

The opposite of agape is selfishness, seeking to benefit self at the expense of others, which has a negative influence on the individual and society. Selfishness can be passive in nature, consisting of self-absorption that leads to failure to even give others consideration.

Agape is a relational term. God designed us to live in multiple relational settings such as families, organizations, and societies. Above all, He designed us to live in relationship with Him. Our ultimate purpose in life resides in the display of agape within the context of these relationships.

THE SCOPE OF AGAPE

In what circumstances of life are we called to display agape? The Apostle Paul answers that question in 1 Corinthians 16:14: "Let all that you *do* be done with love." Everything we do can be done either with other-centered intent (agape) or a self-centered objective (selfishness). Every thought, attitude, word, or act (or failure to act) will be characterized by either agape or selfishness.

When I encounter someone, I can greet her with a cheerful "hello," mutter a halfhearted greeting, or ignore her altogether. Even "mundane" acts such as this one have as their objective benefiting others or self.

Dr. Jerome Motto told the story of a man living in the San Francisco area who left his apartment one evening, walked to the Golden Gate Bridge, climbed over the four-foot guardrail, and plunged to his death in the waters 220 feet below. Dr. Motto reports,

"I went to this guy's apartment afterward with the assistant medical examiner... The guy was in his thirties, lived alone, pretty bare apartment. He'd written a note and left it on his bureau. It said, 'I'm going to walk to the bridge. If one person smiles at me on the way, I will not jump.'"[3]

Every dimension of life—big and small, mundane and critical, possesses the capacity to display either agape or selfishness, can be done either with the intent to benefit others or self. God designed and commands us to intentionally and aggressively pursue the former.

THE DEMANDING NATURE OF AGAPE

Agape does not insinuate a touchy-feely approach to life. In fact, it calls us to do hard things. Agape took GIs out of landing crafts and onto Normandy Beach, some of them so scared they were throwing up. It drives couples to work out their differences even when loving feelings are gone— when powerful negative feelings have replaced them. Displaying agape often demands courage, discipline, and character.

COMPONENTS OF AGAPE

Agape is comprised of two components: morality and grace. Understanding agape requires a working knowledge of these components and how they relate to each other.

Morality

Morality entails giving others what we owe them, that is, dealing with them fairly. This also includes the negative—*not* treating others in harmful ways they do not deserve such as taking their possessions or harming them physically. Synonyms might include *righteousness* and *ethical behavior*.

We tend not to think of morality as a form of agape, but it obviously is. It is more loving to be fair and honest than to be unfair and dishonest. A just society is more loving than an unjust one. The Apostle Paul draws the connection between morality and agape in Romans 13:9-10: "For the commandments, 'You shall not commit adultery, you shall not murder, you shall not steal, you shall not covet,' and any other commandment, are summed up in this word: 'You shall love your neighbor as yourself.'"

Since agape consists of seeking the benefit of others, morality—or giving them what we owe them—constitutes its foundational expression. Loving them requires that we benefit them at least to that extent.

Morality serves as the gears that make society work. Government, business, family, educational institutions, and the interaction between neighbors and friends all depend on the exercise of morality. For example, it is virtually impossible to maintain a good relationship with a person who lies or steals. The absence of morality results in relational chaos and disintegration.

We can see how immoral behaviors such as murder, stealing, and the like fail to display agape. But what about sexual behaviors such as cohabitation and homosexuality? If these relationships are consensual, in what way do they deprive others of their just due and are therefore unloving?

The First Commandment requires that we love God. Maintaining His moral instructions regarding sexuality comprises love toward Him—love on the vertical plane.

On the horizontal plane, maintaining God's moral standards produces agape because His standards provide the greatest benefit to others whether it is evident to us or not. It is obvious, though, in most cases how maintaining God's commands benefits others while disregarding His directives causes harm. For example, cohabitation fails to make the lifetime commitment to another commensurate with sexual intimacy. Thus, even though sexual relations are consensual, failure to make that commitment takes something very precious from persons without giving them due compensation. This arrangement also robs children born into that relationship of the stable home life that parents owe them and that marriage provides.

Grace

While morality comprises the foundational component of agape, its highest expression resides in grace. We have defined morality as giving others what we owe them. Grace consists of giving others what we do not owe them. This also includes forgiveness—not exacting from them what they owe us.

Your neighbor is sick, so you mow his lawn. You have no moral obligation to do so. Therefore, this action represents an act of grace, going beyond what you owe. Giving to charities embodies grace. History's greatest expression of grace is found in the cross, in Christ's dying for our sins, providing us with forgiveness, eternal life, and countless other blessings we do not deserve.

While morality constitutes the gears that make society work, grace provides the oil that lubricates those gears, preventing them from overheating and enabling them to work smoothly and without friction. If we were all perfect, we could do just fine in a society characterized solely by morality. Human limitations and flaws, however, require the oil of grace for us to get along.

Most of us have made mistakes in our checkbook that have resulted in our being overdrawn. The results can be brutal, costing $35 or so for each bounced check. Our agreement with the bank gives it the moral right to charge that fee. Then banks introduced overdraft protection, grace that provides oil to the financial gears. Grace is the overdraft protection that God extends to human beings and that God calls us to extend to our spouses, children, friends, and even enemies.

The Relationship Between Morality and Grace

Because morality comprises the foundational expression of agape, it is wrong to extend grace at the expense of morality, e.g. to neglect paying my electric bill in order to give to a charity. Doing so in essence is stealing from the electric company to help others. Agape requires that we meet our moral obligations first. We must pay creditors before giving others what we do not owe them.

We possess a strong temptation to extend grace at the expense of morality because grace always seems to be magnanimous whereas enforcing morality can appear to be harsh or unkind. In addition, the unpleasant aspects of maintaining moral standards appear immediately, whereas we can only see the benefits later. In contrast, grace extended at the expense of morality tends to appear magnanimous in the present, but its negative consequences take time to surface.

If we do not maintain morality as the required foundation for agape, instead displaying grace at the expense of morality, our individual lives and society will quickly descend into chaos, inflicting harm on everyone. The gears of society will cease to operate properly, and we will be left with a puddle of the oil of grace on the floor.

At times our society displays grace at the expense of morality by extending grace to criminals who have evil intent. Doing so is unfair to victims and potential victims, which includes society as a whole. Recently a judge released a convicted gang member who then murdered four people.

The principle that grace must not be extended at the expense of morality leads to a second factor in the relationship between morality and grace. Morality requires that someone must pay for grace. The cross provides the ultimate example of this principle. God did not provide grace, forgiveness for our sins, by sweeping them under the carpet. That would have been unjust—grace at the expense of morality. Rather, He paid for them at the cross. Grace comes at a cost. The grace displayed by the Good Samaritan cost him effort, time, and financial resources. If I mow my neighbor's lawn, I am paying the price for this expression of grace with the expenditure of my time and energy.

The Apostle Paul taught, "Let the thief no longer steal, but rather let him labor, doing honest work with his own hands, so that he may have something to share with anyone in need" (Ephesians 4:28). Paul was instructing this man to earn the resources necessary to manifest grace. When we display grace we must be willing to pay the price.

The Combined Impact

When morality and grace are combined biblically, these components of agape make relationships and society work well and produce success. The reason agape engenders success is explained in the next chapter.

Chapter 2

Humans Were Designed to Display Agape

We should display agape not only because God *commands* us to do so but also because God *designed* us to do so. God created human beings to function as agape-producing organisms. That should be the ultimate objective and output of our lives. When it is, we will function as God intended and consequently will enjoy successful, meaningful, and happy lives.

An automobile operated according to the manufacturer's design will function well and achieve its intended purpose. Because the Manufacturer of the human being designed our lives to produce agape, doing so will result in optimal individual and societal well-being. In contrast, an individual or society that experiences love deprivation will encounter sickness and failure.

Proof that we were designed to produce agape lies both in the exalted characteristics inherent in agape and the positive impact of agape on every aspect of human existence.

Agape Encompasses All Admirable Expressions of Humanity

Agape encompasses virtually every other admirable human trait. For example, fidelity is an expression of agape, infidelity, of selfishness. Courage reflects agape while cowardice is born of concern for self over
others. Likewise with virtue versus vice; responsibility versus irresponsibility; compassion versus cruelty.

These qualities that express agape are the dominant characteristics of historic American society. Today we find increasing

21

displays of those characteristics that express selfishness.

We often refer to the expressions of agape listed above as *humane* behaviors, connoting that they reflect humanity at its best. We describe the negative characteristics on the list as *inhumane*, failure to function at a human level. Therefore, agape encompasses all of the highest expressions of humanity, engendering life at a fully human level—the level at which we were designed to function. The opposite qualities are ugly, destructive, and debilitating. Agape edifies while selfishness destroys.

Agape Enhances All Elements of Life

Because agape constitutes God's design for living and encompasses all of the noblest human qualities, it optimizes every aspect of life.

Positive Relational Outcomes

A marriage characterized by agape expressed in qualities such as fidelity, kindness, patience, consideration, responsibility, and compassion is far more functional, meaningful, and enduring than one characterized by the opposite qualities. An employer/employee relationship in which both parties consistently function based on agape toward each other will be characterized by harmony, mutual benefit, stability, and success. Likewise, agape enhances all relationships.

Positive Emotional Outcomes

A life characterized by agape will engender emotional health and vitality for both the person expressing it and the person receiving it, while selfish living stirs up emotional turmoil in both.

Displaying morality, fidelity, responsibility, and other expressions of agape eliminates guilt and produces a clear conscience, a sense of internal integrity, and the resulting peace. Showing compassion rather than cruelty engenders feelings of wholeness in the giver and joy in the receiver. Agape tends to minimize strife, thus promoting emotional tranquility.

Positive Physical Outcomes

Love for God motivates us to be good stewards of the body He has given us. Likewise, love for others prompts us to care for our health so that we can have vitality and longevity to serve them.

Positive Financial Outcomes

Agape calls us to be good stewards of our finances since money becomes a major means of expressing agape to others. Therefore, stewardship promoted by agape leads to financial well-being. Loving choices also tend to be less expensive than selfish ones. Consider the cost of a DUI or a divorce.

Agape Feedback Circuit

Each of the expressions of agape described above enhances the other. Good relationships promote emotional, physical, and financial well-being. Financial responsibility, emotional well-being, and healthy choices can in turn enhance relationships. We see, then, that the impact of agape on the various components of life forms a mutually supportive feedback circuit that raises all of life to the highest level. Selfishness engenders mutually destructive outcomes. A DUI can result not only in financial expense but also missed work and conflicted relationships.

The Societal Benefits of Agape

Society constitutes a network of relationships. Therefore, by optimizing the relationships that comprise a society agape engenders health in society as a whole.

If our politicians were committed to function based on agape rather than selfishness they could easily save billions of dollars and reduce taxes, which in turn would boost our economy.

Individual commitment to agape would reduce divorce, crime, drunk driving, and a host of other very expensive, disruptive, and painful societal maladies. The stability agape engenders in marriage would enhance the health and well-being of our children. A society characterized by agape would require fewer police, result in lower insurance rates, and produce an endless number of other societal benefits. Those advantages would all reinforce one another, increasing the overall well-being of our nation immensely.

We can see the opposite impact inflicted by the selfish orientation of a banana republic where bribes constitute a way of life. We observe these same results of selfishness in the cold, harsh, uncaring communism of the Soviet Union and Mao's China, which were responsible for the murder of millions of their own citizens and inhumane treatment of untold others.

Agape brings beauty, joy, and success to society, and without it people are consigned to a lonely world characterized by cruelty and despair— the heartless existence described in George Orwell's *1984*. This conclusion leads to the question of how agape is produced. We will address that topic next.

Chapter 3

Management Produces Agape

If life characterized by agape consistently engenders success and other benefits listed above, why don't human beings consistently choose it? The answer begins with the reality that God did not create humans like animals, with an instinctive drive that spontaneously produces optimal living.

Though at times humans display agape spontaneously, most of the time we must intentionally manage the resources God has given us in order to produce maximum agape. This intentional management of our lives includes employing our mind to determine what course of action will most benefit others and employing our will, our volition, to implement that agenda.

The Role of the Mind in Managing for Agape

In the town where I live, individuals can be found standing on street corners holding up cardboard signs asking for money. In searching for the agape response, my first impulse is to lower the car window and hand out a few dollars. Further thought, however, prompts me to wonder why these people are not availing themselves of the scores of government programs designed to help them or why they do not reach out to a local rescue mission. This line of reasoning leads me to ponder whether giving them money will enable them in a lifestyle not in their own best interests.

This situation demonstrates how displaying agape requires employing the mind with which God has equipped us. Virtually every opportunity to display agape requires analysis. The Apostle Paul makes this point in Philippians 1:9-10. "And this I pray, that your love (agape) may abound still more and more in knowledge and all discernment, that you may approve the things that are excellent...." Paul teaches that agape requires knowledge and discernment.

We need to engage our minds not only in identifying whether a particular action will produce agape but also in projecting whether it will produce the most agape. Do I give money to the man on the street corner who seemingly is not working, or do I add those dollars to the tip for the needy single mom waiting on my table who is working?

We must also employ our minds to answer the "how much?" question. Sometimes these quantitative type questions are the most difficult to answer. Do I empty out my wallet to help the waitress, or do I just enhance the tip by an extra two dollars and use the rest of my funds for other purposes? The same questions also confront us in the allocation of other resources.

Decisions about allocating resources must also consider the issue of morality vs. grace discussed earlier, requiring that priority be assigned to obligations first.

Often well-intentioned people seek to display agape without effectively engaging their minds, which leads to wasting resources and even hurting those they are seeking to help. This sort of misguided agape is addressed in Marvin Olasky's book *The Tragedy of American Compassion.*[4]

All of these factors and more underscore the significant role of the mind in managing our lives to maximize agape.

The Role of the Emotions in Managing for Agape

By emotions I am referring to the full range of the subjective side of our human nature such as desires, feelings, affections, and subjective inclinations.

Our emotions or desires serve numerous positive functions. They provide impetus for many of our actions. At times our concern for others motivates us to help them. Emotions can also bring much joy to life. Without feelings we would be consigned to a cold, drab existence.

Though emotions can provide motivation and joy, they are not designed to provide guidance. God designed the mind, not the emotions, as the human GPS. Success in life requires guidance in keeping with reality. For example, one reality of life consists of the need to limit spending so as not to exceed one's financial resources. The mind has the capacity to grasp that principle, identify those

26

limitations, and make commensurate decisions. The emotions possess no such capability.

In addition, emotions pull us down wrong paths, especially those that provide immediate gratification such as spending beyond our budget. Therefore, our emotions are not only incapable of determining our spending limits, they also encourage us to exceed them, which makes their choice as a guidance system especially destructive.

If for just one day we devoted ourselves totally to following our desires, we would probably not survive till noon. The typical person might begin that day by sleeping in, not feeling like going to work. Finally rolling out of bed at about 10:30, he would consume a 4,000-calorie breakfast and then speed to the nearest mall, totally ignoring traffic laws (who feels like stopping at traffic lights?). Upon arrival he would take whatever he wanted from mall stores without paying, which he would not feel like doing. Chances are, a person who operated totally based on desires would be dead or in jail within hours.

Some might contend, however, that many human emotions can motivate us toward loving behaviors. This happens at times, but even these positive emotions need supervision by the mind.

Relationships tend to move through a cycle that begins with a "honeymoon period," when the parties feel like displaying agape, and then proceed to a time of strife (often instigated by power struggles), before finally reaching a state of maturity characterized by harmony and stability. These stages are often referred to as *forming*, *storming*, and *norming*.

For example, Community Church welcomes its new pastor, who is the most wonderful pastor ever, which is only fitting since he has come to the most wonderful congregation ever. During this honeymoon phase, emotions tend to produce a rather high level of agape, with both pastor and congregation being motivated to be a blessing to one another. Perhaps God designed this honeymoon phase as a means of getting relationships off to a good start. This emotional surge, however, will not see the relationship through. Soon it will move on to the "storming" stage during which at least some negative emotions will probably arise. This phase of the relationship demands guidance by the mind rather than the emotions to enable its survival to the mature phase.

Even during the honeymoon stage, however, when it appears that emotions are providing agape-producing guidance, these inclinations of the emotions must be managed by the mind. For example, the heightened emotional state during those times may lead the church to make unwise decisions, such as failing to establish healthy boundaries and guidelines. "He is such a caring pastor that there is no need to discuss specific working arrangements or responsibilities." The church learns over time, however, that he plays 18 holes of golf five afternoons a week, prompting the leadership to realize that they should have allowed their minds to guide their well-intentioned emotions during the honeymoon stage.

In many decisions the input of the emotions is helpful and even essential such as when choosing a dessert or a spouse. Even in those cases, however, the mind needs veto power. Some relationships that the emotions pursue powerfully are a very bad idea and need to be banned by the mind—and some desserts also. Therefore, though emotions might play some role in management, the mind must have the final word.

The Role of the Will in Managing for Agape

The third human component, the will, serves in the role of referee between the mind and the emotions in managing for maximum agape.

We concluded above that management to produce agape requires that the mind and not the emotions provides guidance. Our emotions, however, have not signed on to that program and instead demand that we follow their dictates. The influence of the emotions is especially powerful because though the intellect knows best, the emotions feel best. Though our mind may be correct in telling us that a second helping of tiramisu is not a good idea, the emotions can be very persuasive. The will is thus stuck with the unenviable task of playing referee between the mind and the emotions, rejecting the demands of the emotions for immediate gratification and instead implementing the realistic guidance of the intellect.

Life is good when the intellect and the emotions are in agreement. Vacations are great in large measure because during those times the intellect and emotions often are in sync. It's okay to sleep in. It's even okay to ignore our normal diet. We enjoy the same congruity between the mind and emotions when we relax in the evening after a hard day of work. During these times the will does not have to do the hard work of arbitrating between the mind and the emotions because they are in agreement.

Success or failure in life, however, is often determined at those times when the struggle between the mind and emotions is greatest, such as when you feel like telling off the boss or a customer or a spouse or when emotions tell a student that going out for a fun evening is actually the best preparation for an exam—"I will be fresh and relaxed." When temptation is greatest, yielding to emotions is usually most costly. It is the job of the will to prevent that from happening.

Given our natural self-orientation, most expressions of agape require that we engage the will in resisting the pull of the emotions. The ongoing need to say "no" to our desires in order to display agape demands a high level of volitional strength. This requires the development of self-discipline and character.

Self-discipline and character are developed primarily through the disciplinary training of others, especially those in positions of authority such as parents, teachers, coaches, military drill instructors, and supervisors. As these authority figures require individuals to discipline themselves, and as those individuals respond, their capacity for self-discipline, their volitional strength, will increase. Societies valuing discipline and character produce members with the volitional strength to choose agape over selfishness.

Managing for Agape Matters

How important is it for us to make the hard decisions necessary for the production of agape? Why not just relax and float downstream with the tide of selfish desires? These choices are of ultimate importance because they will determine whether we will ultimately be losers or winners at life.

Losing at Life

I mention the negative first because our society tends to believe that this category does not exist. A Christian song from a decade or so ago proclaimed, "In heaven's eyes there are no losers." Hearing that song often made me wonder whether the writer had considered Judas Iscariot, Adolf Hitler, or the child pornographer. Contemporary American society, both secular and evangelical, tends to reflect the philosophy of Dodo in *Alice in Wonderland*: "Everybody has won and all must have prizes." Any rational analysis of life, however, tells a different story.

By losers at life I am not referring to those who tried their best and failed, the Super Bowl team that came in second, or even a team that gave maximum effort but ended the season with an 0-18 record. I am referring to the person who opts for selfishness over agape as the pattern of his existence.

One overwhelming aspect of life is the prospect that we can approach our last days realizing that we were losers in the one life that was ours, that we had used it for selfish ends rather than for the benefit of others.

Added to the personal devastation of being a loser at life is the harm it inflicts on others, especially those closest to us. Unfortunately, we all hurt others to some extent. That is part of being a flawed human, the part I find most agonizing. Thinking back on pain I have caused others can be almost overwhelming. Sometimes there is simply no way even to try to compensate or express regret, but even when we can, doing so still does not undo the reality that we inflicted pain on another human being. That reality underscores the seriousness of our human capacity to choose either agape or selfishness, to choose either winning or losing.

Winning at Life

A happier but equally serious reality resides in human potential for good. Life holds for us the capacity to make choices that will benefit loved ones and society as a whole. We can show love both in daily interactions and in the more macroscopic endeavors of life such as through long-term relationships, a meaningful occupation, and a trail of kindnesses. I think of the contribution of John Wesley, whom some historians credit with saving England from the atrocities inflicted on France by the French Revolution. Susanna Wesley, his mother, displayed a pattern of agape through her diligent and thoughtful maternal efforts that contributed significantly in molding John into the man he became.

Recently I have been especially impressed when attending the funerals of some seemingly ordinary individuals to hear about the uncommonly profound contributions their lives made. Their legacies demonstrate that we all have the capacity to be winners at life.

Losing as a Nation

We are confronted with the challenge of winning or losing not only as individuals but also as a society. National loss results when a significant number of people in a society pursue selfishness rather than agape.

Currently America is losing as a nation. Enough individuals in our society are producing selfishness rather than agape to send America into serious agape deficiency. As a result we are rapidly becoming a losing society, both by inflicting ourselves with moral decay and also by exporting our immorality to other nations.

Though being a loser as an individual is tragic, being a loser as a nation is far more so. Losing as a nation could lead to serious economic devastation that could deprive us of even the basic necessities of life and result in societal meltdown. Even worse, losing as a nation often results in military loss, which usually leads to murder of men, rape of women, and enslavement of children—that is if a nuclear attack does not occur first. Consider the rape of Nanking or the fate of the nations of Eastern Europe who were left to the not-so-tender mercies of the Soviet Union after World War II. National loss can produce horrific results.

Most Americans who end life on the losing side are still surrounded by a supportive society: rehab programs, welfare assistance, hospitals, and in many cases families who provide support. These support systems help deaden the pain. Losing as a nation, however, results in the destruction of those support systems, exposing vanquished people to unthinkable horror devoid of mercy.

It is therefore of utmost importance that Americans come to grips with the awful costs of losing as a nation and identify and implement a strategy for winning. That is the objective of this book.

As I have emphasized, winning or losing is determined by whether or not a society values and displays agape. The next chapter identifies one of the most powerful forces in producing that result.

Chapter 4
The Power of Culture

By culture I am referring to the totality of beliefs, attitudes, values, behaviors, and institutions of a people group. But culture refers less to these entities per se than it does to the imprint they make on the psyches of those within a population, especially children, as they internalize and perpetuate them. Culture in large measure makes people who they are. Consequently, next to God, arguably culture is the second most powerful entity in the universe.

Contributors to the Power of Culture

Culture wields vast power because for most human beings culture determines truth. A man who was born in Saudi Arabia to a Muslim family believes that an Islamic worldview embodies truth. If you try to tell him that a woman should be allowed to decide how she dresses, your chances of persuading him hover right at zero. Likewise, attempts to convince a college student in Kansas raised in a middle-class American family to consider suicide bombing as a career choice will probably fail. The distinction between these two people does not reside in their intellectual ability or genetic makeup but in their culture. Had they been mistakenly switched at birth and raised in the alternate culture, their concepts of truth almost assuredly would also be reversed. Though some people manage to rise above their culture, they represent a tiny segment of society rather than the norm.

Adding to the power of culture is the oblivion of people to its sway over their minds and lives. They mistakenly believe that their worldview and lifestyle stem from rational analysis. Awareness of cultural influence would encourage us to examine the cultural messages we receive. Lack of awareness of the overpowering influence of culture and our specious confidence that our beliefs are

33

rationally derived result in lack of analysis, which to a great extent makes us victims of culture's influence.

Human beings are not victims of culture in the absolute sense, since they have the capacities to analyze and then either accept or reject cultural messages. Most human beings, however, are too unaware of their capitulation to culture, too consumed with the activities of daily life, too immobilized by inertia, too constrained by fear of being different to evaluate and confront destructive cultural concepts or to board a Mayflower and sail to a new world so that they and their offspring can establish their own culture.

They prefer life inside their cultural prison to the unknowns and risks of the world outside. Beyond that, their unevaluated assumption that their cultural prison walls are constructed of truth, that their culture prescribes *the right way* to think and live, leads them to believe that their culture does not consign them to a prison but rather houses them in a temple.

American Capitulation to Culture

As Westerners, heirs of the Enlightenment, we possess confidence that we have transcended the confines of culture, that our worldview and lifestyle are genuinely the products of empirical evidence and logic, i.e. rational analysis. Muslim or Hindu nations may be chained by culture, but not us.

We can, however, marshal countless examples demonstrating that we also are captives of our culture. Consider our penchant for saving whales while killing our own babies. What exercise of the scientific method has brought us to those conclusions? It is culture rather than empirical evidence and reason that also shapes the American mind-set.

This American blindness to the molding influence of culture on our thinking, attitudes, values, and behaviors prevents us from suspecting that our culture is the cause of our current societal problems. While we might believe that something has gone terribly wrong in America, we remain convinced of the validity of our culture. And like the man in Saudi Arabia challenged regarding the right of women to choose their mode of dress, we tend to become defensive rather than analytical on those rare occasions when someone might present rational challenges to our core cultural beliefs.

All Cultures Are Not Created Equal

Multiculturalists propagate the view that all cultures are created equal. But what if they are not? Multiculturalism would leave individuals and societies vulnerable to adopting and remaining in a misery-inducing culture without evaluating that choice.

In the previous chapters, we considered the superiority of cultures that promote maximum agape as opposed to ones that engender selfishness. Cultures that encourage suicide bombing or the burning of widows or genocide or other inhumane behaviors get low scores for agape production. Though no culture is perfect, it is apparent that some cultures do a better job of promoting agape than others.

Multiculturalists, in a desperate attempt to validate their theory, enjoy pointing out the few weak spots in good cultures while overlooking glaring problems in bad ones. We witnessed this inclination when President Obama offered a critical analysis of Christianity as compared with Islam by dredging up blights on the church from centuries ago while overlooking Muslim atrocities that occur almost daily in the present. Any fair-minded assessment, however, reveals that some cultures are significantly superior to others in producing agape.

Cultural Tilt

The National Football League (NFL) consists of two conferences, the American Football Conference (AFC) and National Football Conference (NFC). Imagine if the NFL drew up a schedule in which every game would have an AFC team playing against an NFC team. They would also tilt each field 5 degrees and require that the AFC teams always played uphill and NFC teams played downhill.

Although both teams would be doing essentially the same things: running, passing, blocking, tackling, kicking, etc., everything would be a little harder for AFC teams and easier for the NFC teams. Though the AFC teams might win a few games, on average they would lose more often. Many fans, tired of losing, would stop coming to AFC home games, resulting in the AFC teams being tight for money while NFC teams would become rich from growing attendances. AFC players would get discouraged from losing, playing to empty stands, and getting paid less. Perhaps the AFC would be able to stay in business somehow, but they would always be a second-rate, struggling conference. All of this would result from a mere 5-degree tilt of the field.

Culture is a lot like that. If we visited homes of families at a middle-class economic level in different cultures around the world, for the most part we would find them all engaged in generally the same activities: eating, sleeping, doing laundry, earning money, and caring for children. Yet, the tilt resulting from their different cultures over time would exert its influence so that those living in agape-engendering cultures would do better relationally, economically, physically, emotionally, and in virtually every other way.

It is important to understand this because cultural differences are virtually never black-and-white in nature. In any given society we find moral and immoral people, those who are kind and others who are not so kind, hard workers and shirkers, intact families and those that have fallen apart. The differences tend to be in the intensity and percentages and their effect over time. This cultural tilt can make all the difference in affluence, safety, order, education, sanitation, morality, a favorable business climate, good healthcare, and other quality-of-life issues.

Of course, outcomes are even more pronounced when the cultural field is tilted 10% or 20%.

AMERICAN CULTURE

The long-term significant influence of cultural tilt takes us to a major theme of this book. Past American culture produced high levels of agape, which engendered success. Adoption of a different culture is causing agape deprivation and the resulting precipitous societal decline. The chapters ahead identify our past and present cultures and evaluate why our past culture produced agape and success while our current culture encourages selfishness, resulting in serious decline.

Chapter 5

The Culture that
Made America Great

Practically every negative symptom currently confronting America took root in the 1960s when our society began the transition from a Christian to a post-Christian culture. (I will support this assertion statistically in a later chapter.) This development indicates that America was made great by its past Christian culture and has declined because it has abandoned and replaced it. This chapter explains why Christianity made America great.

America Was Christian Culturally

Some argue that America never was a Christian nation. Whether or not it was depends on one's definition of "Christian nation." Obviously we never were a Christian nation in the sense that we acknowledged Jesus as our King or the Bible as our Constitution. Various scholars, however, have made the case convincingly that America possessed a strong Christian orientation culturally from its founding up until we arrived at the post-Christian era of the 1960s. It is revealing that even those who have coined the term "post-Christian culture" in so doing confirm that our previous culture was Christian.

We find compelling evidence of our Christian founding in expressions to that effect in the constitutions of practically every one of the original 13 states ratifying our national Constitution. For example, the Constitution of Delaware declared:

> Every person ... appointed to any office ... shall ... subscribe ... 'I ... profess faith in God the Father, and in Jesus Christ His only Son, and in the Holy Ghost, one God, blessed

for evermore; and I do acknowledge the Holy Scriptures of the Old and New Testament to be given by Divine inspiration.

Maryland's Constitution asserted:

> No other test or qualification ought to be required, on admission to any office ... than such oath of support and fidelity to this State ... and a declaration of a belief in the Christian religion.

South Carolina's Constitution required:

> No person shall be eligible to a seat ... unless he be of the Protestant religion. ... The Christian Protestant religion shall be deemed ... the established religion of this State.[5]

America maintained this same cultural orientation throughout its history up until the 1960s. In response to the terrible death toll resulting from the Bataan Death March, in his address on April 9, 1942, General MacArthur sent this message to the American people: "To the weeping mothers of its dead, I can only say that the sacrifice and halo of Jesus of Nazareth has descended upon their sons, and that God will take them unto Himself."[6]

In *The Closing of the American Mind*, Allan Bloom observed, "In the United States, practically speaking, the Bible was the only common culture, one that united the simple and the sophisticated, rich and poor, young and old...."[7]

Robert N. Bellah wrote:

> The Bible was one book that literate Americans in the seventeenth, eighteenth, and nineteenth centuries could be expected to know well. Biblical imagery provided the basic framework for imaginative thought in America up until quite recent times and, unconsciously, its control is still formidable.[8]

Up through the 1950s in many areas of the country every school day began with Bible reading and prayer. In the small industrial town in which I grew up, located about 30 miles northwest of Philadelphia, not known for being especially religious, on Good Friday from noon until 3pm businesses were closed, a sacred hush descended on the town, and practically the only activity consisted of people going to and from the three-hour community church services. This was the case in many towns across our nation.

I mention these anecdotal expressions to give a sense of the extent to which Christian culture permeated life in the United States prior to the 1960s. It is difficult for those born since then to grasp the profound practical impact Christianity had on our society throughout that era.

Asserting that America has been Christian culturally does not mean that the majority of Americans were genuine believers. Many were not. But even those people, living in an environment shaped by Christian culture, reflected that influence in their values, attitudes, and behaviors.

Other Causes Credited for American Greatness

Some have attributed American success to sources other than our Christian culture such as our founding documents and the freedoms we enjoy.

One problem with attributing America's success predominantly to these sources is that they seem too limited to account for the American character and the tremendous attainments our nation enjoyed in every aspect of life. Can a constitution—even one as brilliant as the U. S. Constitution—alone produce such broad-based success? That seems to be a stretch. The French Revolution attempted to achieve a similar goal but based on a worldview that eliminated God. They even possessed America's Constitution as a model. That revolution nonetheless produced disastrous results, for years engendering economic deprivation and societal chaos, one form of government quickly replacing another, with the party in power reigning in terror by employing the guillotine to eliminate its enemies.

A fascinating little book entitled *The 'Jesus Family' in Communist China* records how a Christian community in communist China during the late 1940s and 1950s achieved success in virtually every aspect of life, far surpassing surrounding non-Christian villages.[9] This success came without a constitution similar to ours or the freedoms we enjoy. A good constitution has been a blessing for America but cannot be credited as the primary source of American achievement.

Another problem with attributing American success to our constitution and freedoms is found in the many indications that these assets themselves must be attributed in large measure to the Christian culture that permeated the colonies.

A major mistake many social analysts make is assuming that the beautiful and beneficial qualities historically found in the American character are rooted in the goodness of humanity. Such a conclusion manifests gross naïveté, failing to appreciate the rather obvious human tendency toward selfishness.

This error of crediting humanism as the source of American agape-oriented character is reflected in a passage from Barack Obama's autobiography, *Dreams from My Father*. When the family was living in Indonesia, Barack Obama's mother, realizing that the Indonesian culture was not having a good influence on Barack's character, decided to return him to America. Here is his recollection of her concerns:

> "If you want to grow into a human being," she would say to me, "you're going to need some values." Honesty— Lolo should not have hidden the refrigerator in the storage room when the tax officials came, even if everyone else, including the tax officials, expected such things. Fairness—the parents of wealthier students should not give television sets to the teachers during Ramadan, and their children could take no pride in the higher marks they might have received. Straight talk—if you didn't like the shirt I bought you for your birthday, you should have just said so instead of keeping it wadded up at the bottom of your closet. Independent judgment—just because the other children tease the poor boy about his haircut doesn't mean you have to do it too.[10]

Obama's mother in effect wanted her son to embrace American virtue. Tragically, this was her perspective regarding the source of American virtue as he recalls it:

> My mother's confidence in needlepoint virtues depended on a faith I didn't possess, a faith that she would refuse to describe as religious; that, in fact, her experience told her was sacrilegious: a faith that rational, thoughtful people could shape their own destiny. In a land where fatalism remained a necessary tool for enduring hardship, where ultimate truths were kept separate from day-to-day realities, she was a lonely witness for secular humanism, a soldier for New Deal, Peace Corps, position-paper liberalism.[11]

Her conclusion that virtues not present in Indonesia but prevalent in America were the result of secular humanism, of position-paper liberalism, reflects a serious flaw in her analysis of American culture. If she were alive today she would see (if she would admit it) that as secular humanism and position-paper liberalism have come into full bloom they have not produced the qualities she desired for her son. How different our nation might be today if she had realized when Barack Obama was a boy that the character qualities she desired for her son were the product of our Christian culture.

The Link Between Christian Culture and American Greatness

Clay Christensen, Professor at Harvard Business School, made a video in which he shared a conversation he had with a Marxist economist from China who had come to America on a Fulbright Scholarship. Professor Christensen asked this man whether he had learned anything surprising while in America. He responded by sharing his discovery of the essential role of religion in sustaining our democracy and free markets. He realized that historically most Americans regularly attended a church or synagogue. He concluded that these people followed the laws of our society not because they were accountable to the government but because they were accountable to God.

This conclusion left this Chinese communist concerned about the future of American democracy in light of our post-Christian orientation in which church attendance is declining. He observed that America is living on past cultural momentum that is in the process of winding down.

Christiansen concluded the video with the observation that American religious decline is leading to disaster "because if you take away religion, you can't hire enough police."[12] This is a profound observation. Christiansen is asserting that a religious culture brings success in part because it produces a citizenry that obeys the laws because of internal, spiritual motivation. Societies where law must be maintained solely through law enforcement tend toward a grim, cruel, and chaotic existence that ultimately fails. Consider, for example, the Soviet Union. Dr. D. Vaughan Rees, the author of *The 'Jesus Family' in Communist China*, in analyzing the reason for the success of this Christian community as compared with the deplorable conditions of surrounding villages observed, "(I)t is not laws that are needed in a land, but good citizens who obey the laws, those who fear God and keep His commandments."[13]

Obedience to laws comprises only a narrow spectrum of the

contribution of Christianity to society. By its promotion of agape, Christian culture instills a full range of society-enhancing inclinations and therefore produces a strong cultural tilt toward success.

In a more extended video, Professor Christiansen added his own analysis to the observation of this Chinese man by asserting that any religion, or at least any religion that teaches morality, is able to provide the human impetus necessary to keep the law. He theorized that such a religion must teach people that they must follow all the rules, be honest, and respect the property of other people.[14]

There is a tendency among Americans because they are big-hearted, open-minded, and largely isolated to believe that all religions are essentially the same in terms of promoting virtue. This naivety revealed itself in the aftermath of 9/11 when President Bush and other American leaders were quick to describe Islam as a "religion of peace."

In seeking to find a religion that advocates and does an effective job of promoting the qualities listed by Professor Christiansen, one is hard pressed to discover any outside of biblical Christianity and Judaism. It is easy to make the mistake of believing that the nature of virtue is rather self-evident and therefore all religious writers and leaders whose hearts are in the right place will advocate for moral, loving positions. This, however, is *not* the case.

Vishal Mangalwadi, who was born and raised in India, authored *The Book That Made Your World: How the Bible Created the Soul of Western Civilization*. He makes the case that the Bible possesses the unique capacity to engender a virtuous and successful society.[15] His book demonstrates that the pursuit of a religion of the nature described by Professor Christiansen reduces the options to those based on Scripture, that is, those with a Judeo-Christian foundation.

Taking the case one step further, not just any form of Christianity will produce a well-functioning society. This requires that a society adopts a biblically-based form of Christianity. Just like a doctor must accurately read a CAT scan, likewise the production of a virtuous and successful society requires an accurate understanding and application of Scripture. This is an important point because people tend to cite atrocities resulting from unbiblical manifestations of Christianity as proof that it does not work. A solid case can be made, however, for the assertion that cultures shaped by those attempting to faithfully follow the teachings of Scripture have produced the greatest success in the broad spectrum of societal issues. Therefore, search for a religion of the nature described by Dr. Christiansen leads us to a biblical form of Christianity.

Why Christian Culture Produces Success

It is difficult to dispute that across the past several centuries until the 1960s America was the greatest nation on earth by practically every measure. Though its critics accentuate its flaws, any fair-minded person will acknowledge that compared with other nations America has displayed superiority. What produced this outcome?

America's Christian culture produced success because it promoted significant levels of agape through various means.

The Centrality of Agape in Scripture

Agape is the chief attribute of Christian living and therefore the primary value of a Christian culture. Loving God and neighbor comprise foundational elements of both the Old Testament and New Testament, the core concept of the First and Second Great Commandments and the New Commandment given by Christ. The noun form of agape is present 117 times in the New Testament and the verb form occurs 144 times. Not only are these terms found frequently, but they are used in critical passages, making this concept the central theme of Scripture.

Agape is taught in Scripture not only in passages that use the term but also in countless other passages describing, commanding, and illustrating agape. Jesus tells the story of the Good Samaritan in support of His teaching on love, and yet the story never uses the word "love."

The emphasis of Christianity on agape resulted in Americans making the production of agape a major objective, which in turn encouraged its prevalence and engendered American success.

In addition, Scripture discourages us from following selfish emotions, thus providing valuable guardrails for Americans living under its influence. Our current culture has removed those guardrails.

Promotion of the Components Comprising Agape

Christianity produces abundant agape because Christianity promotes the two components of agape identified earlier: morality and grace.

Until recently it may have been easy to assume that American morality was not the product of our Christian culture but merely a reflection of human goodness—an assumption Barack Obama's mother made. As America has abandoned its Christian roots, however, we have observed a drastic decline in morality, indicating that our past Christian culture was its source.

Scripture also promotes grace, the highest expression of agape. We noted that grace comprises giving others what we do not owe them. Even though by definition we may have no obligation to others to display grace toward them, Scripture, and thus Christian culture, accentuates our obligation to God to show grace to others.

Think of the story in Luke 16 of the rich man who died and found himself in Hades. In this story Jesus nowhere indicates that this man did anything immoral. Rather, his sin was failure to extend grace to Lazarus, a beggar who spent time at his house seeking help. Although this rich man had no obligation to Lazarus, he did have an obligation to God to help Lazarus. Likewise, the man who built bigger barns did nothing immoral. His sin lay in his failure to use his resources to extend grace to others. Because of this scriptural emphasis, our Christian culture has motivated the display of grace in our society.

American society has displayed substantial quantities of Christian grace through the creation of hospitals, rescue missions, and other relief efforts, and also in its generosity to poorer nations and in treatment of conquered enemies.

Christian Culture Encourages Effective Management

Our Christian culture has also produced agape because it encourages and enables the employment of our minds and wills to manage our lives for maximum production of agape.

It may seem intuitive that human beings should employ their intellect to determine how best to live and should exercise their wills to follow that guidance. This is not the case. As we consider in future chapters the new culture America has adopted, we will discover that it discourages employment of the mind and will, which leaves the lives of many Americans unmanaged and unproductive.

Intellectual Advantages of Christian Culture

Scripture provides valuable information for the intellect by offering major insights into reality that would otherwise be out of our reach. For example, it enables us to know who God is, who we are, how we got here, how we can have a relationship with Him, how we should live while we are here, and where we are going when we leave. Scripture provides us with an understanding of the forces guiding history and the direction it is headed. It tells us what lifestyles work and where the pitfalls are located.

Apart from Scripture, human beings even when advantaged by substantial education lack the capacity to understand many significant aspects of God's design, especially in regard to the functioning of human nature, leaving them incapable of making valid decisions. Consider the miscalculations communism makes regarding human functioning. It is taught, nonetheless, in many universities. The need for biblical input is also graphically illustrated by the bad choices being made by post-Christian American society such as allowing biological males in women's bathrooms and shower rooms.

Scriptural insights proved invaluable in the establishment of our government. For example, biblical teachings on fallen human nature informed our founders of the need for separation of powers.

Likewise, biblical teaching regarding God's design for sexuality, marriage, and family provided our nation with the most effective and economical configuration for these relationships. In *The Case for Marriage: Why Married People Are Happier, Healthier, and Better Off Financially,* Linda J. Waite and Maggie Gallagher in making the case for the beneficial nature of marriage conclude their book with the following assertion:

> Decades of social-science research have confirmed the deepest intentions of the human heart: As frightening, exhilarating, and improbable as this wild vow of constancy may seem, there is no substitute. When love seeks permanence, a safe home for children who long for both parents, when men and women look for someone they can count on, there are no substitutes. The word for what we want is *marriage*.[16]

Conversely, in his book, *The Marriage Problem: How Our Culture Has Weakened Families,* James Q. Wilson discussed how the deteriorated family is creating a wide variety of societal problems that are having a devastating impact on our nation. For example, he reports that "[t]he homicide rate for children in stepfamilies is seventy times higher than it is for those living with both biological parents."[17]

Scriptural insights into God's design provided the cognitive foundation that led to the production of significant levels of agape by Americans and the resulting success.

Volitional Advantages of Christian Culture

We have noted that agape production requires volitional strength. Christianity motivates the will by a number of means.

The Bible is filled with exhortations (motivational speech) that encourage and challenge people to live according to biblical principles. Therefore, the custom of Americans in the past to read Scripture strengthened their resolve to develop and display character.

Christianity also motivates people to love by its teaching that the life of agape yields success while selfishness produces failure. Scripture affirms that the person who is honest and responsible will be more successful than the person who is not. Fidelity in marriage brings greater joy to life than infidelity. The message that agape produces success encourages people to exercise the discipline necessary to produce it. Likewise, Christians are motivated volitionally by scriptural teachings regarding reward and punishment in both this life and the next.

Traditionally, a large segment of Americans attended church regularly where they were motivated by sermons and Sunday school lessons to pursue agape. The Bible's instructions to parents, government, and the church to discipline those under their authority also contributed to the strengthening of the will of the individual and development of American character.

The Holy Spirit, who takes up residence in the believer, provides an even more potent resource for strengthening the will, therefore supplying spiritual power for the production of agape.

American Cultural Tilt toward Agape

An almost endless list of other agape-producing aspects of our past Christian culture could be cited along with the benefits they produced. In addition, this agape orientation of American citizens resulted in institutions that possessed and encouraged the same values. Fairness, honesty, and decency in government, business, and other institutions contributed significantly to American achievement. Though America did not manifest agape to perfection, it produced an overflow of agape that made it the most successful nation on earth on practically every count.

FORCES DRIVING AMERICA'S DECLINE

Why has such a great nation declined so quickly? Because our American Christian culture that produced success has been replaced with one that actively erodes agape. It is important to grasp that dual negative factors are at work accelerating American decline. Not only has America lost its agape-producing Christian culture but it has replaced it with one that breeds selfishness. We have replaced the goose that laid the golden eggs with a coyote that is eating the eggs.

The chapters ahead describe the nature of this new culture, the means employed to impose it on America, and its agape-devouring nature.

SECTION TWO

IDEOLOGY OF SELFISHNESS

We can only win the culture war if we possess a working knowledge of the culture of the Left. This section and the next provide a basic understanding of the worldview of the Left, how it has infiltrated our society, and why it is producing a destructive outcome.

Chapter 1

Precursor to the Ideology of Selfishness

The Advent of Materialism

Though America was predominantly a Christian nation cultural at its founding, Deism, the belief that God created the universe and then left us to our own devices, also maintained a presence. This worldview offered the advantages of both providing an explanation for origins and conveniently getting God out of our way so that those not desiring to acknowledge Him could approach life on their own terms.

Those who held this orientation and others seized on the publication of Charles Darwin's *On the Origins of Species*, in 1859, as an opportunity to divest themselves of God completely, asserting that evolution had provided a scientifically validated explanation for origins that eliminated the need for belief in God.

The resulting worldview, which I refer to as Materialism, postulated that only matter and energy exist, eliminating from the universe any non-material component, including the human soul.

Though Materialism is not the predominant worldview in contemporary America, we must address it because it played a major role in paving the way for our current culture and continues to be a force in our society.

The Promise of Materialism

Materialists asserted that science would provide solutions to our most challenging problems. Agricultural advances would end hunger; medicine would eliminate sickness and perhaps even death; psychology would resolve emotional, behavioral, and relational problems; social studies and other disciplines would bring in world peace; and education would develop human intellectual capacities to achieve all these objectives. In short, human rational capacities applying the scientific method would bring in utopia.

Deficiencies of Materialism

We have noted that success in a society results from significant levels of agape, which are generated by engagement of the mind to develop a plan for its production and employment of the will to implement that plan. Materialism failed to develop necessary intellectual and volitional capacities to produce adequate levels of agape.

Materialist Deficiencies of the Mind

Materialism viewed itself as advocating pure science—human reason applied to empirical data using the scientific method in order to produce a scientific worldview. Therefore, those rejecting Materialism were branded as unscientific.

But what if God did create the universe? In that case the scientific evidence would point toward the existence of a Creator. In that case materialists would need to reject those scientific findings, i.e. abandon science, to maintain their commitment to a solely material universe.

This is in fact the situation with Materialism. The Intelligent Design movement has amassed evidence demonstrating that the complexities of the universe require intelligent origins. Nonetheless, materialists, to maintain their exclusion of all non-material entities, have had to cling to their less cogent and therefore unscientific positions.

Consequently, this pseudo-scientific system produces unscientific results not only by what it denies (the existence of the immaterial world) but also by the theories it proposes to explain origins without intelligence.

Let's say that Joe won the lottery 10 times in a row. The probabilities of this outcome occurring by chance are for all practical purposes right at zero. A reasonable person might suspect that Joe has some inside connections with the lottery agency. But since the lottery agency does not allow for that conclusion, they must come up with another explanation. Joe must have somehow evolved to a higher level of existence that includes a subconscious attraction to winning tickets. Rejecting a rational analysis of the evidence necessarily leads to irrational explanations. Materialism frequently displays this tendency, especially regarding issues of origins.

Because Materialism excludes the existence of the supernatural, it rejects the validity of Scripture, robbing those under its sway of Scripture's important intellectual insights.

Therefore, though Materialism places great emphasis on the mind, by advocating an erroneous understanding of the universe and rejecting the valid understanding of the universe found in Scripture, it leaves those under its influence ill-equipped intellectually to make valid decisions, especially as related to the understanding of human beings and the importance and production of agape.

Materialist Deficiencies of the Will

As mentioned, Materialism's rejection of the non-material world results in the elimination of the human soul, reducing the human being to molecules and energy, capable of functioning only at the level of a biological machine—a robot incapable of genuine choice. In short, humans lack a will. Consequently, all human decisions result from societal programming, placing human beings, as described by psychologist B. F. Skinner, "beyond freedom and dignity." The absence of volition leaves robotic human beings devoid of agape producing capabilities, unable to generate qualities such as courage and fidelity.

Eradicating the Possibility of Agape

Evolution positions human beings on the top rung of the evolutionary ladder, in essence assigning humanity the role of deity. Although this heady status may have initially blinded Americans to the serious downside of the materialistic position, in the aftermath of two world wars, the development of the bomb, and the fears generated by the Cold War, college students and others began to recognize that Materialism had stolen their humanity as they considered these materialist positions:

- Humans consist only of molecules and energy—depriving them of a soul.
- Humans differ only in degree and not in kind from animals.
- Human beings possess no unique value. Therefore, abortion has no moral implications but neither did Hitler's social engineering objectives, viewed as helping along the

53

evolutionary process by advancing the master race and killing off those viewed to be inferior.

- The relative value of human beings.declines across their lifetime through disease, aging, and other forces, leaving older individuals as liabilities to be eliminated, a status toward which all human beings are headed.
- The elimination of God leaves humans without help beyond themselves. The threat of nuclear annihilation has turned the entire world into a foxhole and human beings as anxious atheists without a God to whom to pray.
- Humans are temporal creatures, devoid of eternal hope.

Ultimately the human being as a biological machine is incapable of producing agape. Any behavior that may appear to be motivated by agape is merely produced by biological or social forces. While it may seem that a husband loves his wife, this appearance of agape actually is comprised only of robotic responses to societal programming. Reading anything more into the appearance of agape is wishful thinking.

This is really bad news not only because it renders us incapable of producing agape but also because it makes it impossible for someone else to love us. Therefore, Materialism consigns human beings to a cold, drab, lonely existence reflective of Soviet-era unpainted concrete apartment buildings, where agape does not and cannot exist.

Materialism not only robs human beings of the capacity to display agape but nullifies any motivation to express agape. Why should an individual seek the benefit of a being that consists of nothing more than a temporal biological machine? With no spiritual world, no God, no soul, only molecules and energy, why should anyone feel motivated to love others?

Consequently, Materialism provides no substantive basis for making decisions other than selfish ones, an orientation antithetical to agape. We may seek to benefit others because of the resulting benefit we derive (being kind to my spouse may make life happier for me), but no basis exists for decisions and behaviors that have the other person as the ultimate beneficiary.

By distorting the individual's worldview, including his perspective on agape, by reducing the individual to a biological machine lacking the capacity to produce agape, by depriving the human being of any value and thus eliminating any reason for extending agape to him, Materialism leads to an agape-deprived society incapable of success.

The Marginal Acceptance of Materialism

Because of its self-designation as the exclusive embodiment of reason, Materialism became the dominant force in higher education and gained inroads into public school curricula. The materialist perspective also exercised vast influence over mainline Christian denominations, whose hierarchies sought to gain intellectual respectability by adopting materialist perspectives while at the same time attempting to hold onto a semblance of Christian beliefs.

Despite these inroads, most Americans continued to believe in the existence of God and many tenets of Christian doctrine. It seems that Materialism with its dehumanizing teachings simply did not have enough appeal to captivate the American soul and replace Christian culture, though it succeeded to some extent in shaping the American mind. Many Americans maintained a vague belief in the materialist concepts they were taught in school while continuing to embrace the tenets of Christianity, largely unaware of the dissonance embodied in their belief system.

Broken Promises

The global conflict ushered in by World War I provided a major indicator that Materialism may not be living up to its utopian promise. Materialists managed to put a good face on this global tragedy by declaring it "the war to end all wars," a learning experience that would prevent its recurrence.

With the advent of World War II, the development of the atom bomb, and the threat of annihilation via the Cold War it became evident that the promised paradise was out of reach of Materialism— that under its influence we were moving in the wrong direction.

Intellectual Uncertainty and Materialism

In addition to its other failures, concerns also began to surface regarding whether reason (scientific analysis) could provide knowledge with absolute certainty. Could science connect us to reality? Intellectuals were responding increasingly in the negative. Consider that what appears to be a solid wall is comprised primarily of empty space. This raises the question regarding what exactly is reality, and can we know its essence? If we cannot draw concrete conclusions regarding a concrete wall, how can we possibly speak with certainty regarding the more abstract and yet more significant elements of existence such as morality, the purpose of life, etc.

Similar uncertainties arose regarding communication. One individual does not define words to mean exactly the same thing as another, as evidenced by countless misunderstandings. These failures suggest that accurate communication, a function necessary for the development of a rational worldview, is impossible.

As a result, the intellectual community began to view the mind as an inadequate tool for determining and dealing with reality. Though these concerns were not on the minds of the mainstream American, they engendered discussion in academia where the cultural direction of society is often formulated. These concerns prompted academics to seek an alternative worldview to Materialism. Since Materialism placed total confidence in reason, they pursued an option that did not.

The Alternative to Materialism

Having rejected Christianity and then having assessed reason to be inadequate, intellectuals viewed subjectivity rather than objectivity as the basis for determining reality. Immediate experience and feelings comprised the only means of achieving knowledge with certainty. My intellectual conclusions about the wall may be wrong, but I can be certain of my subjective experience of it—if I run into it headfirst I feel pain. So Americans began to look to emotions, feelings, subjective experience as the only reliable means of determining reality and guiding their lives. This commitment to the subjective was expressed in the 1970s slogan "If it feels good, do it."

Before we discuss the nature of this non-rational, feelings-oriented worldview that America adopted, we must first ask how the well-educated society of the greatest nation on earth, made great by a Christian culture, was convinced to trade in that culture of success for an irrational one. We will examine this question next.

Chapter 2

Weapons of Cultural Transformation

American culture up to the 1960s maintained a strong commitment to reason through the influence of both our founding Christian culture and Materialism. With this prior rational cultural orientation, how could Americans suddenly adopt an irrational worldview? This transition was made possible largely by technological developments that possessed a special capacity for propagating irrational concepts.

Technological Developments

The 1950s brought us the small and cheap transistor radio, which changed the dynamic in the home from the family gathered around the radio in the living room to kids having their own radios in their own rooms. This allowed for the propagation of a distinct teen music culture, one largely beyond parental supervision.

This arrangement enabled those controlling this communication channel to shape the minds and attitudes of young people. As we consider the major role music plays in molding culture (think about its impact in spawning the hippie culture), we realize the profound significance of this technological advance and the power it assigned to those controlling this medium.

Soon after, television became a common fixture in the family living room, providing a means of injecting cultural values through news, sitcoms, and other programming. A recent survey indicates that Americans over two years of age watch television 34 hours per week on average.[18]

These technological developments were quickly followed by the VHS player, the Walkman, the DVD player, the Internet, iTunes, the iPod, video games, smart phones, the iPad and other tablets, Netflix and Amazon movies, social media, and almost countless variations of the above.

Though the movie industry had existed for a long time, its reach was multiplied through the advent of the movie outlets listed above. Added to that, the technology currently available for producing and viewing movies enhanced substantially its capacity to influence minds and emotions. Consider color, graphics, high and ultra-high definition, CGI (computer-generated imagery), increased sound quality, and advanced expertise in production techniques designed to influence audiences.

The availability and proliferation of these devices gave conveyers of culture almost unlimited access to American society, allowing them to promote their ideas, attitudes, and values.

Children and teenagers were especially accessible to those promoting cultural concepts because they tend to have more time to use these media, possess more malleable minds, and are driven by peer pressure to tune into these cultural channels. I know some young people who have their iPods streaming music into their ears all night while they sleep. Imagine the almost unlimited power the controllers of these outlets exercise in shaping impressionable minds.

POWER TO PROMOTE THE IRRATIONAL

The Power of Pictures

Added to the capacities these technologies provide for imposing culture, they possessed a unique power to implant irrational cultural concepts because of a factor Neil Postman identified in his book *Amusing Ourselves to Death.*

Postman asserted that "photography and writing ... do not inhabit the same universe of discourse."[19] One reason is that a picture gives a snippet of information severed from any context, therefore leaving us with trivia rather than real knowledge, which is useful only for entertainment.[20] Of greater significance, while language demands rational engagement, pictures resist it.

Language, of course, is the medium we use to challenge, dispute, and cross-examine what comes into view, what is on the surface. The words "true" and "false" come from the universe of language, and no other. When applied to a photograph, the question, Is it true? means only, Is this a reproduction of a real slice of space-time? If the answer is "Yes," there are no grounds for argument, for it makes no sense to disagree with an unfaked photograph. The photograph itself makes no arguable propositions, makes no extended and unambiguous commentary. It offers no assertions to refute, so it is not refutable.[21]

Consequently, while writing and other verbal communication elicit rational analysis, pictures possess the capacity to bypass our rational processes and embed unprocessed concepts directly into the mind.

Note how many of the technological advances described above communicate through pictures or allow pictures to be transmitted more easily and effectively. Consequently, based on Postman's insight these technological advances have unleashed vast capacities to inject concepts into the minds of Americans that escape rational analysis. Consequently, they possess the capacity to inject into the American intellect irrational concepts and an irrational worldview.

Postman especially saw television as a threat to rational discourse, both because of its primary emphasis on pictures and because it has invaded our homes, this becoming the primary conveyor of our culture.[22]

The capacity to implant unprocessed concepts into our minds takes on unbridled power when all these media convey the same set of messages that converge into a unified worldview. The Left has employed American media to do just that.

The Power of All Non-Rational Communication

Not only pictures but all forms of non-rational communication possess the power to bypass rational analysis and insert their messages directly into our minds. Virtually all entertainment fits this description. Though the lyrics of music and plots of movies and television entertainment use words, their message is not presented in a context in which recipients rationally analyze the message. We listen to music and watch sitcoms and movies to be entertained, not to learn. Consequently, the listener often absorbs the message without thinking about, much less questioning, its validity.

Few if any young people analyzed the lyrics of John Lennon's "Imagine" to ponder the validity of its message that Heaven and Hell do not exist or that globalism would eliminate killing. Yet these concepts embedded themselves directly into their belief system. Adding to the influence of rationally unprocessed lyrics is the vast number of times a young person is likely to listen to a popular song. Beyond that, because of the emotional impact of music, it implants the lyrics even more indelibly into the psyche. All of us can easily remember lyrics of songs from decades ago and even experience the emotions attached to those songs.

As a result of young people hearing the lyrics of popular songs that conveyed distinct ideological messages, the unprocessed concepts conveyed by these lyrics became an integral part of their worldview and culture. Many of these concepts would have been rejected had the message been presented rationally. However, these concepts bypassed their rational scrutiny and entered directly into their minds, influencing their perspective on life and the resultant values, attitudes, and behaviors.

Reinforced by movies and television entertainment, irrational cultural messages began to stick, transforming the cultural orientation of American youth from an objective, rational perspective to a subjective, irrational one.

In light of the capacity of these media to implant irrational concepts, it is no accident that just as those promoting an irrational culture became armed with these weapons of mass indoctrination in the 1960s, the American post-Christian, irrational worldview began to emerge.

Cultural Control by the Left

Liberal Control of Technology

The power possessed by these tools for implanting irrational perspectives directly into minds leads us to wonder who gained control of these media.

It is evident from the content communicated through these media that the American Left took possession of and maintains dominant control over them, using them to convey its message, especially to young people. Though occasionally movies and entertainment television will include programming with family-friendly content, for the most part the material propagated through these media promote liberal-oriented themes such as sexual promiscuity, homosexuality, anti-American propaganda, anti-Christian perspectives, content that undermines parental authority, programming that promotes violence, etc.

One might wonder why conservatives did not adopt these tools to propagate their message. I wonder about that myself. Maybe because they are, in fact, conservative. One of the great tragedies of our time has been the success of a relatively small contingent of liberals in selling their message because they recognized the propaganda capacities of these new technologies, seized the initiative, and consequently used them to advance their agenda, while conservatives looked on and complained.

One avenue of communication that conservatives have utilized is talk radio. It is of special interest that liberals have not been able to gain traction in this arena. Postman's theory explains why. Since talk radio uses words conveyed in a rational context, its message must be rational. Since liberal ideas are largely irrational, they do not come across well in this rationally-oriented medium. They can only be sold through channels of communication that bypass the reason.

Though talk radio has made an impact, unfortunately it does not have sufficient entertainment value to reach the broader population, thus limiting its influence. Though it has given conservatives a rallying point, it has made only limited inroads into liberal populations. In other words, virtually everyone watches television and movies, which for the most part convey liberal concepts, while talk radio attracts only a limited, predominantly conservative audience.

Fox News and a fledgling Christian/conservative movie industry also provide an alternative. Though these media outlets have proved helpful, they are no match for the juggernaut of established mainstream media controlled by the Left. They have been effective at preaching to the choir but lack the reach to influence the congregation.

One means of communication in which conservatives have a more equitable representation is the Internet. Liberals continue to look for ways to control that medium, but to date they have been largely unsuccessful.

Nonetheless, with little presence in the preponderance of media, conservatives find themselves at a distinct disadvantage in shaping and controlling attitudes, values, and beliefs of American society. That limitation represents a major factor in their losing the culture war.

Liberal Employment of Television News

No objective person can deny that the mainstream news media advocate for the Left. Their unfailing support of President Obama and virtually every liberal cause makes this conclusion undeniable. This raises the question of how liberal television news manages to promote its irrational message to the American people since news tends to be verbal.

This is where television's pictorial capability comes into play. The mainstream media allow pictures that promote the agenda of the Left while excluding those that would advocate against it. For example, the mainstream news media assiduously avoided showing pictures or videos related to the recent exposé of Planned Parenthood (implicating the organization in the sale of baby parts), though these pictures were readily available. Nonetheless they found it easy to procure video footage of lions in the wild to promote the story related to the killing of Cecil, which promoted animal rights, a pet agenda item for the Left.

Also, presenting issues in sound bite length segments enables the news media to easily present a biased perspective. Numerous means of slanting a story along with more traditional propaganda techniques such as controlling the narrative, telling only one side or positioning the favored perspective last, and other such techniques enable those controlling television news to propagate the Left's non-rational culture.

Liberal Dominance in Education

Liberal control of educational institutions, especially higher education, has provided them with a platform to impose a non-rational culture on malleable minds in the classroom, thus indoctrinating new generations with their worldview. Though teaching is a verbal media, liberals are able to use educational institutions to propagate non-rational ideas because teachers for the most part are older, hold a position of almost dictatorial authority, have imposing academic credentials, are generally much more knowledgeable than their students, are often protected by tenure, and are sheltered from scrutiny by the walls of the academy.

In his book *Slouching Towards Gomorrah*, the late Robert Bork spoke of the espousal of irrationality in the academic world by "the rejection of the very idea of rationality." [23] Bork made reference to "the astounding claim that rationality itself is neither possible nor legitimate...." These academics assert "that what counts as rationality is socially constructed, that there are different ways of knowing, which means that reality has no stable content, not even in principle."[24] Bork wrote of "the denial that rationality, now routinely derided as 'logocentrism,' is legitimate or perhaps even possible...."[25]

John R. Searle reports that problems in academia are confined "not just to the content of the curriculum but to the very conception of rationality, truth, objectivity, and reality that have been taken for granted in higher education, as they have been taken for granted in our civilization at large."[26]

The promotion of irrationality in educational institutions serves to divide universities into two separate compartments. One compartment includes the teaching of subjects that require empirical content and reason such as physics, chemistry, engineering, and medical research. The other compartment embodies courses such as social studies, philosophy, history, counseling psychology, education, and other areas that serve as the natural habitat of liberal ideas, fields where the irrationality of ideas is not easily demonstrated and failure of those irrational ideas is not immediately exposed. This same dichotomy is found in our society in general.

In his book *Hard America, Soft America*, Michael Barone recognizes this dichotomy, hard America consisting of fields where rational thought is required while soft America is bound by no such constraint. He exposes the impact of this arrangement on the education of American young people. "Americans at 18 have for many years scored lower on standardized tests than 18-year-olds in other advanced countries."[27] He sees this outcome resulting from our young people residing primarily under the influence of soft America that dominates our educational system.[28]

The Bottom Line

Liberals possess almost sole proprietorship of the channels of influence over young people, controlling schools, the music industry, television entertainment and news, and movies. Consequently, with each passing year, as the conservative element of society ages and the liberal-indoctrinated younger generation emerges, the irrational concepts of the Left gain increasingly greater traction in American society.

Liberals, taking advantage of the capacities of new technologies for implanting irrational ideas, and utilizing other means of communication that they control such as education, were quick to employ these resources to market their irrational worldview to the American public. The next chapter describes the nature of the ideology that they have sold to America.

Chapter 3

Cultural Invasion

The Hippie Movement

America was invaded in the 1960s, not militarily, but culturally. Having been shaped by a Christian culture throughout its history, America in large measure discarded that cultural orientation for a new one. Of course, many Americans continued to adhere to the former Christian culture, but the new one became the cutting edge and since then has become the dominant orientation of our nation, so that even those who continue to embrace traditional American Christian culture manifest some degree of infiltration by the new one. Those contending that we live in a post-Christian era are correct.

The hippie movement embodied the initial manifestation of this culture shift. Some authors make the case for the culture shift beginning in the 1950s. Trends during that decade did prepare the way for the 1960s, but the actual American cultural transition began in earnest in the mid-1960s.

Mention of the hippie movement conjures up scenes of the British Invasion with the Beatles' tour of America in 1964-65, the Summer of Love in San Francisco in 1967, the yippie protest at the Democratic National Convention in Chicago in 1968, and Woodstock in rural New York in 1969. It brings to mind unconventional dress and hairstyles, rock music, drugs, the "sexual revolution," and communal living. It also calls to remembrance certain characters such as Timothy Leary on the East Coast, Ken Kesey on the West Coast, and Norman Mailer who became a major literary inspiration to the movement. The popularity of this phenomenon was reflected in the Summer of Love attendance estimated at 100,000 and Woodstock drawing an estimated 400,000.

Though this countercultural movement may seem like ancient history now, the concepts that drove it form the dominant cultural orientation of America today. Cultural observers tend to divide living Americans into six generations: the World War II Generation, the Silent Generation, the Baby Boomer generation, Generation X, Generation Y (the Millennials), and Generation Z. Though each of these generations reflects distinctive characteristics, our educational system, news media, and especially the entertainment media for the most part have imposed the hippie orientation on them all, making that the dominant lens through which America sees life. In fact, we can trace virtually every major theme in American post-Christian culture to the hippie movement. In more recent years, social commentators are acknowledging that our current culture is merely the 1960s culture come of age.

The majority of the American public, including many Christians, sense an emotional connection with the hippie movement as representing *their* culture Therefore, they view it in positive terms— young people advocating for peace and love instead of war, with various cool happenings such as Woodstock representing "the good old days." This comes as no surprise since, as we noted in an earlier chapter, culture becomes deeply embedded in the psyches of young people, and this is their culture.

The concepts embodied in the hippie countercultural movement, however, were not of the innocent, altruistic type many perceive them to be. An examination of the underpinnings of this movement reveals its aggressively anti-agape character. It turns out that the movement not only fails to promote agape but actually militates against it. Our examination will reveal that the hippie movement, labeled by some as "the love generation," in reality spawned a culture of selfishness.

Its Motivating Force

We ended the chapter on Materialism by highlighting the sense of personal emptiness created by that worldview. How satisfied can people be when they find themselves reduced to matter and energy, classified as animals, and deprived of the capacity to make real choices? All this renders them devoid of unique value, dignity, and purpose.

Now also confronted with the failure of Materialism to produce utopia or to provide an effective means of identifying reality, they needed an alternative. Academia had long since rejected Christianity. Having eliminated the spiritual and now the rational, what was left? They found the solution in a non-rational, subjective, feelings approach to reality.

The typical American on the farm and in the factory, the electrician, accountant, and engineer, did not find themselves agonizing over these issues. Rather, these were primarily the musings of the academic class. Therefore, it comes as no surprise that the hippie movement was spawned among college students whose worldview was being shaped by professors and campus culture. Consequently, mainstream Americans did not originally embrace the perspectives described below. That came later. We will see why and how that occurred in future chapters. The views described below took root in the hippie subculture promoted by liberal academics.

FoundAtionAl Concepts

We possess a penchant to label things, and this urge prompts us to put a tag on the hippie perspective. Some may refer to it as existentialism. Others view it as having morphed into postmodernism. Yet others may contend that neither label fits. One problem with both existentialism and postmodernism is that both resist definition. There seems to be almost universal disagreement on a precise meaning of both terms, and one may even argue that both perspectives defy precise meanings.

What really matters is identifying the core beliefs that drove the hippie movement and continue to dominate secular American culture today. The term "Subjectivism" best captures these concepts. Miriam Webster defines subjectivism as follows: "1a: a theory that limits knowledge to subjective experience; b: a theory that stresses the subjective elements in experience; 2a: a doctrine that the supreme good is the realization of a subjective experience or feeling (as pleasure); b: a doctrine that individual feeling or apprehension is the ultimate criterion of the good and the right."[29] In other words, Subjectivism identifies feelings, subjectivity, as the ultimate measure of reality and therefore the ultimate basis for determining values and making decisions. We will discover that this concept embodies the foundational principle dominating the hippie movement and the culture it spawned. Therefore, I will use Subjectivism to refer to that cultural orientation.

The beliefs of the hippie movement were embodied in three concepts.

Do What Feels Good

The foundational tenet of Subjectivism is found in the hippie mantra "If it feels good, do it." Note that this crucial concept calls for viewing and responding to life totally on a subjective basis.

In his book of collected works entitled *Existentialism*, Robert C. Solomon states: "Norman Mailer has given us the first explicit formulation of what might well be called American existentialism.... (I)t is undeniable that Mailer's writings offer us the best American expression of the existentialist attitude we have to date."[30]

Mailer's essay "The White Negro," published in 1959, describes the "Hip" person, from which came the name "hippie." Mailer's thesis in this essay was that American existentialism is the merging of the rebellious white person with "a black man's code," hence the "White Negro."[31]

Mailer described the distinctive element of the Hipster's approach to life as:

> (t)he psychopathic element of Hip which has almost no interest in viewing human nature, or better, in judging human nature, from a set of standards conceived a priori to the experience, standards inherited from the past. Since Hip sees every answer as posing immediately a new alternative, a new question, its emphasis is on complexity rather than simplicity.... Given its emphasis on complexity, Hip abdicates from any conventional moral responsibility because it would argue that the results of our actions are unforeseeable, and so we cannot know if we do good or bad....[32]

Mailer was asserting that life's complexities render impossible the development of an objective, rational basis for understanding life and consequently for establishing morals. In other words, empirical information and reason are incapable of telling us with certainty anything about the world beyond our immediate feelings, especially as related to moral issues.

Mailer provided added reasons for denying a rational understanding of reality in asserting that the universe consists of

> ... a changing reality whose laws are remade at each instant by everything living, but most particularly man, man

raised to a neo-medieval summit where the truth is not what one has felt yesterday or what one expects to feel tomorrow but rather truth is no more or no less than what one feels at each instant in the perpetual climax of the present.[33]

Note first that Mailer, in keeping with our first principle of Subjectivism, identified truth with feeling. Mailer views truth to be different for everyone and constantly in flux. A person goes to sleep in one world at night and wakes up to a whole new reality in the morning. Thus, the understanding of the world that we held when we went to sleep does not apply to the world that we experience when we wake up. This universe lacks the stability necessary to support objective knowledge and therefore moral principles. This perspective annuls the validity of all principles, rules, or morals since these require a stable universe .

This absence of a stable, external, objective reality leaves internal, subjective reality as the only valid basis for viewing life and making decisions.

It is difficult to get one's arms around the vastness of the implications of this shift from a reason-based approach to a feelings-based approach to reality. The immensity of this transition will become apparent in the discussion ahead.

Do It Now

Another hippie slogan, "Do it now," captures the second underlying tenet of this movement, which flows out of the first one. Employing feelings as a basis for identifying reality and making decisions limits the individual's outlook and decision-making criterion to the present moment since one's feelings cannot feel yesterday or tomorrow but only the immediate present. Recall Mailer's assertion above that "...truth is no more or no less than what one feels at each instant in the perpetual climax of the present."

This perspective eliminates consideration of any commitments made yesterday. Likewise, the future constitutes a rational abstraction and thus not a concern for feelings. Consequently, all decisions should be based exclusively on what makes one feel good in the immediate present. In other words, this approach to life advocates for immediate gratification as the only criterion for all decisions.

Drugs as mind and mood-altering substances were a significant aspect of the hippie movement. Recreational drug use makes no sense if we are identifying reality rationally. If, however, we are using feelings and the corollary of immediate gratification as the basis for decision-making, drugs become an optimal choice for maximizing present feelings. The current trend toward legalizing drugs in some states reveals our continued embrace of Subjectivism.

The Right to Do Your Own Thing

The third tenet of the hippie philosophy finds expression in another popular hippie cliché, "You have a right to do your own thing." This concept nullifies all external authority, assigning total authority to the individual, granting him full autonomy.

The term autonomy is derived from two Greek words meaning law and self. The autonomous individual is a law unto himself. This precisely describes the perspective of the hippie movement. The state, the police, the university, the military, parents, and even God were viewed as having no right to impose their will on the individual. A hallmark of the hippie movement was an antiauthoritarian, antiestablishment attitude, graphically communicated by the hippie reference to police as "pigs."

It should be further noted—and this is significant—that Subjectivism not only assigns all authority to the individual but further restricts authority to the individual's feelings, nullifying any authority that might be exercised by the mind, the will, or even the conscience. Granting the individual autonomy while calling on him to use his mind and will as the basis for exercising autonomy would at least have provided some guardrails for his choices. Granting all authority to the emotions, however, even removes those guardrails. This arrangement is a recipe for disaster since as we noted earlier the emotions serve not merely as an ineffective guidance system but one that promotes irrational and destructive behaviors.

A Rational Explanation of the Irrational

Though Subjectivism, the hippie philosophy just described, is non-rational, the analysis that follows seeks to make some rational sense of it.

Feelings Are the Foundation

The subjectivist mindset makes sense once we adopt the foundational concept of Subjectivism, that feelings comprise the basis for determining and responding to reality.

As we observed, Mailer made the case for using feelings as a basis for determining reality by asserting that our immediate subjective experience provides life's greatest certainty. I know what I am feeling now. That is all I know for sure. Therefore, from the hippie perspective and that of our current society as it has adopted Subjectivism, viewing my feelings as my greatest certainty represents the only reasonable starting point in developing an approach to life.

I once counseled a lady who had been living with a man but moved out because he had consistently taken advantage of her. During our session she listed numerous destructive aspects of this relationship that made any thought of returning irrational. During the next session she shared with me that she had listened to a song that week that urged her to "follow her heart." She felt her heart telling her to move back in with him, and so she did. This woman's subjective decision-making process vividly reflects the orientation of contemporary American society.

This position manifests itself in many ways in our current society. For example, for decades now commercials have been devoid of factual content, instead selling products based on emotions. I saw an automobile commercial recently that showed a family having a good time riding to various places across the country. This commercial provided no objective reasons for buying this car—fuel efficiency, safety ratings, J. D. Power reports. Rather, it sold the car based solely on the good feelings the car elicited as depicted in the commercial. A rational analysis would have revealed that virtually any car could have carried the family to those same places, therefore producing the same feelings. Advertising agencies get paid large sums to sell products. Apparently they know that the American public rather than being insulted by this rationally vacuous pitch will instead respond by purchasing cars because of the emotions it elicits.

This feelings orientation shows itself in the transgender issue. The dominant perspective of our society is that one's feelings rather than the objective fact of genetic and biological makeup should determine reality, even to the extent of giving a biological male feeling like a female entrée into girls' bathrooms and shower rooms.

To understand and assess Subjectivism, we must adopt this starting point that feelings comprise reality. Once we have done so, we will see that the rest of this worldview makes sense.

I Am the Only Real Person

Since Subjectivism determines reality by feelings, and since I can only feel my own feelings, I am the only reality and consequently the only real person. All others who exist are merely objects that I experience on the monitor of my mind. Since my feelings are the only measure of meaning, the only value of those objects in my field of experience resides in their capacity to make me feel good.

Of course, no one actually holds objectively the position that he or she is the only real human being and that all others are objects, but Subjectivism is not about objective positions but about feelings and their implications for behaviors. So although few sane people would proclaim themselves to be the only real person, this conclusion nonetheless permeates attitudes and values and induces actions in our society.

Barbara Defoe Whitehead recognizes this inclination toward reducing the universe to the experiencing individual in her book *The Divorce Culture*. Whitehead observes:

> (T)he notion of divorce as the working out of an inner life experience casts it in far more individualistic terms than in the past. Because divorce originated in an inner sense of dissatisfaction, it acknowledged no other stakeholders. Leaving a marriage was a personal decision, prompted by a set of needs and feelings that were not subject to external interest or claims. Expressive divorce reduced the number of legitimate stakeholders in divorce to one, the individual adult.[34]

Here we see this perspective of the individual as the only real person not just being applied to a real-life situation but to one of life's most significant ones. The irrationality of Subjectivism may seem to be too strange to actually be employed in real life, instead being better suited for a philosophy class questioning whether a tree falling in an unpopulated forest makes a sound. Whitehead's observation, however, reveals that people in our society actually do function based on subjectivist perspectives, even one as bizarre as the individual viewing himself as the only real person.

Although, in a superficial sense, being the only real person in the universe may seem like a great arrangement, the downside is that it consigns the individual to isolation—an existence of solitary confinement. No one else has access to the individual's universe at a meaningful level, as a person, because there is no other person. Consequently, Subjectivism eliminates relationships as a philosophical and psychological possibility. Whitehead's description above reflects the impact of this perspective on marriage, and later we will see its broader application to relationships and the resulting damage it inflicts.

It is not difficult to find a logical connection between seeing oneself as the only real person, which entails the individual committing himself to a lifetime of solitary confinement, and the current escalation in the suicide rate.

A marriage relationship, though perhaps intimate physically, cannot be genuinely intimate when one's spouse does not afford him or her the status of actual personhood. It is not only difficult but dangerous to develop too much intimacy within this arrangement because, as Whitehead observed, one's spouse senses no obligation to remain in the relationship if his feelings direct him elsewhere. And if a spouse is not given consideration as a real person in the decision to divorce, imagine how much less consideration he or she is given in other aspects of the relationship. This inclination of the individual to view himself as the only real person has led to the escalation of cohabitation, a sort of non-relationship relationship that limits one's vulnerability.

The Right to Autonomy

Since feelings are my only basis for determining reality, and since on that basis I am the only real person possessing the only real value, I obviously have a right to do my own thing. No one else exists to say otherwise or to have opposing claims. Therefore, autonomy constitutes the necessary conclusion.

Some might assume that Subjectivism establishes limits to the autonomy of the individual when the welfare of another human being comes into play (i.e., my right to throw my fist ends where another person's nose begins). Notice, however, that nothing in the subjectivist theoretical construct supports that position. There is no other person, and therefore no other nose exists at the end of which my rights terminate. All of the other noses are only theoretical ones, not real ones deserving of consideration other than what they can do for me.

Our society reflects this conclusion of Subjectivism that the rights of the individual are in no way limited by the welfare of others in practices such as in abortion, which denies babies even the right to live if they present an inconvenience to the experiencing individual. Likewise, the rights of the transgender biological male are not limited by privacy concerns, fears, or even the safety of women posed by his presence in their shower room.

Since the individual constitutes the only real person with the right to do his own thing, in effect he is cast in the role of god. Though few people would identify themselves as god, many in our society under the influence of Subjectivism convey that attitude with the attendant rights and behaviors.

Rationale for Pursuing Pleasure

Since feelings are the basis of reality, and since I have the right to do my own thing, these conclusions necessarily lead to making choices that maximize good feelings—produces the most pleasure. These choices are made solely on the basis of feelings without consideration for rational analysis or practical outcomes.

Rationale for Immediate Gratification

As already noted, feelings know nothing about yesterday or tomorrow. They only have awareness of the present. Therefore, basing reality on feelings makes the only reasonable choice doing that which brings maximum positive feelings in the present—immediate gratification. Commitments made yesterday or deferred gratification in hope of a better tomorrow are not considerations. Some sacrifice now might bring far more pleasure tomorrow, but such calculations are the product of reason and consequently not part of a subjective worldview.

Authentic Living

Subjectivism insists that only this feelings-oriented approach to life constitutes authentic living, and any other approach to life fails to achieve fully human existence, instead comprising a betrayal of one's humanity. Consequently, "doing what feels good now" embodies the only moral principle of Subjectivism.

That this represents the bottom line of Subjectivism was graphically depicted by events such as Woodstock, where the only consideration was maximum immediate pleasure. Any consequences such as the trashing of Max Yasgur's farm were of no concern. That contemporary society embraces the same feelings-based value is revealed by the fact that when people bask in the glow of Woodstock, they hardly ever consider the damage done and the flagrant selfishness exhibited.

FEELING OUR WAY

Since Subjectivism is founded on feelings rather than reason, America embraces its tenets emotionally rather than rationally. In other words, Americans do not hold most of the ideas presented above at a conscious, rational level but rather at a subjective, attitudinal level.

It is significant that academics refer to the period since the 1960s as a "post-Christian era," identifying our current culture by what it is not rather than by what it is. It would seem to make more sense to identify our culture based on what we believe now rather than on what we used to believe. This reticence to identify our current cultural beliefs stems from the fact that few in our culture can objectively identify contemporary American cultural beliefs; that is, they are incapable of verbalizing them.

Communists are able to identify their beliefs, as are socialists, Muslims, and Hindus. But contemporary secular Americans are at a loss if asked to verbalize their core beliefs. Instead they usually respond with a litany of unrelated clichés that sound like they are reading from the walls of a serendipity shop such as, "I believe that everything happens for a purpose," without having given much thought to who makes everything happen for a purpose or why it does or why they believe it.

Yet another reason for not objectively identifying our culture by its basic beliefs is that those beliefs are irrational and make no objective sense. One can understand why people are hesitant to list the unrealistic concepts cited above as representing their belief system. It is one thing to hold these concepts at the subjective level but something quite different to express them out loud in public. Imagine asserting to your boss or spouse that you have a right to do your own thing and plan to do what feels good whenever the feeling arises and have a right to do so because you are the only real person.

Nonetheless, even though few Americans are able to express the essence of Subjectivism and despite its irrational nature, this worldview exercises dominant influence over American values and behaviors.

I am not suggesting that every American is totally committed to Subjectivism. Just as many Europeans are committed to socialism to varying degrees or not at all, and likewise with communism in China, so also Americans have been influenced by Subjectivism to varying degrees. However, just as in Europe and China socialism and communism provide a powerful shaping force, likewise Subjectivism exercises significant influence in molding American society.

For example, American elections are decided predominantly by feelings rather than by the objective qualifications or platform of the candidate. "Hope and change" feels good even when the hearer is given no objective basis for hope and no rational explanation of what will be changed. Countless other examples could be marshaled to demonstrate that even though the ideology above is not consciously held or objectively expressed by Americans, it nonetheless represents the driving force behind the value system of our culture.

Subjectivism in the Real World

The fact that this worldview has a degree of internal cohesion does not make it valid. The error of its foundational thesis—that feelings comprise an effective instrument for determining and responding to reality—renders it an unworkable approach to real life.

Subjectivism might work for a brief time for college students who are in relatively good health, are supported by their parents, live in a safe country that provides a wide array of social services, and are not responsible for a family and children. These circumstances circumscribe a bubble of unreality within which a person who employs this feelings approach to life can survive to a limited degree for a limited time.

Even for those sheltered by this protective bubble, however, this approach to life quickly unravels. The devolving scene in the Haight-Ashbury district of San Francisco during the Summer of Love as Larry Eskridge describes it provides a grim display of this reality.

> The free and easy hippie celebration of sexuality also manifested itself in all sorts of unforeseen "bummers." Venereal diseases were rampant in the Haight, and hippies seeking treatment for syphilis, gonorrhea, and herpes combined with drug overdoses [served] to overwhelm the Free Clinic and the city's health department. Even more troubling was the generally degrading effect life in the Haight had on the young runaway girls who came to the Bay area. As one young teenage girl named Alice told early Jesus People figure David Hoyt, "Girls didn't have any trouble finding a place to spend the night" if they were willing to pay the right price. Others turned to full-fledged prostitution to feed themselves and their drug habits. Sexual violence

toward women was also a grim reality. As early as April 1967, one hippie broadside lamented the situation: "Rape is as common as bullshit on Haight Street." In general, by midsummer 1967, women in the Haight were at risk for all sorts of emotional and physical violence from their male counterparts.

While these discomforts and hardships were daunting enough, the hippies' fervent belief in the spiritual and personal blessings of drug use was responsible for perhaps the largest share of trouble. Besides growing harassment from the police, overdoses, bad trips, and the hyperaggressiveness associated with speed were a constant of life in the Haight. These problems multiplied as overcrowding grew and the drug supply's safety and quality were increasingly compromised. A closely related problem was a dramatic increase in assaults and robbery (rip-offs) in the hippie district as a new attempt to control its hitherto free-and easy drug trade overwhelmed the Golden Rule ethos of the counterculture. As one author described it, "The flower movement was like a valley of thousands of plump white rabbits surrounded by wounded coyotes." When two popular hippie drug dealers were found brutally murdered in separate incidents late that summer, it became clear to many that the bloom was off the hippie rose.[35]

No doubt one reason for the short duration of the movement in its original form is found in this disconnect between its ideology and reality. The unrealistic choices prompted by emotions could only be sustained for a very short time, even in this artificial environment propped up by real world parents and social services.

Subjectivism encounters even greater problems when it is practiced outside this type of bubble of unreality and is confronted with the realities of normal life. Imagine a father and mother with a family seeking to run a business to support themselves trying to approach life based on Subjectivism. Untenable results would quickly set in.

Subjectivism's ultimate conflict with reality resides in its eradication of agape and the corresponding production of large quantities of selfishness, a problem we will examine next.

CHAPTER 4

AGAPE DESTROYING CULTURE

Replacing the Production of Agape with the Pursuit of Selfishness

Producing agape for the most part must be intentional whereas selfishness usually comes naturally. Nothing about Subjectivism encourages agape. Doing one's own thing, doing what feels good *now*, gives no consideration to the well-being of others. In fact, making the experiencing person the only person eliminates the possibility of agape altogether by eliminating any genuine other toward whom the individual can display agape. Agape is a relational term. Subjectivism leaves no other real person out there with whom to have a relationship—to benefit.

Subjectivism not only eradicates the prospect of agape, but promotes the antithesis—selfishness—by encouraging the individual to do his own thing, to consider *only* himself.

This selfishness is further promoted by instructing the individual to make his own thing that which feels good. If the mind were employed to determine the individual's thing, at least there would be a chance that he might select as his thing behaviors that would benefit others, since doing so might also produce benefit for self in return. Employing the emotions to determine one's thing, however, makes the likelihood of a selfish choice almost a certainty. And specifically identifying what "feels good" as the emotion to pursue virtually ensures selfishness.

As we saw above, Barbara Defoe Whitehead concluded that doing one's own thing inclined people toward divorce, and Larry Eskridge described a host of destructive outcomes from the same selfish orientation in the Haight-Ashbury district during the Summer of

Love. The Summer of Love graphically demonstrated the "forming, storming, norming" process described earlier, with the tendency of emotions to produce loving, though at times misguided desires during the honeymoon stage of a relationship or situation, only to burn out after the initial euphoria wears off. This seems to have been the case with the hippie movement. The love generation, though briefly displaying flickers of altruism, quickly morphed into a generation characterized by selfishness.

Subjectivism further militates against agape by making selfishness a virtue. As we noted above, doing one's own thing, "being real," is the only moral obligation of Subjectivism. Under its influence people pride themselves on their selfishness, announcing proudly, "I did this just for me," as if such behavior constitutes an expression of august nobility deserving high praise, which in fact it does when viewed through the lens of Subjectivism. This further encouragement of the natural human tendency toward selfishness has unleashed the darkest aspects of human nature.

Whitehead reports that beginning in the 1960s selfishness as a virtue became the dominating element of our society's view of divorce:

> People began to judge the strength and "health" of family bonds according to their capacity to promote individual fulfillment and personal growth.... Once the domain of the obligated self, the family was increasingly viewed as yet another domain for the expression of the unfettered self.... Once regarded mainly as a social, legal, and family event in which there were other stakeholders, divorce now became an event closely linked to the pursuit of individual satisfactions, opportunities, and growth.[36]

Whitehead concludes that all obligation to others has been replaced by obligation solely to one's self.

> (O)ne's first obligation in the dissolution of marriage was to oneself.... If expressive divorce excluded the idea that there are other parties at interest in the "divorce experience," it also overturned earlier notions about one's moral responsibilities to others. An individual's right to divorce was rooted in the individual's right to have a satisfying inner life to fulfill his/her needs and desires. The entitlement to divorce was based on the individual entitlement to pursue inner happiness.... No one, including the divorcing

individual's children, had a "right" to intervene in this intensely private experience or to try to disrupt the course of an emotionally healthy journey toward divorce. Nor were there morally compelling arguments for considering the interests and claims of others in the marriage. If divorce was an entirely subjective and individual experience, rooted in a particular set of needs, values, and preferences, then there was no basis for making judgments about the decision to divorce. The new ethic of divorce was morally relativistic: There could be no right or wrong reasons for divorce.... If the divorce experience was an inner journey of the sovereign self, what right had anyone to place impediments in the way?[37]

Framing selfishness as a virtue renders Subjectivism's definition of character antithetical to the traditional one. Historically, character consisted of subordinating one's self-interests to those of spouse, children, neighbor, and country. "America the Beautiful" extols those who "more than self their country loved, and mercy more than life."

These thoughts are foreign to the mind-set of contemporary society, which considers acting selfishly to be noble. Whitehead notes that the core principle underlying Emily Post's well-known book on etiquette was the obligation of the individual "... to please others, to place the comfort and interests of others above one's own."[38] Now such chivalry is not only dead but we consider it to be wrong.

Pac-Man like, Subjectivism also devours agape by encouraging people to be takers and not givers. Almost invariably the immediate gratification promoted by Subjectivism necessitates the consumption of that which someone else has produced. As the report of life in the Haight-Ashbury district during the Summer of Love reveals, those encountering physical problems from promiscuous sex and drugs went to the government health facility for help, that is, they used taxpayer money, earned through the labor of others, to support their selfish behavior.

We find this same subjectivist inclination at work today in the popular support for Bernie Sanders in the presidential primaries. His socialistic platform entails taking from others what they have earned and giving it to his constituency. His followers display the subjectivist ethic of viewing others as existing merely to enable them to feel good. They function not as producers but consumers, devouring whatever they can politically wrest from others.

If we evaluate a marriage relationship in terms of a bank account, viewing acts of agape as deposits and acts of selfishness as withdrawals, Subjectivism quickly puts a marriage relationship into an overdrawn condition, failing to produce agape while manufacturing large quantities of selfishness. This overdrawn condition often leads to marital bankruptcy. Likewise with selfish politicians who are bankrupting and otherwise destroying our nation through self-serving choices rather than decisions that benefit the people.

Subjectivism's Impact on Morality and Grace

As noted earlier, agape is expressed at two primary levels: morality, its foundational expression, and grace, its ultimate expression. It is evident that both expressions of agape have suffered at the hands of Subjectivism.

The Demise of Morality

We defined morality as giving others what we owe them. Having a right to do one's thing eradicates all obligation to others. In addition, since the experiencing individual is the only real person, no one else exists with rights to claim, thus eliminating even the possibility of obligation.

Many hippie behaviors such as drug use were harmful to others. More recently, the takeover of the Wisconsin capitol building by liberal protesters, the contemporary purveyors of the hippie culture, included trashing the facilities with such behaviors as urinating in public areas of the building, a blatant disregard for the rights of others. Most interesting was the lack of media attention assigned to this behavior, suggesting that selfish practices hurtful to others are now being accepted as a cultural norm, a protester's prerogative, especially when the protesters represent the Left. The point here is that granting the individual the right to do his own thing nullifies all consideration of others, completely eradicating any basis for morality.

This abandonment of morality was displayed graphically in the riots in Ferguson, Missouri, and Baltimore, Maryland. Lawless rioters were permitted to burn buildings and loot stores. The media showed no concern for their lawlessness but instead called to our attention the rioters' feelings of rage, which the media viewed as justification for their lawlessness, regardless of how baseless these feelings were, instead compelling the rest of society to understand. The question of whether their feelings of rage were rooted in reality seemed never to enter the discussion, even though in almost every case the stipulated reasons for the rage turned out not to be valid. In our Subjectivism-driven society such objective facts and related rational analysis are irrelevant. Only feelings count.

The only immorality Subjectivism acknowledges is found in calling something or someone immoral since doing so denies the individual the right to do his own thing. Hence, this culture views Christianity in its biblical form as immoral because it teaches morality.

This elimination of morality as a category finds expression in our society practically everywhere one looks. For example, cohabitation is no longer thought to be immoral. Most Americans no longer consider viewing pornography as immoral. I constantly hear radio advertisements offering to help spenders avoid paying credit card debt. It seems that many in our society no longer consider it a moral responsibility for people to pay for things they have purchased.

The Demise of Grace

We defined grace as extending to others benefits that we do not owe. It appears that on this count Subjectivism shines, in effect displaying total, ongoing grace to the individual. Assigning him the right to do his own thing in essence makes grace an absolute. Though society owes him nothing, it grants him everything, including the right to take advantage of every resource while granting pardon for every harmful consequence of his actions. The subjectivist individual exists in a bubble of absolute grace.

At first blush this arrangement seems to be quite magnanimous, extending to the individual unlimited and perpetual grace. It is even given an air of nobility because this absolute grace eliminates judgmentalism and condemnation, which are viewed as characteristics of narrow-minded conservatives.

Closer examination, however, reveals that the grace Subjectivism grants in reality comprises only pseudo-grace. The artificial nature of this grace shows itself in three primary ways.

First, grace must be granted by another person, whereas the practitioners of Subjectivism grant grace to themselves. Note that the cliché is usually framed in self-oriented terms: "I have a right to do my own thing." This indicates that the individual has conferred this prerogative on himself, which does not amount to grace but rather to self-conferred selfishness.

A second factor that makes the grace extended by Subjectivism pseudo-grace is found in our previous recognition that grace must not be granted at the expense of morality. The absolute grace of Subjectivism, as we have noted, leaves no place for morality. Granting grace to the pregnant woman to deal with her "problem" in the most convenient way does so by eliminating any moral obligation to the unborn child. The grace extended to the rioters mentioned above was also granted at the expense of the moral obligation of rioters not to destroy the property of others. This arrangement of offering absolute grace at the expense of morality constitutes an unworkable formula that is causing societal meltdown.

A third problem with the pseudo-grace of Subjectivism lies in its failure to designate a means of payment. We have noted that grace must be paid for by the person extending grace. Subjectivism makes no such arrangement. The right extended to the individual to do drugs will be paid for by the person he mugs to get drug money and by society, which must cover the cost of his lack of productivity and need for medical and psychological help.

Consequently, though Subjectivism might appear at first blush to represent the quintessence of grace, in reality it constitutes pseudo-grace and anti-grace, an arrangement that does not produce agape but consumes it through selfishness.

An unintended consequence of this pseudo-grace resides in the harm it does to the recipient. Human beings cannot handle this total grace and the autonomy it grants. Lord Acton observed, "Power corrupts, and absolute power corrupts absolutely." Absolute grace in effect grants absolute power. Empowering the individual to do his own thing quickly becomes a corrupting force. Or to state the case in different terms, absolute grace frees the inherent selfish nature of the human being to express itself, which not only harms others but exerts its debasing influence on the perpetrator.

Subjectivism Undermines Management for Agape

As previously observed, producing agape requires managing our resources by employing our mind and volition. Subjectivism is destructive because it replaces the intellect and will with the emotions as the basis for decision-making and related behaviors.

Suppressing the Mind

Subjectivism's devaluing of the intellect in favor of emotional guidance undercuts interest in and efforts toward intellectual development. Developing our minds requires hard work, and applying the mind in analyzing the situations of life is equally laborious. Thus, the belief that this work is unnecessary results in the tendency not to bother.

This devaluing of the mind has negatively affected our educational system by deemphasizing the importance of factual content and the development of rational thinking skills. We find evidence of this in school curricula that replace rigorous academic disciplines with courses that contain minimal intellectual content and require little effort.

We have heard much in recent years about "low-information voters," people who lack sufficient knowledge to make intelligent choices in the voting booth. A Subjectivism-dominated educational system has produced millions of low-information voters, a large segment of our electorate (perhaps approaching a majority). But beyond the lack of essential information, many in our society lack the skills necessary to rationally analyze whatever information they do possess because the educational system has not developed their rational problem-solving and critical thinking capacities.

Subjectivism not only views the employment of the mind as nonessential but goes a step further and views it as the enemy. If my thing is drugs, my mind may raise red flags, cautioning me about the costs, health risks, legal troubles, and the like. These cerebral warnings may inhibit me from doing my thing—from being *authentic*. Rational analysis of facts revealing that "Hands up, don't shoot" actually did not occur in Ferguson has been viewed negatively, as blocking expression of emotions generated by belief that it did happen. Therefore, rational analysis can serve as the enemy—a weapon used to inhibit emotional expression.

This deactivation of the American intellect is exemplified in the superficial argument made for abortion—that a woman has a right to do what she wants with her own body. This argument disregards the obvious fact that the unborn baby is not her body and therefore deserves consideration. The willingness of our society to overlook such obvious irrationality reveals the American preference for emotions over mind as the guidance mechanism of choice.

As this example of abortion shows, Subjectivism's preference for emotions over mind results almost invariably in the production of selfishness rather than agape.

Disconnecting the Will

Directing our lives by our emotions leaves no role for the will since doing what one feels like doing requires no exercise of the volition. Swimming upstream demands constant, vigorous exercise of the will, but floating downstream requires no volitional engagement. Therefore, Subjectivism's call to do what feels good allows the individual to disengage the volition and drift downstream with the tide of his desires.

Subjectivism is injurious to the will not only because it calls for its disengagement but also because, as a consequence, it never requires its exercise, leading to its atrophy rather than its development, leaving people in our society weak-willed, lacking self-discipline and character. We see the evidence, for example, in the significant and growing problem of obesity among Americans. Though in some cases obesity results from physical pathology, in most cases it does not, instead revealing a weakness in American discipline and character.

In addition to eliminating the need for self-discipline, Subjectivism discourages societal disciplinary practices such as discipline in schools and even in the home, which previously served as venues for developing the will and character.

This deficiency in development of the volition is of special concern in an affluent society. More primitive settings demand human discipline just to survive. Many in developing countries must carry water from sources miles from their home. They must work the land, chop wood, and perform other laborious tasks that require the exercise of discipline for survival, resulting in the development of self-discipline.

Instead of chopping wood to keep warm, most Americans need only to touch a thermostat. Therefore, even the natural challenges of life that demand discipline for survival have been eliminated for most Americans, leaving a large segment of Americans bereft of volitional muscle.

This undeveloped volition renders the individual incapable of expressing agape, which often requires the exercise of the will. Consequently, when confronted with the choice between the more difficult option of producing agape or the easier option of displaying selfishness, often the individual's will is too underdeveloped to make the difficult but loving choice, even when the person might *prefer* to display agape.

Subjectivism's Influence on Societal Management

Replacement of our Christian culture with Subjectivism has been tantamount to the owner of a company firing a well-qualified manager and replacing him with a 16-year-old who has a reputation for partying. The result of course would be the dismantling of the company's organizational structures and replacing them with unruly practices, resulting in chaos and bankruptcy.

Likewise, Subjectivism has reduced a nation of relatively well-managed individuals and institutions to disorganization. Our significant stockpile of resources has been squandered, in short order reducing us to a debtor nation. Agape requires resources and their effective use. Subjectivism's elimination of management is preventing our society from producing agape.

Culture Devoid of Agape

What are the practical effects of this drain on agape resulting from America's adoption of Subjectivism?

The Demise of Virtue

In describing the benefits of agape we noted that nearly all other virtues flow out of it. For example, fidelity is a specific expression of agape. Subjectivism by promoting the opposite of agape not only eradicates virtues of all kinds but actually promotes the corresponding vices.

The Decline in Fidelity

Under the influence of Subjectivism, we have witnessed a drastic decline of fidelity in American society, not only in failure to keep marital commitments but also in the unfaithfulness of politicians to their constituency and to the nation as a whole. Our president has displayed infidelity regarding his commitment to uphold the Constitution and to promote the welfare of the American people.

Demise of Responsibility

Fyodor Dostoevsky stated in *The Brothers Karamazov*, "If God does not exist, everything is permitted."[39] Permitting everything leaves the world without God in moral chaos.

The other half of this truth, however, is equally devastating: If God does not exist, nothing is required, i.e., responsibility has also been eliminated. If the individual has a right to do his thing, he in effect has been exempted from responsibility. Therefore, Subjectivism permits everything and requires nothing. It kills agape with a two-edged sword.

Under the influence of Subjectivism, Americans no longer tend to sense responsibility. If you bought a house beyond your means, you are not responsible. It is the bank's fault for lending you the money, and therefore the bank should bear the responsibility. If you bore multiple babies out of wedlock, you should not have to bear responsibility for supporting them. The government should. You are not responsible for finding a job. Unemployment benefits should extend indefinitely. You are not responsible for drug abuse. It is a disease.

One outcome of the demise of responsibility is seen in the decline of American financial responsibility. A very obvious and troubling manifestation of this eradication of responsibility resides in the fiscal irresponsibility of the federal government as well as many states and cities. Individuals also reflect this financial irresponsibility in buying beyond their means, maxing out credit cards, and putting little into savings. Lack of financial responsibility also manifests itself in the significant numbers in our society who feel no responsibility for meeting their own financial obligations but rather as a matter of course expect the government to achieve that for them.

In 2009 the federal government waived a state responsibility that food stamp recipients perform some minimal work. This dismissal of the work requirement resulted in a significant increase in those participating in the food stamp program. The states of Kansas and Maine decided to reinstitute the work requirement, which produced the following results:

> Once work requirements were established, thousands of food stamp recipients moved into the workforce, promoting income gains and a decrease in poverty. Forty percent of the individuals who left the food stamp ranks found employment within three months, and about 60 percent found employment within a year. They saw an average income increase of 127 percent. Half of those who left the rolls and are working have earnings above the poverty

level.[40]

These results demonstrate that many of those receiving government entitlements could assume responsibility for their own needs but choose not to do so, nor does the government in most states require them to do so. Our subjectivist culture has undermined commitment to responsibility.

Perpetual Adolescence

Children are inclined to allow their emotions to take charge while maturity requires the employment of mind and will in managing our lives. The transition to adulthood does not come easily, requiring work to develop the intellect and strengthen the will. As noted above, Subjectivism fails to develop and employ the mind and will but instead inhibits it. Therefore, Subjectivism breeds immaturity.

Maturity also requires growing out of the self-centeredness of adolescence and growing into the consideration for others (agape) related to adulthood. Marriage requires shedding selfishness as does virtually every other dimension of adult life. In replacing agape with selfishness, Subjectivism promotes perpetual adolescence, which prevents people from successfully fulfilling adult societal roles.

Various sociological observers have identified perpetual adolescence as a trend among American individuals and society as a whole. As we examine marriage, government, and almost every other aspect of American society, we find that many filling these roles lack the maturity to make these institutions function as they should. What does it tell us about the state of America's maturity when a United States president engages in a sexual encounter with an intern in the White House?

In her book *The Death of the Grown-Up*, Diana West documents our societal tendency to get stuck in immaturity.

> More adults, ages 18 to 49, watch the Cartoon Network than watch CNN. Readers as old as 25 are buying "young adult" fiction written expressly for teens. The average video gamester was 18 in 1990; now he's going on 30. And no wonder: The National Academy of Science has, in 2002, redefined adolescence as the period extending from the onset of puberty, around 12, to age 30. The MacArthur Foundation has gone further still, funding a major research project that argues that the "transition to adulthood" doesn't end until age 34.... (O)ne-third of the 56 million Americans

89

sitting down to watch *SpongeBob SquarePants* on Nickelodeon each month in 2002 were between the ages of 18 and 49.[41]

Tying the perpetuation of adolescence with the decline in agape, West observes the following:

> What has also disappeared is an appreciation for what goes along with maturity: forbearance and honor, patience and responsibility, perspective and wisdom, sobriety, decorum, and manners —and the wisdom to know what is "appropriate," and when.[42]

How could it be otherwise? What else can a culture that discourages the development of the mind and will and advocates the pursuit of doing what feels good be expected to produce?

Inhumanity

Perhaps the worst outcome of Subjectivism lies in its fostering of inhumanity—attitudes devoid of human sympathies and the resulting behaviors. Viewing the experiencing individual as the only real human being eradicates empathy toward others, thus promoting inhumanity.

This desensitization of human sympathies reveals itself in divorce, not only in regard to the pain victimized spouses feel but also the cruelty it inflicts on children. Should human compassion not compel us to work through our differences to spare our children the negative consequences divorce inflicts, as many studies reveal?

Isn't the tax burden laid on the hardworking American by our government inhumane? I see a plumber in his truck returning to his home late at night after working hard for 11–12 hours so he can feed, clothe, and house his family, only to have the government take an unconscionably large proportion of his earnings. This requires him to work on weekends or necessitates that his wife work also, all to secure the reelection of politicians. Have these politicians no heart for their constituency, no human feelings toward them? Obviously not.

Or think of a government that pays its workers salaries and benefits well above the national average for similar jobs while many of those in the military, who endure hardship and risk their lives for our safety, qualify for food stamps. What human sense of fairness would permit this?

Although I am grateful for the work of organizations that care for those injured while defending our nation, at the same time I am incensed by the need for such organizations. Can it possibly be that a government that wastes billions cannot find money to provide every possible benefit for those who have given so much for us? This situation reveals an inordinate depth of inhumanity.

These callous displays of inhumanity and countless others are the product of Subjectivism—the dearth of agape and the abundance of selfishness it produces. Although selfishness and inhumanity have always been present in society, a culture that fosters these darker characteristics of human nature elevates the quantity of inhumanity to dangerous levels.

The most tragic dimension of American inhumanity resides not in the cruelty it inflicts on others, but rather in the inhumane nature Subjectivism breeds in those who perpetrate such acts. Bearing acts of inhumanity is terrible; being inhumane is worse.

Choosing Who Gets to Do Their Thing

During Subjectivism's early years, it preached the message that people have a right to do their own thing. Back in those days we found Jesus People asserting that their thing was Jesus, and that was okay. They had a right to do their thing, too. I was attending NYU at the time, and I experienced the same openness to my embrace of biblical Christianity from the faculty and other students, even though few shared my position.

Since the Left-wing purveyors of this philosophy have gained power, however, they have changed the rules. Only they have the right to do their thing. Those who disagree must knuckle under. If your thing is cohabitation or homosexuality, that's okay. If your thing is killing a baby that has been conceived as a result of sexual promiscuity, that is okay also. If your thing is to adhere to traditional biblical principles, however, that is not okay. Conservative speakers invited to college campuses should be uninvited or shouted down. The free-speech advocates have morphed into the political correctness tyrants—the real fascists in our society. Though the Left has not yet succeeded in totally subjugating Christians, it has advanced substantially in that direction.

This result has produced the worst of all possible worlds: empowering people driven by selfish desires to do their thing while denying the same latitude to those desiring to promote agape.

If Subjectivism is so devastating, why doesn't our society reject it?

And since this orientation is so destructive, how are we managing to survive at all? We will address these questions next.

Chapter 5

Embracing and Surviving Subjectivism

The Subjectivist Faith

As the Baby Boomer generation reached adulthood, Subjectivism went mainstream, becoming the dominant force in our culture, which is the status it holds today. What reason do adherents of Subjectivism have for believing that individuals and society can survive under its influence in the face of overwhelming evidence to the contrary? The operative word here is "reason." As we have seen, Subjectivism assigns no role to reason and is instead totally driven by emotion. Therefore, our society needs no rational basis for embracing it.

The AIDS virus destroys the defense mechanism of the body, allowing it to continue its destructive work. Likewise Subjectivism in establishing feelings as the basis for determining reality disarms our natural individual and societal defense mechanism of rational analysis. Subjectivism is irrational, but reason has been excluded as a basis for evaluation, consequently allowing the virus of Subjectivism to remain in the American body politic and to continue its destructive work. Subjectivism constitutes cultural AIDS.

Subjectivist hope is rooted not in reason but in faith, specifically the belief that human beings set free from external authority, assigned total autonomy, will emerge like butterflies from their cocoons as beautiful individuals, collectively creating a beautiful society.

Adherents to the subjectivist faith claim that human selfishness is a product of authoritarian establishments that have dominated society across the centuries, inhibiting human growth and warping human personality. If only human beings had been given autonomy,

93

the right to do their own thing, they believe the results would have been radically different. If given autonomy now, healing would take place producing healthy human beings who act in a responsible and beneficial manner. Society's fundamental mistake is that it has been asking a fish to function on land—a human being trying to swim on the hard surface of authority. Put the human being in an ocean of autonomy and he will display his innate goodness.

This theory requires faith because substantial evidence demonstrates that granting increased autonomy results in increased chaos, as Woodstock, Occupy Wall Street, and countless other situations demonstrate. Progressive education, which proceeds under the assumption that the autonomous child will behave well and learn much, has been an unmitigated flop. It would only be surprising if it were otherwise. Imagine telling a seasoned teacher who is struggling with discipline problems in the classroom that these unruly behaviors stem from too much authority and that if she would just give students total free rein they would act responsibly.

In the face of overwhelming empirical evidence, Norman Mailer and other secular humanists argue that progressive education has failed because it has never trusted students with total autonomy, that its allowances were always limited. Had these educators displayed the necessary faith in humanity to totally release their grip, the results would have been far more favorable. Mailer conveys his commitment to this subjectivist faith and the related confidence in the positive outcomes of absolute autonomy as follows:

> . . . (T)he nihilism of Hip proposes as its final tendency that every social restraint and category be removed, and the affirmation implicit in the proposal is that man would then prove to be more creative than murderous and so would not destroy himself. Which is exactly what separates Hip from the authoritarian philosophies which now appeal to the conservative and liberal temper—what haunts the middle of the twentieth century is that faith in man has been lost, and the appeal of authority has been that it would restrain us from ourselves. [43]
>
> Hip, which would return us to ourselves, at no matter what price in individual violence, is the affirmation of the barbarian, for it requires a primitive passion about human nature to believe that individual acts of violence are always to be preferred to the collective murders of the State: it takes literal faith in the creative possibilities of the human being

to envisage acts of violence as the catharsis which prepares growth.[44]

History, however, bears out that totally autonomous human beings do not become saints but instead, abusing their absolute freedom, behave selfishly. Therefore, the subjectivist faith that asserts that we are at our best when assigned absolute freedom flies in the face of our personal experience and the experience of humanity throughout history. Maybe a few dictators have been benevolent, but they belong to an exclusive club.

Contrary to this subjectivist faith, William Bennett makes the following observation regarding our society that under the influence of Subjectivism has granted individuals increasing autonomy:

> America is the greatest nation in the history of the world—the richest, most powerful, most envied, most consequential. And yet America is the same nation that leads the industrialized world in rates of murder, violent crime, imprisonment, divorce, abortion, sexually transmitted diseases, single-parent households, teen suicide, cocaine consumption, and pornography production and consumption.[45]

Mailer himself exposed the failure of autonomy to produce sainthood by marrying six times and having stabbed his second wife twice with a penknife.[46] The subjectivist faith turns out to be a leap in the dark with every reason to believe that the landing will not be a happy one.

MEANS of AMERICA'S SURVIVAL

In light of the destructive nature of Subjectivism, how does our society continue to survive its influence? Two factors are temporarily propping America up.

PARASITIC EXISTENCE

America continues to survive Subjectivism because of the vast pool of American resources amassed through the influence of our past Christian culture that it had to draw on. Think of it this way: A person of average means cannot economically sustain a drug habit very long, whereas a person who has inherited many millions can finance his drug use much longer. The Left's takeover of America parallels the latter.

Subjectivism took over a society with the greatest store of resources of any nation in history. Those resources included not only a wealthy economy but also a well-developed infrastructure, a substantial manufacturing base, a great educational system, the world's best healthcare system, the world's most powerful military, an effective governmental structure, and many other valuable assets. In addition, because of our Christian cultural roots, America possessed a vast supply of human capital: people who were moral, well-educated, living in stable family situations, hardworking, responsible, knowledgeable, skilled, and disciplined.

Above all else, like an airplane that has run out of fuel, America has had sufficient Christian cultural momentum to forestall a crash landing for an extended time. As that Chinese communist economist we quoted earlier observed, America is surviving on cultural momentum from the past.

When Subjectivism took over our culture, it began devouring these resources, not only spending those amassed in the past but also borrowing against projected future production. Of course, survival by squandering past resources and borrowing against future ones with no apparent means of repayment entails barreling at full speed down a dead end one-way street with a brick wall at the end.

One aspect of taking such a trip is that as long as the car is moving it feels no different than driving down the interstate. Likewise, as long as our government and other elements of our society can locate and consume pockets of resources, life in America will feel the same as it did when we were actually producing, with the exception that now we don't have to work as hard since we are borrowing these resources instead of earning them. One of the few remaining major pockets of American capital resides in our retirement funds, and the government is already scheming to take control of them.

Since we have become a feelings-oriented society, as long as our situation continues to feel the same or better than in the past, the realities pointing to disaster do not matter—we seem not to notice the brick wall at the end of the street looming ever closer.

A term conservative Americans use frequently is "unsustainable." Those expressing this concern are seeing the brick wall at the end of the street approaching rapidly and are screaming for the government to shift its foot from the gas pedal to the brake. Their voices are being drowned out by the media so that they cannot be heard by low-information voters who continue to consume borrowed resources and enjoy the mirage of "normal American life."

Consequently, Subjectivism continues its parasitic existence by devouring its dying host. That host, however, is now near death, its lifeblood nearly drained. In every direction we look we find evidence of resource exhaustion coupled with societal denial.

Some social analysts make the mistake of viewing our current malaise as an expression of a cyclical pattern that will automatically right itself at some time in the future. "It's just another downturn similar to those experienced in the past." Therefore, they conclude that we will again pull out of it. "We are Americans, and that's what we do." The difference this time, however, is that we have hollowed out our resources and the means of producing them, leaving only a superficial shell.

Even worse, we have killed our Christian culture, the goose that laid the golden eggs, that provided a basis for recovery in the past. In addition, as long as we had a population committed to responsibility, hard work, honesty, courage, fidelity, stable families, and other agape-producing elements, we had the necessary human capital to fight our way back. Now we find that both the Christian culture and the human capital it produced have been largely annihilated.

Therefore, in our present state we are incapable of recovery because we are bereft of the resources and means of producing those resources that recovery requires. America is like Sampson after his hair was cut, confident that he still had his previous strength but self-deluded. On our present course, America will certainly die. The only questions are *how* and *how soon*. America's only hope lies in acknowledging very quickly the disastrous nature of our present culture, developing a strategy for restoring our past Christian culture, and throwing all our energy into implementing that strategy.

Cultural Bipolar Disorder

As we have noted earlier, an individual or society that approached life purely on the tenets of Subjectivism could not long endure. Because this outcome is so obvious, hardly anyone has ever attempted to live purely on the basis of Subjectivism.

Consequently, America has adopted a bipolar culture. It embraces the manic inclinations of Subjectivism to the greatest extent possible, but when forced by reality it retreats to the depressive Christian culture of rationality, responsibility, and morality in order to survive and to restock resources for the next manic binge.

This societal bipolar disorder showed itself at the macroscopic level when as a result of the disastrous manic Jimmy Carter years our society realized it must endure what the Left views as the depressive Ronald Reagan era so that it could restock its economic and military resources. But after refueling during Reagan's watch, it was time to return to the manic presidency of Bill Clinton and ultimately to Barack Obama. This same bipolar approach to life shows itself at the microscopic level in the individual American lifestyle. We spend to the max in the pursuit of good feelings but then revert to a sufficient degree of responsibility to prepare for the next manic phase.

One might ask whether this bipolar formula—pursuing all the good feelings possible and exercising rational thinking and discipline only when necessary—is not merely the way people function regardless of their culture. Don't we all strive to maximize good feelings and discipline ourselves to function rationally only when necessary? Haven't people always gone to work because they had to and gone on vacation whenever they could? This is a valid question since this superficial analysis makes our contemporary aspirations seem no different from those of Americans prior to the 1960s.

This assessment fails to recognize the underlying shift in values since the 1960s. Compare the current goal of maximizing good feelings while minimizing the disciplines of rational living with the goals of people living during our previous Christian culture. In our previous cultural environment people prized virtues such as hard work, responsibility, financial stability, marital fidelity, etc. My parents sacrificed for their children and were glad to do so. Their goal was not to feel good as much as possible but to be people of character. This was the case with a majority of pre-1960s society. The ultimate value did not reside in good feelings but in honest, decent, respectable living.

As we have noted, being a person of character constitutes one of the ultimate expressions of agape. My parents' self-sacrifice provided a graphic display of agape, as did their willingness to stay together, to serve others in various ways, to maintain financial responsibility, to live moral lives, to give, to be good neighbors, and to make a contribution to the world. These were their goals—the kind of persons they strove to be, and objectives they achieved in large measure. Their values and behaviors reflected our previous Christian culture as a whole.

Liberals love to mock "Leave it to Beaver" as if that existence is not possible—was only a made-for-television mirage that never existed in real life and therefore constitutes false advertising for the 1950s. It is necessary for them to revise and distort this piece of history in order to prevent exposure through comparison of the disaster they have created.

But families filled with love in the full-orbed meaning of that term were the norm prior to the 1960s debacle, even though the creators of our current self-centered society cannot imagine human existence so abounding with decency and kindness, responsibility and discipline, morality and grace, and other manifestations of agape. The agape-deficient culture that the propagators of Subjectivism have produced is so far beneath our previous Christian society that they must conclude that such a society could not and did not exist. They are wrong.

Of course, I am not suggesting that people in the pre-1960s era consistently pursued agape and invariably reached this goal. The Left enjoys setting up the straw man of perfection and then mocking our previous Christian culture because it did not achieve it. Though agape was not realized to perfection, it was their goal, and because it was their goal and they earnestly pursued it, they achieved it to a great extent—so much so that Tom Brokaw referred to those of the World War II era as the "greatest generation." Aspiring to the goal of agape as opposed to the objective of contemporary Subjectivism to feel as good as possible for as long as possible explains the difference in outcomes between then and now.

Note some of the differences: the absence of drugs vs. widespread drug abuse; marriage and fidelity vs. the immediate gratification offered by cohabitation, extramarital affairs, and no-fault divorce; desire for children vs. voluntary childlessness so as to realize more freedom and fun without them; disciplined spending to achieve financial responsibility vs. four cars, big homes, and maxed-out credit cards; and the list could go on and on.

A recent Congressional Budget Office report revealed that ObamaCare would result in the loss of the equivalent of 2.5 million full-time jobs. The Democratic Party's response suggested that loss of jobs represents a good thing because employment constitutes an evil blocking the path to feelgood pursuits. This response vividly displays the values of Subjectivism. In his article entitled "ObamaCare freeing the job-locked poets?" Jonah Goldberg reported on this exuberant Democrat attitude toward job loss by noting:

Democrats insist this is a boon. Indeed, many are talking about it as an act of liberation (which reminds me of an 11-year-old headline from The Onion: "IBM Emancipates 8,000 Wage Slaves").

House Minority Leader Nancy Pelosi says the CBO report vindicates ObamaCare, because "this was one of the goals. To give people life, a healthy life, liberty to pursue their happiness. And that liberty is to not be joblocked, but to follow their passion."

Pelosi is particularly invested in this view. She's been mocked for years now for her repeated claims that ObamaCare is an entrepreneurial bill because it would let Americans quit their jobs to, among other things, "write poetry."[47]

Americans who were products of our previous Christian culture would view such attitudes emanating from government leaders with utter disbelief.

We are like those people suffering from bipolar disorder who don't take their medication because they enjoy the manic phase too much. Those suffering from bipolar disorder when going through the manic phase seem not to believe that it will ever end—but it does. So it will for America.

This bipolar approach to life is dangerous because it takes very little manic behavior to produce very disastrous consequences. One incident of manic behavior such as trying heroin, telling off a boss, unleashing road rage, or buying a house or boat beyond one's means can destroy an individual's life and that of others. Because life can't tolerate much mania, America's quest for as much mania as possible is wreaking havoc. It is amazing that the plethora of resources America amassed by discipline and hard work across centuries has been squandered by the manic behavior of our present society in a few decades. I have made reference to cultural tilt, but Subjectivism has tilted our society so severely that we are now in freefall.

Note that mania is invariably antithetical to agape just as an explosion tends not to create useful products. Manic living is selfish living. Those suffering from bipolar disorder while living in the manic phase hurt themselves and others, especially those closest to them. American mania is in the process of destroying countless individual lives and relationships and an entire nation.

Absence of Awareness and Intention

The embrace of Subjectivism in general and the bipolar approach to it just described in particular have occurred largely without awareness or intention. Therefore, I am not suggesting that Americans have consciously decided to abandon their previous Christian culture for Subjectivism or are even aware that they have done this. For the most part, they have not. It is true that leaders of the Left in various fields such as education, news, and entertainment have pushed this agenda and have developed strategies for marketing it. But those strategies for the most part do not advance the tenets of Subjectivism rationally, which would be a hard sell and out of sync with the nature of Subjectivism. Instead they do so primarily through the non-rational means described in an earlier chapter such as movies and lyrics of music.

Most Americans are not hard-core, self-conscious Subjectivists but rather hold these attitudes, values, and beliefs largely at a subliminal level. Therefore, in speaking of the bipolar approach to life described above, I am not suggesting that the majority of Americans are intentionally living for all the good feelings they can possibly derive from life and then consciously exercise the necessary discipline to earn enough resources to go on another subjectivist binge. Rather than being calculated, this approach to life takes form as a spontaneous response to subjectivist values and attitudes. Couples today don't opt to honeymoon in Paris or the islands instead of the Poconos or the Catskills as a result of rational analysis but because of cultural values.

That said, however, subjectivist culture nonetheless possesses a powerful grip on our society, resulting in decision-making being guided far more by feelings than by empirical data and reason. Our nation manifests a strong cultural tilt in that direction, ultimately making a huge difference in every aspect of our society from morality to the economy and everything in between.

Embracing Subjectivism

It is easy to see the attraction of Subjectivism. Our human tendency is to want to do our own thing, to pursue immediate gratification, to function as god. Therefore, Subjectivism constituted an offer that Americans, especially college students, simply could not refuse. As those students grew into adulthood, they carried the hippie culture with them. Hippies morphed into yuppies, carrying

Subjectivism from Haight-Ashbury and Woodstock to suburbia and boardrooms and ultimately to the White House, arriving with the presidency of Bill Clinton and coming to full expression with Barack Obama. Though Subjectivism has shed some of its external manifestations, its underlying concepts remain embedded in American psyches, values, and attitudes and have worked their way out in our behaviors.

One would think that as Baby Boomers became adults they would have become concerned that Subjectivism really does not work in the real world, that Mailer's leap into the dark does not provide a workable strategy for adult living, that ultimately doing one's own thing, doing what feels good, would produce disaster. They did not.

A major factor in dispelling these rational fears emerged in a psychological theory that seemed to provide assurance that Subjectivism does work in the real world. We will examine that theory in the next section.

SECTION THREE

PSYCHOLOGY OF SELFISHNES

Chapter 1

The Theory That Dominates America

Carl Rogers: Father of Psychological Subjectivism

Though, as we have seen, Subjectivism makes little sense in the real world, the theory of psychologist Carl Rogers provides it with academic credibility.

Rogers was born around the turn of the 20th century in a suburb of Chicago. After college, he attended Union Theological Seminary to train for a career in ministry but transferred to Columbia University where he earned a PhD in psychology. He taught at Ohio State, set up a counseling center at University of Chicago, taught at University of Wisconsin, and finally accepted a research position at a think tank in La Jolla, California, where he remained until his death in 1987.

Rogers' Personality Theory

Rogers' evolutionary perspective led him to the belief that all organisms, including human beings, possess what he referred to as a "self-actualizing tendency," a subjective mechanism that intuitively leads the individual to optimal development and behavior. Animals following their self-actualizing tendencies seem to be well-adjusted and live relatively stress-free. We don't find depressed or schizophrenic squirrels or armies of deer seeking to destroy one another. Rogers believed that humans fail to enjoy such tranquility and optimal functioning because they lack the freedom to follow their self-actualizing tendency.

The reason, Rogers postulated, is that individuals need acceptance by significant others such as parents, teachers, and friends. If that acceptance is granted conditionally ("I accept you *if* you act in a certain way"), then the person will be able to accept himself only if he meets those conditions of acceptance. Therefore, his behavior will be guided by a quest to meet those conditions rather than by his self-actualizing tendency. This pursuit will produce emotional, behavioral, and relational problems because it does not embody who he really is.

If, however, this person receives unconditional acceptance from significant others ("I accept you just as you are, without imposing my standards on you"), then he will be able to accept himself unconditionally, which will free him to follow the guidance of his self-actualizing tendency. This will lead him to become a fully-functioning person who will experience success.

This theory might be diagrammed as follows:

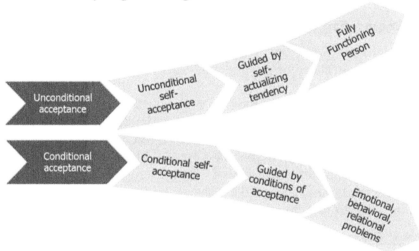

For example, a high school student may be academically inclined but not enjoy athletics. His father, who had a reputation as a great athlete at the local high school, conveys to his son that there is no need for him to emulate his father's athletic achievements. Rather, Dad is proud of him unconditionally, i.e., regardless of what direction he pursues. As a result, this young man is able to accept himself unconditionally, which frees him to follow his self-actualizing tendency to pursue academics. As a result, he is happy and successful and will develop into a well-adjusted person.

If instead this father conveys to his son that he will accept him only under the condition that he follows in his footsteps, excelling in athletics, this young man will be able to accept himself only by meeting this condition of acceptance. As a result, rather than following his self-actualizing tendency toward focusing on academics, he joins the football team, is miserable, and fails to do well. This misery and failure engender emotional struggles that lead to behavioral problems, which ultimately produce relational issues.

This illustration of Rogers' theory casts it in the most favorable light, making it seem valid because the son has productive aspirations. However, as we will discover, this theory has a dark side in that it requires a father to accept unconditionally not only a son with a preference for academics, but also one with inclinations to party and do drugs, asserting that if the father displays unconditional acceptance even in the face of these negative aspirations his son will develop wholesome desires. Later, we will explore whether this theory works.

At the heart of this theory we find two concepts: (1) the self-actualizing tendency that subjectively guides the individual to live optimally and (2) unconditional acceptance that frees the individual to follow the guidance of the self-actualizing tendency.

Unconditional acceptance serves as the change agent. Rogers believed that if all humans were accepted unconditionally, humanity would display the same tranquility and effective functioning found among squirrels and deer. We would be well-adjusted as individuals and form societies characterized by peace and productivity.

Rogers' Therapeutic Approach

In keeping with his theory, Rogers proposed that to help those struggling with emotional, behavioral, and relational problems the therapist must first develop a relationship with the client, thus becoming a significant other. From this platform, the therapist-as-significant-other conveys unconditional acceptance to the client. This is accomplished by the therapist guarding against interjecting his own values or opinions during therapy sessions, but instead communicating acceptance toward the client regardless of his behaviors or intentions, an approach labeled non-directive therapy.

Using this approach, the therapist enables the client to accept himself unconditionally, that is, to feel good about himself regardless of his intentions or behaviors. This frees the client to be guided by his self-actualizing tendency, which in turn will lead to the resolution of his problems and his development into a fully-functioning personality.

Conveyance of unconditional acceptance by the therapist is achieved in large measure by reflecting back to the client his own meaning and feelings. This approach lets the client know that he has been understood, which encourages the client to explore for himself a solution to his problem.

For example, if the client conveys that she is afraid of flunking out of school, the therapist might respond by saying, "So then, you are concerned that you may not do well academically." Note that this approach excludes any sort of rational discussion related to the client's problem such as, "Have you done poorly in times past?" "Have your teachers told you that you are flunking?" or "Why do you feel that you will not do well in your studies?" And it certainly omits questions that may suggest a judgment or accusation such as, "How much time do you spend studying?" or "Do you feel you are doing your best in preparing for your classes?"

The client, sensing unconditional acceptance and experiencing the resulting freedom to be guided by her self-actualizing tendency will explore her situation and discover her own solution. This student might conclude, "You know, I think I'm struggling because I really don't like this marketing major. I enrolled in it because my best friends did, and I thought it would be great to be in classes together with them. But as I have been freed to explore my feeling regarding this choice, the reality of actually working in this field is setting in, and I think I am better suited for being a teacher."

Rogers' therapeutic approach does not allow objective input since optimal guidance is believed to come only from the individual's self-actualizing tendency, and therefore no one else is capable of giving adequate direction. The only legitimate task of a therapist (or anyone else) is to provide an environment of unconditional acceptance that will set the person free to discover her own solution.

Likewise, parents, teachers, and others, rather than attempting to interact rationally and objectively regarding problems confronting children, students, and others, need to reflect unconditional acceptance in order to provide an environment in which their self-actualizing tendencies can lead them to resolve their own issues.

Applications

Rogers believed this theory works when applied to virtually every type of problem, including struggles with depression, anxiety, various types of behavioral issues, and relational problems. Consequently, it found application not only in psychotherapeutic settings but in the family, in education, and in other venues.

Rogers also envisioned that his theory would help even healthy people by maximizing their potential. For example, unconditional self-acceptance could give a major-league batter the confidence needed to increase his batting average. Therefore, it found application to everyone in all areas of life.

In addition to individual applications, Rogers believed his theory could help social groups and society as a whole. Whatever the problem, conditional acceptance represents the foundational cause and unconditional acceptance provides the remedy.

I will refer to this theory as Rogerianism.

Equating Acceptance and Love

Under the influence of Rogers' theory, our society has come to equate love and acceptance, or at least it views acceptance as being a necessary component of love. Loving someone entails accepting them. In discussing a client being loved in the context of a therapy session, Rogers states, "'Loved' has here perhaps its deepest and most general meaning—that of being deeply understood and deeply accepted."[48] Later he even more directly links acceptance and love in saying regarding this client, "Here she finds complete acceptance—or love, if you will...."[49]

As a result of Rogers' influence, to love means to accept. It may mean more, but it must include acceptance. This reality is seen even more clearly when viewed from the negative, that in today's society not to accept a person or his behavior is perceived to be unloving and even hateful.

This definition applies to unconditional love and unconditional acceptance. These terms have come to be reviewed as synonyms. Both terms are used frequently and seldom if ever do we find anyone differentiating between the two. To love unconditionally means to accept unconditionally and vice versa. As we will see later, the equating of these terms holds significant implications.

Reasons for the Dominance of Rogers' Theory

Writing in 1985, William Kirk Kilpatrick observed:

> "Carl Rogers is ... one of the most important social revolutionaries of our time. He is the father of the human potential movement and is arguably the world's most influential living psychologist."[50]

Rogers' theory has exercised dominant influence on American

society across the past half-century, not only in venues such as therapy and education but across the broader spectrum of society. Ultimately, unconditional acceptance has become the core concept of American culture.

Below are the various factors that helped catapult Rogerianism to this dominant status.

Compatibility with Subjectivism

Similarities

An analysis of Rogerianism reveals that it constitutes Subjectivism packaged in psychological language. Subjectivism calls us to do what feels good, i.e., to be guided by our subjective inclinations. Rogerianism likewise advocates guidance by the self-actualizing tendency, our subjective proclivities. Subjectivism asserts that the individual possesses the right to do his own thing. Rogerianism by accepting the individual unconditionally extends him the right to do his own thing. Unconditional acceptance removes all basis for objecting to any behavior, thus freeing the individual to live as he pleases. Likewise, Rogers' encouragement of unconditional *self-*acceptance enables the individual to give himself permission to do his own thing. He can feel good about himself regardless of how he lives.

Subjectivism believes that doing what feels good represents the natural human condition, and therefore giving individuals the right to do so will produce positive results. This belief was seen in Norman Mailer's assertion that humans given absolute autonomy will ultimately experience growth. Rogers' theory displays the same confidence, asserting that the self-actualizing tendency set free by unconditional acceptance will produce a positive outcome—a fully-functioning person.

As we have already emphasized, culture for most people represents truth. Since Rogers' theory was compatible with the culture of Subjectivism, in essence comprising a psychological expression of it, Americans embraced it as being valid. The inroads of Subjectivism prepared the American psyche to feel at home with Rogerianism.

The Major Difference

The major difference between Subjectivism and Rogerianism is found in Rogers' claim of scientific evidence that accepting a person unconditionally, allowing him to do his own thing, would yield productive results.

Hippies needed little encouragement to believe that they had a right to do their own thing, especially when that thing consisted of doing what feels good, so they were happy to accept by faith that good things would result, even in the face of a tsunami of empirical evidence pointing in the opposite direction. American adults bearing the responsibilities of grown-up life in the real world, however, were more hesitant to believe that a perpetual Woodstock would somehow be productive.

Rogers' theory provided Subjectivism with the promise of psychological validity. He asserted that research demonstrates that people accepted unconditionally, freed to do their own thing, will become psychologically healthy and productive. Therefore, giving the individual permission to do his own thing does not portend individual and societal meltdown but instead paves the way to optimal individual functioning and societal success. Americans did not have to take Mailer's leap of faith to embrace their new culture but instead could rely on the assertion of scientific research by a noted psychologist.

The synergy between Subjectivism and Rogers' theory resulted in the wide and profound acceptance of Rogerianism. The correspondence of their messages reinforced their influence, establishing them as foundational ideologies of American post-Christian culture.

Irresistible Appeal

Another very powerful factor that motivated Americans to embrace unconditional acceptance lay in its appeal. Subjectivism extended an offer to American society it could not refuse because of its legitimizing of self-gratification. Rogers actually improved on this offer by promising that doing one's own thing paves the path to individual and societal optimization.

How great it would be to wake up every morning knowing that I would be—or at least should be—accepted that day regardless of my attitudes, words, and actions. If others do not accept me unconditionally it is their problem and not mine. Equally as appealing is the promise that as I am accepted unconditionally, I will be able to accept myself unconditionally, resulting in my morphing into the optimal me. A chapter in what might be considered Rogers' major book, *On Becoming a Person*, is entitled "To Be That Self Which One Truly Is" identifies this promised outcome.[51]

Yet another aspect of the appeal of unconditional acceptance is freedom from blame and hence guilt. If I do develop problems or behave in ways some may consider inappropriate, it is not my fault. I would be my optimal self if people would accept me unconditionally. Therefore, others are to blame and not me.

Maybe the ultimate appeal of unconditional acceptance is that as with Subjectivism it designates the individual as god because being accepted unconditionally gives him ultimate authority and the resulting autonomy. It allows him to determine his own morality. Whatever his self-actualizing tendency leads him to do is the *right* thing to do. No one has any basis, and therefore any right, to say that what he is contemplating or doing is wrong. Only his self-actualizing tendency can know what is best for him. Consequently, he has total authority to follow its lead. He has absolute autonomy.

Human beings possess a perverse desire to assume the role of deity. It was, in fact, the original sin (Genesis 3). Unconditional acceptance not only places the individual in that role but also facilitates that craving with the promise that as he follows his self-actualizing tendency and does his own thing he will become a healthy, fully-functioning god.

All of these attractions of the Rogerian teaching on unconditional acceptance made it an irresistible offer. As a result, this concept was woven quickly into the very fabric of our post-Christian culture, becoming its central essence, not in an objective sense, but at an attitudinal level, driving American values and behaviors.

Self-Help

Rogerianism also gained nearly universal popularity because it could be utilized as a self-help tool. The Freudian approach to therapy could only be administered by a trained and very expensive psychiatrist, making the cure costly and time-consuming. Using the Rogerian approach, however, people could fix their problems and maximize their personalities merely by reading a book or attending a seminar and applying Rogers' principles. The old warning, "Don't try this at home," did not apply to Rogers' theory. Consequently, the market was soon flooded with self-help books and seminars offered by a variety of psychologists who presented the Rogerian approach each in his own distinctive way.[52]

The Solution to Almost Everything

Subjectivism did not promise to fix or improve anything, but seemed only to find application to love-ins and rock concerts, not especially productive activities. Therefore, this approach to life, though appealing, was not practical.

By way of contrast, Rogers' theory, as previously noted, presented itself as a system that would solve human problems of practically every kind and enhance human development. Later in life, Rogers traveled the globe seeking to apply his theory in the promotion of national and world peace.

Substitute for Christianity

Our previous Christian culture had already ensconced love as the ultimate virtue. Rogerian psychology, building on that cultural base, merely informed American society that the ultimate expression of love is unconditional acceptance.

Consequently, Americans felt comfortable with unconditional acceptance not only because of its correspondence to Subjectivism but also because of this link with our former Christian culture, making it appear to be the best of both of these cultural worlds.

This perceived relationship between unconditional acceptance and Christianity provided Rogerianism with the added benefit of a religious aura. For post-Christian Americans who may have been feeling the absence of a religious dimension in their lives, unconditional acceptance to some extent filled that void by allowing them to feel that they were still practicing Christianity, only without church and ritual. In fact, Rogerianism allowed them to feel that they are above all the trappings of institutional Christianity, instead focusing on love (unconditional acceptance), the heart of the matter. We find a large and growing contingent in our society today who see themselves as very spiritual despite their lack of connection with any church, or perhaps because of it.

An analysis of contemporary American society reveals that in many ways psychology has replaced Christianity by becoming a secular religion. Many roles previously assigned to a pastor or priest are now filled by the psychologist. Previously people took their problems to their pastors, whereas now they seek help from therapists. Conversely, many pastors now counsel and even preach in large measure from the perspective of psychology. Even when a person has lost a loved one, a scenario in which one might feel that psychology reaches its limitations, people today turn to it for grief therapy to help them through the various stages of grieving. Even the grief therapy groups hosted by churches predominantly approach the issue psychologically. Functioning as a secular religion has provided Rogerianism with even greater cultural power.

The Magnanimous Image of Unconditional Acceptance

Unconditional acceptance is also appealing because it gives the appearance of comprising the ultimate expression of agape. While failure to accept appears invariably to be unkind and even hateful, what could be more loving than accepting unconditionally? In fact, the term hateful is frequently leveled by the media and others at anyone who fails to accept unconditionally any person or behavior. Those objecting to homosexual marriage or those concerned over illegal immigration (i.e., not accepting illegal immigrants unconditionally) are frequently characterized as haters.

In the mind of the typical American, love and unconditional acceptance have become indistinguishable just as failure to accept has become synonymous with hate. Therefore, a person objecting to unconditional acceptance is perceived to be opposing love.

Unconditional Acceptance as Our Cultural Foundation

Since accepting unconditionally has come to be viewed as incontrovertibly beneficial and loving, and since failing to accept unconditionally is now considered to be undeniably harmful and hateful, Americans have concluded that it is always moral to accept unconditionally and always immoral not to accept unconditionally. Consequently, unconditional acceptance has become established as our only but sufficient cultural moral principle and core cultural value.

Because unconditional acceptance, the operative element of Rogerianism, promises to provide the solution to the broad range of human problems and to optimize the capacities of individuals and society as a whole, it soon became adopted not only as a psychological theory and our foundational moral principle but also as a way of life. With it life runs as it should. Without it, in a culture characterized by conditional acceptance, individuals and society will be broken. If we would all just learn to accept one another unconditionally, we would develop into healthy personalities and our society would become peaceful and productive.

Brendan Eich, the creator of the JavaScript programming language, worked at Mozilla for 15 years and was named CEO in 2014. It was discovered, however, that back in 2008 Eich had made a $1,000 contribution in support of Proposition 8 in California, which called for the confining of marriage to one man and one woman. Many in the company viewed Eich's contribution to this cause as a failure to accept gays, thus violating our culture's compelling moral principle of unconditional acceptance. This resulted in a movement within the company to have him removed as CEO. This pressure ultimately led to his resignation.[53]

One can hardly imagine a more tepid expression of non-acceptance than a $1,000 contribution made six years earlier toward a cause that did not condemn homosexuality per se but merely circumscribed the definition of marriage. Yet this transgression of our cultural moral code of unconditional acceptance was sufficiently egregious to force the outing of a CEO of a major company despite his very significant previous accomplishments and contributions to the company. This incident demonstrates graphically the power of unconditional acceptance as our society's dominant moral principle and core cultural value.

The ultimate indication that unconditional acceptance has become America's core cultural concept can be found in any attempt not to accept. Any hint of non-acceptance of any group on any basis is met with hostility. For example, the major concern following any incident of Islamic terrorism is that our society does not respond with non-acceptance of Muslims—"Islamophobia."

The one exception to our cultural mandate of unconditional acceptance is found in the non-acceptance of evangelical Christians and conservative Jews. Our society rejects these groups because it views biblical morality as an expression of non-acceptance. Therefore, those committed to biblical values are viewed as a societal cancer.

Identifying Our Post-Christian American Culture

Many scholars have correctly observed that we now live in a post-Christian America, indicating that the essence of our culture is no longer Christian but something else. That something else is Subjectivism, especially as expressed in Rogerianism, which within the last half century has gained dominance over our previous Christian culture.

This dominance shows itself in countless ways within our society. For example, our news and entertainment media produce content that predominantly reflects unconditional acceptance rather than Christian morality as its guiding principle. Nudity, profanity, fornication, adultery, and homosexuality are all accepted. A person who is unwilling to accept them unconditionally will quickly be shamed and silenced with such labels as judgmental, close-minded, bigoted, discriminatory, self-righteous, and the like. We find the same commitment to unconditional acceptance in government policy with the acceptance of abortion, illegal immigration, granting welfare benefits virtually unconditionally, and in numerous other policies and practices.

The embrace of unconditional acceptance by the secular world is perhaps most flagrantly displayed in the current insistence by the Left that transgender biological men should be permitted in the bathrooms and shower rooms of girls. It is not even enough to provide them with their own bathrooms and shower rooms because this may prevent them from feeling accepted by society in general and by the girls with whom they now identify. No other consideration, the safety of girls and women, their sense of modesty, fears they might experience, or other factors, must be allowed to supersede our society's foundational commitment to unconditional acceptance.

Though some exceptions to unconditional acceptance obviously exist, non-acceptance even of these remaining holdouts is being diminished with time. For example, even non-acceptance of a practice as repugnant as pedophilia is being eroded through means such as the lowering of the age of consent and assertions by some that sexual relations between adults and children are not harmful to children. In theory leftist American culture accepts everything unconditionally. Our practices continue to move toward that theoretical ideal.

The Compelling Question

America has embraced the concepts of Rogerianism as embodying a valid, research-supported understanding of the human personality and therefore as an effective approach to dealing with human problems and optimizing human potential. Beyond that, we have adopted Rogers' central principle of unconditional acceptance as our core moral concept, our basic societal value, and a way of life.

The question remains, though, whether Rogers was right regarding his theory and its scientific support. If so, by embracing

Rogers' theory and installing unconditional acceptance as our foundational moral principle our culture has taken a major step forward. If, however, Rogers' theoretical construct is not valid, Americans have made a serious mistake in embracing Rogerianism and the post-Christian culture based on it.

Next we will examine an experiment that provides compelling indicators regarding whether America has made the right choice.

Chapter 2

The Experiment

The Setting

There is good reason to believe that the best measure of the validity of Rogers' hypothesis is found in one of his major attempts to apply this theory on a large scale. In this chapter we will examine an experiment Rogers conducted in the context of a Catholic school system in California. This school system, operated by the Sisters of the Immaculate Heart of Mary (IHM), comprised 60 schools including a college. The order at the outset of the project was run by 560 nuns. Rogers appointed William Coulson, a colleague who worked very closely with him for many years, as project coordinator.

This experiment provided a good test of the effectiveness of Rogers' theory for a number of reasons. It came after Rogers' theory had opportunity to mature. The project began in 1966 when Rogers was about 64 years old, perhaps at the prime of his career. He had been doing therapy for about 35 years, had taught for 23 years, and five years earlier had published perhaps his most significant book, *On Becoming a Person: A Therapist's View of Psychotherapy*. By this time his ideas and skill in applying them were well seasoned.

This experiment also represented Rogers' theory well because it applied his ideas on a large scale and in various settings such as in groups, with individuals, and with an organization as a whole. If the experiment had comprised only a small study, one could conclude that some quirk might have influenced its outcome, but the magnitude of this effort provided a fair opportunity for the application of Rogers' theory.[54]

An additional reason this setting provided an optimal test of

Rogers' theory is that the Immaculate Heart of Mary school system was reputed as being one of the more liberal entities within the Roman Catholic Church, thus providing a more welcoming audience for Rogers' ideas. Beyond that, this experiment took place in Southern California in the late 1960s when Subjectivism was especially gaining momentum in that area of the country. This no doubt provided a hospitable environment for Rogers' ideas, giving them optimal opportunity to work.

This experiment also represents a good indicator of the effectiveness of Rogers' ideas because of the dramatic nature of the results. As you will see, the findings were *not* ambiguous.

Beginning in 1966 the Sisters of the Immaculate Heart of Mary (IHM) allowed Rogers, Coulson, and 58 facilitators to organize encounter groups within the school system.[55] Administrators, teachers, and students participated.

The function of these groups was to provide a non-threatening Rogerian environment of unconditional acceptance that would encourage the participants to be aware of and express their feelings, that is, to experience "non-directive self-exploration."[56] In a later publication, Rogers wrote of

> an exploration of increasingly strange and unknown and dangerous feelings in oneself, this exploration proving possible only because the individual gradually realizes that he is accepted unconditionally.[57]

The Results

The short-term results looked quite positive. Coulson recalled:

> Rogers and I did a tape for Bell and Howell [the project sponsors] summarizing that project; and I talked about some of the short-term effects and said that when people do what they deeply want to do, it isn't immoral.[58]

That is, as these people were freed by unconditional acceptance to be guided by their self-actualizing tendency, initial indications were that they behaved appropriately. Here it seems that we find the process described in an earlier chapter in which the euphoria of the honeymoon stage can produce spontaneous agape. As we noted in that discussion, this initial enthusiasm with its positive results tends only to be temporary.

Coulson later reflected, "we hadn't waited long enough."[59] Soon the picture changed dramatically. Coulson reported that within a year, 300 of the 560 nuns "were petitioning Rome to get out of their vows. They did not want to be under anyone's authority, except the authority of their imperial inner selves."[60]

Coulson cites "a tragic book called *Lesbian Nuns, Breaking Silence*, which documents part of our effect on the IHM and other orders that engaged in similar experiments...."[61] The book recounts lesbian activity among nuns resulting from the influence of these groups. Coulson reflects:

> An older nun in the group, "freeing herself to be more expressive of who she really was internally," decided that she wanted to make love with Sister Mary Benjamin. Well, Sister Mary Benjamin engaged in this; and then she was stricken with guilt, and wondered, to quote from the book, "Was I doing something wrong, was I doing something terrible? I talked to a priest—"[62] Coulson explained:
> Unfortunately, we had talked to him first. "I talked to the priest," she says, "who refused to pass judgment on my actions. He said it was up to me to decide if they were right or wrong. He opened a door, and I walked through the door, realizing I was on my own."[63]

Coulson also speaks of "seductions in psychotherapy, which became virtually routine in California,"[64] which Coulson attributed to the fact that "we had trained people who didn't have Rogers' innate discipline from his own fundamentalist Protestant background, people who thought that being themselves meant unleashing libido."[65]

Coulson cited a book entitled *Hollywood Priest*, which described how one of the nuns from the IHM order "got in the spirit of Rogerian non-directive encounter"[66] and propositioned a priest. Therapists were assigned to nuns who opened up too much in the encounter groups.[67] When the priest refused, the nun became sexually involved with her Rogerian therapist.

Coulson reported:

> He got her involved in sex games, in therapy. Rogers didn't get people involved in sex games, but he couldn't prevent his followers from doing it, because all he could say was, "Well, I don't do that." Then his followers would say, "Well, of course you don't do that, because you grew up in an earlier era; but we do, and it's marvelous; you have set us free

to be ourselves and not carbon copies of you."[68]

In other words, these therapists could assert the right given them by Rogers to be accepted unconditionally.

This development and Coulson's analysis of it are significant in that they demonstrate that unconditional acceptance really does grant autonomy to the individual, the right to do his thing whatever that may be. Here we find therapists' becoming sexually involved with clients who are nuns, a betrayal by these therapists of an institution to which they were invited as guests. In addition, in the practice of psychology, sexual involvement with a client is viewed to be unethical, sometimes leading to loss of licensure. Therefore, in addition to being promiscuous, this behavior comprised a serious breach of professional ethics. Despite the multiple ethical violations represented by this behavior, unconditional acceptance granted these therapists and nuns the moral right to participate in it since unconditional acceptance establishes itself as the only morality, eradicating all others.

The ultimate result of this project was the closing of all but one of the schools, including the college. Of the 560 nuns, Coulson estimated that there may have been only a few dozen remaining. Coulson recalled: "(We) called off the study after two years because we were alarmed about the results. We thought we could make the IHM better than they were; and we destroyed them."[69]

Rogers himself was troubled by the results. Coulson taped an interview with him in 1976 in which Rogers shared his feelings about the project:

> I left there feeling, Well, I started this . . . thing, and look where it's taking us; I don't even know where it's taking me. I don't have any idea what's going to happen next. And I woke up the next morning feeling so depressed that I could hardly stand it. And then I realized what was wrong. Yes, I started this thing, and now look where it's carrying us. Where is this going to carry us? And did I start something that is in some fundamental way mistaken and will lead us off into paths that we will regret?[70]

The cause of the upheaval at the Immaculate Heart of Mary school system has been discussed by various sources across the years. Coulson and others have noted that the work of Rogers' experiment did not serve as the only contributing factor to the disastrous outcome for the school system. For some time, a struggle had been brewing between the Order and the Archbishop, Cardinal McIntyre, the order pushing toward more liberal tendencies while Cardinal McIntyre was conservative in his views. In an article in the *Journal of the History of the Behavioral Sciences,* Robert Kugelmann places more responsibility for the destructives outcomes on those tensions than on the work of Rogers.[71]

Though Coulson recognized the other forces at work, he viewed the experiment as the prime contributor to the outcome. I believe his assessment to be correct for several reasons. The timing would suggest this. Though the tensions noted above had been brewing for a while, the explosion occurred contemporaneously with Rogers' experiment, which seemed to serve as a catalyst, inciting an anti-authoritarian attitude that escalated the conflict. In addition, Rogers' work produced other negative consequences for the school system such as major dissension between those favoring and those opposing the encounter groups, those pushing for more unstructured classes who were opposed by some teachers who believed that their lectures provided a more effective means of teaching,[72] and the moral problems mentioned above. It also seems that Coulson, a recognized professional who oversaw the project and who was himself a Catholic, was well positioned to make an accurate analysis. In addition, we might not expect that Coulson would assume responsibility for the calamitous results unless he had good reason to do so. Also, in Coulson's interview with Rogers cited above, Rogers reflects that it was the experiment that had produced the negative results. If any plausible reason existed for attributing those negative developments to some other cause, it is doubtful that Rogers would have assumed responsibility. The fact that Rogers called off the experiment because it was having a negative effect on the organization also indicates that it was largely responsible for these outcomes. Therefore, strong support exists for adopting Coulson's analysis cited above.

This was not the only project that misfired for Rogers. Coulson reported that five additional educational projects were unsuccessful.[73]

Apparently, even Rogers ultimately developed doubts about his theory. Toward the end of his life, speaking to the Association of Humanistic Psychology, Rogers lamented, "I hope Rogerian therapy goes down the drain ... Yes, you can try to grow to be more often empathic, and more often feel an unconditional regard for this person, but it is not something you should do."[74]

Rogers' hope that Rogerian therapy would go down the drain has gone unrealized. Rather, his ideas represent the most dominant force in contemporary American society.

In the next chapter we will examine the reasons for the devastating outcomes described above.

Chapter 3

The Major Miscalculation

What Should Have Happened

According to Rogers' theory, the environment of unconditional acceptance developed through his cadre at IHM should have served to liberate the self-actualizing tendencies of those within the school system to provide them with optimal guidance, enabling the participants to discard emotional, behavioral, and relational pathologies and to blossom into fully functioning personalities, developing good relationships and knitting themselves together into a caring, harmonious community.

Rules, conditions of acceptance, would no longer be needed. The giving of grades should not be necessary to motivate students to study. They would do so spontaneously. The school should have become a model for all of academia and for greater society. Even if these ideal results did not emerge fully, if Rogers' theory were accurate we would have anticipated significant progress in these directions. No doubt this was the outcome Rogers and Coulson anticipated.

Had Rogers achieved these results it would have comprised a breakthrough of monumental significance. Rogers would have proved unconditional acceptance to be the mechanism that freed human beings from emotional, behavioral, and relational struggles, possessing the power to catapult humanity to optimal functioning and to transform society.

These desired outcomes were not forthcoming, however, and instead Rogers' experiment produced the antithesis of his expected ideal results. Why? The answer resides in Rogers' erroneous conclusions regarding the two major components of his system. He mistakenly theorized that human beings are meant to be guided by a self-actualizing tendency, and consequently he erroneously concluded that unconditionally accepting individuals would release this self-actualizing tendency resulting in wholesome behavior and growth.

Human Beings and the Self-Actualizing Tendency

Rogers was right in his assumption that those in the experiment who received unconditional acceptance would experience freedom to display their subjective selves. Rogers was wrong, however, in his assessment of the nature of the subjective human component that would be released. He assumed that it would consist of a human self-actualizing tendency that would produce optimal human behavior.

The Humanistic Beliefs System

Those holding humanistic beliefs such as Rogers contend that at the core of the individual is a drive toward productive inclinations just waiting to emerge, but something is suppressing it. Thus, if we can only identify what is blocking the expression of this positive force and remove the barrier, this innate goodness will gush out, inundating the individual and society with goodness.

We observed Mailer's expression of this humanistic beliefs system in his assertion that authority represents the blockage to the release of human goodness, with the solution being total autonomy. Mailer provided no basis for this theory, and empirical evidence points in just the opposite direction.

It is important to underscore not only what the humanistic perspective includes, but also what it excludes. Built on an evolutionary perspective of the human being, it teaches that the human inclination toward goodness waiting to be unleashed is subjective in nature. Just as squirrels and deer are guided not by mind and volition but by instinctive inclinations, likewise humanists contend that humans as products of evolution possess a similar subjective capacity that will guide them toward optimal living.

Rogers' Version of the Humanistic Beliefs System

Rogers was convinced that conditional acceptance formed that barrier blocking the unleashing of human goodness and that unconditional acceptance would remove it. Note the similarity to

Mailer's ideology. He saw the remedy as autonomy and Rogers' identified it as unconditional acceptance, which in essence grants autonomy.

Unconditional acceptance did in fact release human subjective inclinations to express themselves. This release, however, revealed that the force waiting to be unleashed is not a self-actualizing tendency that would guide the individual toward optimal behavior but instead a depraved nature that inclines the individual toward selfishness and destructive behavior.

If any population might have displayed a positive outcome, we might have anticipated that it would have been those engaged in the IHM experiment. We have good reason to believe that going into this experiment the lives of the participating nuns manifested agape at a rather high level. They had chosen a profession that required them to set aside many of the aspects of life that humans tend to enjoy such as affluence, marriage, children, and freedom to live wherever and do whatever they chose. They occupied strategic positions in an educational institution, indicating that they possessed the skills to succeed in secular life had they chosen to do so. Instead, they had given up many of life's enjoyable prerogatives to serve God and others more fully. In other words, these nuns more than most were managing their lives to produce agape.

Therefore, we would expect that if any group were to display positive inclinations when freed by unconditional acceptance to do so, it would have been these agape-oriented nuns. When their natural inclinations were freed by unconditional acceptance to pursue their desires, however, even these nuns displayed not a self-actualizing tendency toward agape but a fallen nature inclined toward selfishness.

For example, the decisions to follow unbridled sexual inclinations provided no benefit to others but instead did them harm. Likewise, abandoning their orders, though freeing them to do their own thing, was harmful to the Roman Catholic Church, the school system, and ultimately the students.

These outcomes reveal that God has not designed humans to follow subjective instincts like animals. We have no self-actualizing tendency but only a fallen nature largely oriented toward selfishness. In creating human beings in His own image, God designed us to intentionally manage our lives to produce agape by employing our mind and will.

When this intentional management process is deactivated and human beings turn over the guidance of their lives to their subjective selves, the outcome is selfishness that produces chaos and disaster. When unleashed even in a community of nuns, human subjective inclinations produced a Woodstock without the music, a Summer of Love without the drugs, but enough promiscuous sex to compensate for them.

CHAPTER 4

The Implications of Unconditional Acceptance

To understand the dramatic outcome of Rogers' experiment, we must grasp the profound implications of unconditional acceptance, its operative principle. Once we recognize the breadth and depth of the influence of this concept, its overwhelmingly consequential nature, its power for destructiveness becomes obvious.

Unconditional Acceptance at Face Value

People seldom consider the actual meaning of the term unconditional acceptance, probably because superficially the term sounds harmless and magnanimous. Closer examination, however, exposes its malignant underside.

The term unconditional acceptance taken at face value means that the recipient can behave however he chooses without adverse attitudinal or behavioral response from others. It assigns him autonomy. It frees him to be guided solely by his subjective inclinations wherever they might lead.

Or, to state the case differently, in practical terms accepting unconditionally means that people other than the individual being accepted unconditionally do not matter, that his feelings are the only consideration. This takes us back to Subjectivism that views the experiencing individual as the only genuine person and therefore assigns that individual the role of god.

To accept an individual unconditionally in the real world populated by 7 billion people is to assign those other 6,999,999,999 people no value, to in essence relegate them to the status of non-persons. To accept the illegal immigrant unconditionally conveys that working Americans under the added tax burden of paying for his benefits do not matter, nor do American children exposed to diseases he may carry, nor do citizens vulnerable to higher crime levels. We also see this perspective at work in the insistence that a transgender biological male be allowed into girls' shower rooms. Only the feelings of the transgender biological male matter. In this issue they are non-persons with no rights.

Or to view unconditional acceptance from yet another perspective, it extends grace to the person being accepted unconditionally at the expense of morality. In the first section of this book, I showed that morality is the foundational expression of agape and that therefore showing grace at the expense of morality is itself immoral and unloving. This is in fact what unconditional acceptance does. It extends unrestricted grace to the individual being accepted unconditionally, even when he is acting immorally, thus eradicating the moral rights of all others.

Though at first blush these assertions might seem extreme, they represent the actual meaning of the term unconditional acceptance and its practical implications. If we genuinely accept a person unconditionally, and if words have meaning—and these words are not ambiguous, then these are their necessary implications.

THE NECESSITY OF TAKING UNCONDITIONAL ACCEPTANCE AT FACE VALUE

Advocates of unconditional acceptance might argue that this term is not meant to be taken at face value. This objection, however, faces serious problems.

- First, unconditional acceptance as described above is exactly what the term means, and therefore when we use the term that is precisely what we are conveying. Understanding it to mean something else requires that the person using it so indicates.

- This leads to the second concern in determining the meaning of unconditional acceptance. Seldom if ever do we find those employing this term putting qualifiers on it, for example saying, "We should accept individuals unconditionally as long as their actions do not hurt other people." Without such qualifiers we must take unconditional acceptance at face value.

- This practical need for qualifiers leads to a third problem. If we place qualifiers (conditions) on unconditional acceptance, it is no longer unconditional. We have contradicted the meaning of the term and therefore using it is erroneous and misleading. If we want to add qualifiers (conditions) we must stop speaking about unconditional acceptance and choose a different term.

- Its application within our society conveys that we are taking the term unconditional acceptance at face value. We have sanctioned murder in the form of abortion and have left the door open wide to euthanasia. We are sanctioning fornication with our acceptance of cohabitation. We now celebrate homosexuality. The use of recreational marijuana is now being legalized. Unconditional acceptance is also manifested in the growing approval of polyamory, defined as "consensual, ethical, and responsible non-monogamy."[75] Notice the term "ethical" in this definition. It is one thing to practice this behavior and yet another to categorize it as ethical. This description supports the assertion above that unconditional acceptance has in effect designated every behavior except non-acceptance as moral, thus eliminating morality as a category. The acceptance of these practices reveals that our society is applying the term unconditional acceptance at face value. This reality is also revealed in the hostility shown toward anyone who dares not accept these and other practices or who refers to any behavior as being immoral.

- The participants and staff in Rogers' experiment adopted a literal view of unconditional acceptance, not viewing any behavior as off-limits. This indicates that they intended the term be taken at face value. Therefore, those initiating and propagating this concept intended it to be taken literally.

As we noted above, the one exception to unconditional acceptance is found in the categorical rejection of those who do not accept unconditionally, a constituency consisting predominantly of Christians. Nonacceptance of this group is not seen as violating the cultural commitment to unconditional acceptance but rather as supporting it. In other words, America's new culture demands the eradication of our previous morality-affirming Christian culture and the condemnation and punishment of those who still embrace it.

Eradicating the Individual's Humanity

As with Subjectivism, the most profound evil of unconditional acceptance is that it deprives human beings of their humanity. To be human at its very root entails the capacity to make consequential choices, employing the person's mind to determine appropriate behaviors and his will to implement them. Asserting that a person's choices do not make him any more or less acceptable conveys that his choices are inconsequential and that he does not matter as a human being. If a person's choices and the resulting behaviors do not matter, his life has no significance. He is no longer a real human being. If character does not count, if a person is equally acceptable with or without it, no human essence remains. We have reduced humanity to an animal level. Humanistic psychology though claiming to rescue humanity from Materialism, is in its own way also destroying the human being.

This loss of humanity can lead to the sense that life does not matter, which creates an environment conducive to depression and suicide, both rampant in our society. If our attitudes and behaviors don't matter, why should we do the hard work of confronting life's challenges? Why not instead just live in the fantasy worlds of movies, video games, marijuana, and pornography? Or, why not just opt out altogether?

Some attempt to maintain a semblance of morality while embracing the concept of unconditional acceptance by accepting the person while rejecting his behavior. The next chapter discusses whether this approach works.

Chapter 5

Accepting the Person but Not His Behavior

Some people, recognizing the moral bankruptcy created by unconditional acceptance, have tried to salvage morality by employing the cliché, "I accept you but not your inappropriate behavior." In other words, if you display inappropriate behavior I will accept you at the feeling level, but I reserve the right to respond to you at the behavioral level with disapproval, discipline, or some other consequence. This perspective allows parents or other authority figures to deal with *behaviors* they deem to be harmful while still claiming to accept the *person* unconditionally. This solution does not work for several reasons.

Non-Rogerian

Accepting the person but not his behavior is problematic because it violates the theory. Rogers would view accepting the person but rejecting his behavior as a breach of unconditional acceptance, as being judgmental, as imposing our values and standards on the other person. We noted previously how Rogers was forced by his theory to accept the behaviors as well as the persons of therapists involved sexually with clients. He did not respond to the sexual promiscuity of these therapists by saying, "I think you are a fine person, but I condemn your behavior." Rather, his non-response to these unethical behaviors demonstrates that his theory requires the accepting of such behaviors as an aspect of accepting the person. Can you imagine a Rogerian therapist telling a client, "I want you to know that I accept you as a person, but the behaviors you have described and even the

133

ones you are displaying now are reprehensible"? That would never happen.

Therefore, though this cliché (I accept you but not your behavior) might offer a way to accept unconditionally while still maintaining a semblance of morality, it does not represent either the theory as prescribed nor the meaning of the term unconditional acceptance, which includes accepting persons and their behaviors.

The Impossibility of Separating the Person from His Behavior

An even more serious problem for this cliché is that accepting the person but not his behavior requires that persons and their behaviors can be separated. Concluding that the person is good even though his behavior is bad is asserting that no moral connection exists between persons and their behaviors. This position conflicts with Jesus' mandate that we should either make the tree good and the fruit good or the tree bad and the fruit bad. Jesus is in effect teaching that we cannot separate persons from their behaviors. This separation is not possible because a person's behavior flows from and reflects his character, the essence of who he is. Therefore, Jesus insists that we cannot separate them.

Jesus taught, "for out of the heart proceeds...." In other words, behaviors do not appear out of thin air. They are rooted in the heart, the character, the core of the personality. The heart and behavior are indissolubly integrated. Therefore, we must either accept persons and their behaviors or reject persons and their behaviors. We cannot find the behavior unacceptable while viewing the person as acceptable.

Eradicating the Significance of Character

If we accept the person of those living selfishly along with the person displaying a pattern of agape, this conveys that the self-sacrifice, responsibility, and discipline that persons of character exercise have no value. Or viewing the issue from the opposite perspective, the character of the selfish person is as acceptable as that of the person who consistently displays agape.

Imagine that parents have two sons. One studies hard and behaves well while the other is on drugs, disregards schoolwork, and engages in sexual promiscuity. These parents, steeped in our culture's guiding moral principle of unconditional acceptance assert that the person, the character, of both of their sons is equally acceptable. Rejecting a relationship between character and behavior communicates to the son who has paid the price of hard work and discipline that these self-sacrificing efforts are valueless in the ultimate sense. This devaluing of character has led to a scarcity of this valuable commodity in American society.

Undermining Discipline

Another problem with this cliché is that it undermines the exercise of discipline by those in authority. We discipline persons—not behaviors. If we accept the person, there is no basis for disciplining him. Saying, "I want you to understand that I am not disciplining you; I am disciplining your inappropriate behavior," obviously makes no sense. It is impossible to discipline behaviors; we can only discipline persons. Therefore, accepting persons while disapproving of behaviors removes any rational basis for discipline. "You don't have to go to your room for timeout, just your behaviors have to go."

Though parents and others probably do not go through these theoretical gymnastics in considering whether to discipline, nonetheless they intuitively sense that accepting the person leaves no legitimate basis for disciplining him, even though they may disapprove of his behavior.

In summary, accepting the person but not his behavior fails to resolve the moral dilemma and practical problems created by unconditional acceptance. Even though we may attempt to make such a distinction, in the end unconditional acceptance requires that we accept both the person and his behavior. Therefore, this tidy cliché resolves nothing. Rather, it is dangerous because it leaves the impression of resolving the moral dilemma embedded in unconditional acceptance when in reality it does not.

In addition to the negative outcomes of unconditional acceptance already described, the chapter ahead reveals its disastrous impact on relationships.

Chapter 6

Destroying Relationships

Relationships Require Conditions

As a result of Rogers' theory, a popular contemporary teaching is that the ultimate relationship consists of people who accept each other unconditionally. The optimal marriage is viewed to be one in which a husband and wife extend to each other unconditional acceptance. The theory asserts that all relationships, and society as a collage of relationships, would experience growth, effective functioning, and fulfillment under this arrangement.

In reality the opposite is true. Conditions comprise an essential ingredient for all relationships, providing them with meaning, structure, and the basis for functioning.

For example, conditions such as a lifelong commitment, displaying love, living together, and sexual exclusivity supply marriage with its meaning. If spouses were free to have sexual relations with whomever they chose, marriage would lose its distinctiveness. If a spouse could live wherever he or she chose, a marriage would lose its structure and capacity to function. Whatever we might call the resulting relationship, it would not comprise marriage as we know it. Note how our societal adoption of unconditional acceptance that strips relationships of conditions allowed the Supreme Court to easily redefine marriage to what it wanted it to be.

This need for conditions to sustain relationships applies to every relationship: employer and employee, the citizen and those who govern, friendships, neighbors, extended family, etc. Each type of relationship has its own unique set of conditions.

Conditions are also necessary to stipulate the boundaries of a relationship, what it does *not* include. For example, a business relationship does not include the right to intimacy. One neighbor has no right to trespass on the property of another without permission. Much emphasis has been placed on boundaries in recent years. People are discovering that relationships without conditions are not working and in response are establishing boundaries, another name for conditions, for the most part being unaware that they are promoting conditional acceptance.

In essence, conditions when well-conceived, merely define agape for a given relationship, that is, they describe how best to benefit the other person in that particular type of relationship. When reasonable and fair conditions are established and met, relationships are well-ordered and fulfill their intended purpose. This results in participants receiving substantial benefit. Without them chaos reigns, people are hurt, and the relationship disintegrates

This is especially true since, as we learned from Rogers' experiment, people freed by the elimination of conditions to follow their desires tend to behave selfishly. We see, then, that conditions related to relationships prevent selfishness and promote agape whereas a relationship characterized by unconditional acceptance produces selfishness, which leads to its breakdown.

In a marriage counseling session, a wife complained that her husband was acting in an inconsiderate way, constantly making messes in the house and not cleaning them up. He responded with, "Aren't you supposed to accept me unconditionally?" Unconditional acceptance liberated him to act selfishly, resulting in an increased burden for his wife and relational strife.

The Need for Non-Acceptance in Relationships

Unconditional acceptance prohibits all expressions of non-acceptance. This includes any attitudinal, verbal, or behavioral expression of disapproval, and any sort of disciplinary action. This, in turn, exposes the person granting unconditional acceptance to hurtful behavior without any recourse. A wife who feels her husband is being verbally abusive is prohibited by unconditional acceptance from saying so. A husband who
feels that his wife is developing a relationship with another man that is getting too personal must not express his concerns. This arrangement, of course, is unworkable.

Unconditional acceptance does not serve well the person being accepted, either. All of us need honest input from others, especially when we are headed in the wrong direction. Sometimes we do not realize we are coming across in an irritating manner or developing a potentially hurtful pattern of behavior. A great blessing of friends comes in the form of gracious but critical warnings. "I notice that you are drinking more than usual lately. I am concerned that you might be developing a problem." "I have noticed that your relationship with Joe has become a lot friendlier. I'm concerned for you and also for your husband and children. Do you think you might need to set some boundaries?"

Disallowing such crucial input robs us of a valuable resource. We read in the book of Proverbs, "Open rebuke is better than love carefully concealed. Faithful are the wounds of a friend, but the kisses of an enemy are deceitful" (Proverbs 27:5-6 NKJV). Of course, non-acceptance can be conveyed in hurtful ways, but when the objective and approach have the other person's best interests in view, conveyance of non-acceptance can constitute one of the most profound expressions of agape.

Results of Relationships Without Conditions

Relationships only provide genuine meaning, possess necessary structure, and function effectively when related conditions are acknowledged and maintained. In a society whose core cultural value is unconditional acceptance, we would anticipate relational disintegration, and that is precisely what we are witnessing in every segment of contemporary American society.

Marriages are disintegrating. Not only is the divorce rate astronomically high, but cohabitation, opting out of the more demanding but more rewarding conditions related to marriage, is increasing. Cohabitation seems to have become the relationship of choice because the prevailing cultural concept of unconditional acceptance does not support a viable marriage relationship. Therefore, many couples today are choosing a type of relationship that requires far less commitment but also offers far less agape and fulfillment.

Without conditions to govern the interaction between children and parents, these relationships are strained at best, resulting in less agape flowing in both directions. This has resulted in couples opting for fewer children or none at all.

Schools are functioning poorly. Educators look every which way for the cause and solution. Establishing traditional student/teacher relational conditions would go a long way to restoring American educational proficiency. But as noted earlier, in seeking solutions we tend never to consider our culture as the problem.

Role-Reversal

In addition to the reasons cited above, the theory of unconditional acceptance breaks down because accepting unconditionally is seldom something humans want to do. A husband who is happy to have his wife accept him even when he is cranky and unreasonable nevertheless prefers to reserve the right to object when *she* is cranky and unreasonable.

Therefore, this preference toward being accepted unconditionally as opposed to granting unconditional acceptance requires that society designates who is responsible for giving the unconditional acceptance and who is assigned to receive it.

Those historically in positions of authority are expected to do the unconditional accepting, while those historically under authority are selected to receive unconditional acceptance. Parents, teachers, therapists, and the like are expected to accept unconditionally whereas children, students, and clients get to receive unconditional acceptance. Note that since we tend not to enjoy doing the accepting, those called to accept unconditionally get paid to do so except for parents. That would explain why parents, who are not getting paid to accept their children unconditionally, are having fewer of them.

Extending unconditional acceptance to persons grants them the right to do their own thing with impunity, which in effect places them in charge of the relationship. Children accepted unconditionally are positioned to run the household, and many do. Unconditionally accepted students control the classroom. Various educational experts view this arrangement as positive, believing that optimal education will result when students guide the education process. The results do not validate this theory.

This arrangement leaves those previously in authority under authority. If a teacher must accept a student unconditionally, that student in effect wields control over the teacher. He can function as he pleases in the classroom, and the teacher has no option but to go along with it.

Therefore, the ultimate outcome of this arrangement is role-reversal. Those previously in authority are now under authority and vice versa. Children are empowered to determine their behaviors while parents are responsible for providing support. Likewise with other relationships.

Experience tells us that this role-reversal does not work. Children are not qualified to advise parents on how they should be raised, nor do students have the knowledge or wisdom to guide teachers in the educational process.

Even worse, this role-reversal grants authority to children, students, and others without assigning them commensurate responsibility. Instead, the responsibility is still placed on the shoulders of those previously in authority, even though they no longer have the authority necessary to meet that responsibility. When the home or educational system begins to fail, no one blames the children or students who are now in authority. Instead, society continues to hold parents and teachers responsible despite the fact that they have been stripped of their authority. In many businesses, especially those considered to be forward thinking, if an employee fails to perform well the supervisor is held accountable.

The resulting arrangement is untenable. Relationships can work only when authority and responsibility correspond. A person given authority without being assigned the commensurate responsibility can abuse that authority and usually does since he is not held accountable. Under this arrangement selfish inclinations tend to kick in, resulting in counterproductive behaviors.

Likewise, assigning responsibility without commensurate authority results in frustration and failure. A teacher recently told me that under Common Core she is held responsible for her students' school attendance, a factor over which she has no authority or control. Their failure to show up results in a reduction in her pay.

Therefore, role reversal introduces a totally unworkable relational structure on several counts and is creating havoc in American homes, schools, and other venues.

Sociopathic Society

The Rogerian teaching on unconditional acceptance produces an even more sinister and devastating by-product. According to Rogers, the purpose of unconditional acceptance is to engender unconditional *self*-acceptance, which will free the self-actualizing tendency to guide the individual.

From all indications, the unconditionally accepted person does develop unconditional self-acceptance. However, this unconditional self-acceptance does not produce the positive outcome anticipated by Rogers but instead promotes a destructive psychological condition.

Deactivation of the Conscience

Unconditional self-acceptance by its very definition involves the deactivation of the conscience. If I can feel good about me regardless of how I live, that means my conscience has no basis for engendering guilt feelings regardless of my behavior. Therefore, in effect unconditional acceptance deactivates the conscience.

Guilt can be a problem when it is invalid or when a person does not deal with it appropriately. However, the conscience and the valid guilt it produces represent gifts from God, an element of the personality we desperately need to keep us functioning humanely.

Some may assert that morality and kindness should be motivated by agape rather than guilt. I agree with the "should be" part of this assertion. That would be the result if we were ideal human beings living in an ideal world. We must, however, deal with the world we live in and ourselves as we are. None of us do all the right things solely out of love. Most individuals, men especially, have to admit that when they drive the speed limit this behavior does not result from altruism but rather from a desire to avoid blue lights flashing in their rearview mirror.

Though a conscience producing guilt may not be the optimal motivation, we and others are better off if we do the right thing out of guilt in response to the work of our conscience than if we choose harmful behaviors. Ask yourself this question: Would I rather have a person not steal from me out of guilt or steal from me? Therefore, the conscience and the guilt it produces play a major role in maintaining a decent society. Imagine a society where no one felt guilty about anything. It would quickly disintegrate into a nihilistic world of chaos and cruelty.

Influencing Society toward Sociopathology

The downplay of guilt in our society resulting from the promotion of unconditional self-acceptance has inclined us toward becoming a sociopathic society.

A major characteristic of a sociopath, a person manifesting antisocial personality disorder, is a non-functioning conscience, the inclination not to feel guilt, even when committing acts that harm others. One definition of sociopathology and psychopathology describes these personality disorders as follows:

> Both psychopaths and sociopaths lack a moral compass. They are generally incapable of sympathizing with the feelings of others, and lack the set of ethics that tend to keep society from dissolving into a chaotic mess where everyone only looks out for themselves.[76]

Unfortunately, we see our society trending toward this description under the influence of unconditional self-acceptance.

The terms psychopath and sociopath are often viewed as interchangeable. The fifth edition of the Diagnostic and Statistical Manual of Mental Disorders (DSM-5), released by the American Psychiatric Association in 2013, lists both sociopathy and psychopathy under the heading of Antisocial Personality Disorders (ASPD).[77]

The distinction between the two disorders makes sociopath a more appropriate diagnosis for our society. Both display the absence of normal guilt feelings, but the psychopath is considered to be inclined in this direction by nature while the sociopath has developed this personality trait under the influence of his environment, e.g., permissive parents.[78]

By disengaging the conscience, unconditional self-acceptance is promoting sociopathic tendencies in both individuals and our nation as a whole. Under its influence our entire culture functions as a permissive parent by accepting unconditionally, thus breeding unconditional self-acceptance leading to the deactivation of the individual and societal conscience. This in turn generates sociopathic personality tendencies within individuals and in society as a whole.

This sociopathic orientation is reinforced by Subjectivism, which grants the individual the right to do his own thing, which also eliminates any basis for guilt feelings. This doubling down on the anti-guilt message by Subjectivism and Rogerianism is desensitizing the American conscience to dangerous levels.

I am not suggesting that every American is a certifiable sociopath. I am asserting, however, that as parents seek to accept their children unconditionally, as teachers do likewise with their students, as therapists encourage clients toward unconditional self-acceptance, as many government policies reflect unconditional acceptance, as the news and entertainment industries convey the right of the individual to be accepted unconditionally, people are internalizing this message and accepting themselves unconditionally, which in turn has a blunting effect on the conscience, making it easier for people to function without guilt.

Those who enjoy a strong Christian background or who by nature are more morally sensitive stand a better chance of maintaining an intact conscience. Under the influences described above, however, most in our society will experience a tilt toward sociopathology to some degree, which will influence their attitudes and behaviors. Individuals especially susceptible to this orientation will be at greater risk of expressing sociopathic behaviors. Although every society includes people with sociopathic inclinations, the promotion of unconditional self-acceptance has increased the prevalence and intensity of this inclination in our society to unsustainable levels.

This blunting of our societal conscience manifests itself in the widespread acceptance of the practice of abortion, in the physicians and other healthcare providers willing to commit these atrocities, and in organizations such as Planned Parenthood that make a business of providing and promoting it.

The deactivation of the conscience is also on display in the seeming utter disregard for truth-telling among politicians. Dishonesty has always characterized politics to some degree, but in our current society lying has become breathtakingly blatant. The same absence of conscience is reflected in politicians who spend taxpayers' money with abandon, displaying no guilt over the economic destruction they are inflicting on our nation or the tax burden they are laying on the shoulders of hardworking Americans and future generations. We observe this same absence of conscience in the prevalence within our society of those engaging in extramarital affairs that devastate spouses and children and lead to divorce.

The more virulent strains of sociopathology show themselves in school shootings, workplace violence, and mass murders that have proliferated in contemporary America. Drive-by shootings and the more recent trend of "knockout games," the random beating and sometimes killing of strangers, also reveal the depths of our societal sociopathology.

Though these more attention-grabbing examples of sociopathology tend to make headlines, perhaps its lower profile but more pervasive manifestations such as dishonesty and irresponsibility do greater overall harm. Like a low-grade fever, the proliferation of this type of behavior occasioned by a diminished functioning of the conscience, results ultimately in the moral degeneration of our nation to a Third World level.

Of all the ways in which unconditional acceptance exterminates agape in our culture, its promotion of sociopathology represents the most lethal. To unleash selfishness is bad enough, but to extinguish the conscience so that selfishness is on the loose without natural human feelings of empathy or guilt is cruel, heartless, and terrifying.

Survival through Bipolar Living

As with Subjectivism, in its embrace of unconditional acceptance American society avoids total meltdown by means of a bipolar approach to life, unleashing the mania produced by unconditional acceptance to whatever degree possible while applying restrictions on immorality when absolutely necessary. In spheres of society such as business, medicine, law enforcement, and athletics, where people see and feel the effects of the outcomes more immediately, conditions are attached to acceptance. Have you ever seen an unconditionally accepting football fan? In areas such as education and government where the results are less obvious, the effects take longer to develop, and accountability is not as readily applied, mania enjoys more latitude.

Our society continues to move toward more unconditionally accepting mania with each passing day, resulting in the increased unraveling of our societal structure and depletion of our resources. At some point we will have lived in the manic phase so long, and depleted our resources to such an extent, that a return to reality will come too late to bail us out.

The chapter ahead identifies how far we have already gone down that road.

CHAPTER 7

THE LARGER EXPERIMENT

Society in Crisis

One day while scanning stations on my car radio, I stumbled across a talk show hosted by a therapist just as a woman named Nancy was sharing her story. "I am divorced and live with my children and a boyfriend, Bill. I just discovered that Bill had molested the children of his previous wife. Now I am worried about the safety of my children. To make matters worse, I am pregnant. What should I do?" As I listened, I felt tears welling up in my eyes, not only for Nancy and her children, but also for the countless other callers with equally troubling stories, and for our nation as a whole, which might be viewed as a composite caller being devastated by the emotional, behavioral, and relational chaos produced by post-Christian culture.

Around the 1990s Americans began to wake up to the depth and permanence of our societal downturn, coming to grips with the reality that our society had made the transition to a post-Christian culture with its corresponding new foundational concepts and related behavioral patterns. It dawned on them that this change did not represent a passing fad but instead comprised the new normal.

Though the hippie movement barely spanned a half decade, its philosophical orientation had taken root, being supported, perpetuated, and applied by means of Rogerian psychology. Although during the 1990s the old Christian culture still had a pulse, it became evident that it was on life support, while the new culture displayed the vigor of youth, continuing to gain power and territory. The Reagan era was over and Bill Clinton, a poster child of Subjectivism and Rogerianism, occupied the White House. Little doubt remained that

147

the new culture had triumphed and would only become more dominant.

It also was becoming apparent by the 1990s that this new culture did not comprise merely a new cerebral orientation but carried with it new behavioral patterns, many of which were troubling. Consequently, that era brought a rash of books describing the negative impact of this new American cultural ideal. The list below, sorted by date, includes just a few of them:

- Allan Bloom: The Closing of the American Mind (1987)

- David Barton: America: To Pray or Not to Pray? (1988)

- James Davison Hunter:

- Culture Wars: The Struggle to Define America (1991)

- The Death of Character: Moral Education in an Age without Good or Evil (2000)

- William J. Bennett:

- The De-Valuing of America: The Fight for Our Culture and Our Children (1992) o The Index of Leading Cultural Indicators: Facts and Figures on the State of American Society (1994)

- The Death of Outrage: Bill Clinton and the Assault on American Ideals (1998)

- Myron Magnet: The Dream and the Nightmare: the 60s Legacy to the Underclass (1993)

- Gertrude Himmelfarb: The De-Moralization of Society: From Victorian Virtues to Modern Values (1994)

- Robert H. Bork: Slouching Towards Gomorrah: Modern Liberalism and American Decline (1996)

- Barbara Defoe Whitehead: *The Divorce Culture* (1996)

These resources and many others graphically portrayed our societal decline, much of which resided in the area of morality but whose impact was much broader, affecting virtually every aspect of our national life including but not limited to emotional and physical health, government, the economy, education, and the family.

Bert M. Farias succinctly describes the devastating decline of our society since the 1960s as follows:

The divorce rate has doubled, teen suicide has tripled, reported violent crime has quadrupled, the prison population has quintupled, the percentage of babies born out of wedlock has risen sixfold, couples living together out of wedlock have increased sevenfold....

There has never been a society in the history of mankind whose moral values have deteriorated so dramatically, in such a short period of time, as those of Americans in the last 50 years.79

Though these numbers do not include the catastrophic decline of our economy, our educational system, and other dimensions of our society, they tell us that in a few short decades America has experienced an overwhelmingly steep downturn in virtually all areas of life, especially those related to morality. Most arresting is Farias' concluding claim that our society has fallen farther, faster than any society in all human history.

This decline did not just occur on its own. These numbers do not represent normal wear and tear. We have argued in this book that the replacement of Christian culture with Subjectivism and Rogerianism has produced this outcome. Ultimately agape deprivation—the cultural promotion of selfishness rather than love promoted by these cultural forces— is the underlying disease causing each of the symptoms listed above.

Linking Societal Decline with Subjectivism and Rogerianism

Some may ask why we should attribute the indications of societal decline listed above to Subjectivism, Rogerianism, and the resulting core cultural concept of unconditional acceptance. Several factors connect these negative developments with post-Christian culture.

Already mentioned are the distinct parallels between the outcome of Rogers' experiment described above and the developments in our society.

Another obvious link is the timing. This decay started to set in at the time when Subjectivism, Rogerian psychology, and the resulting commitment to unconditional acceptance began to assume a dominant role in our society.

In addition to this time link, a rational link ties this cultural decay to unconditional acceptance. If we sanction promiscuous sexual behavior through unconditional acceptance, we should anticipate more illegitimacy and divorce. If we display acceptance toward poor work in the classroom, declining educational outcomes should not surprise us. Accepting cohabitation would lead to its rise. Therefore, since these results occurred specifically at the time when unconditional acceptance gained prominence, it is only reasonable to attribute these outcomes to its influence.

We have also recognized that conditions are necessary for the health and survival of relationships. Therefore, the application of unconditional acceptance to relationships must bear responsibility for relational decline.

The bottom line is that it makes all the sense in the world to conclude that the abandonment of our Christian culture and its replacement with a culture comprised of Subjectivism and Rogerianism are responsible for these dominant behavioral trends in our society. Ideas have consequences.

America Today

Between Two Cultures

Though the American culture shift toward Subjectivism began in the 1960s, it required several decades to transform American society. As we noted above, it was not until the 1990s that many in our nation realized that we had adopted a new normal that was identifying who we are as a nation.

This cultural orientation had not been evenly applied across the nation. Those in the heartland had not become indoctrinated to the same degree as those in the Northeast and the West Coast. Those who had attended college received a strong dose there, and especially those in the softer disciplines that constitute the natural habitat of Subjectivism. Those with a more liberal bent soaked it up like a sponge, while conservatives were more resistant.

Nor has the advance of Subjectivism been uniform. The Reagan years especially brought back a semblance of our previous Christian culture with its responsibility and decency. Reagan's legacy continued to linger during the presidency of George H. W. Bush, keeping alive for another four years the fading embers of our previous culture. Those who were 15 years old in 1992, President George Bush's last year in office, are only 39 today. Therefore, a large segment of our society still has some recollections of the previous culturally Christian America.

A major contingent in our nation finds themselves drawn to that traditional America with its morality, stability, decency, and strength.

They are also attracted by the order and success it engendered. They recognize that America is currently on a path to chaos and destruction, and they desperately want to see our nation reverse course.

On the other side, we find the Left, which controls the news, social, and entertainment media, our educational system, much of the judiciary, and the deep state, imposing its agenda of fundamentally transforming America. They employ their power to impose that transformation on the American people.

The fact that a majority of Americans have not bought into the agenda of the Left manifests itself in the fact that in almost every case where Americans have had the opportunity to vote on traditional marriage, it has prevailed.

Nonetheless, conservative Americans are being oppressed by government and other instruments of the Left. The power of the Left is substantially enhanced by the willingness of the Republican Congress to do its bidding. This leaves the conservative American majority, those who pay our nation's bills and make our nation work, without representation and under domination of the Left.

The result is an America divided, the Left imposing its will, while conservatives are seeking to fight back but not knowing how.

The Trump Effect

Many political observers have been mystified by the rise of Donald Trump. However, the situation just described explains his popularity. Those Americans desiring to see the subjectivist agenda stopped and a return to a common sense approach to governing find themselves without representation. They believe that he will represent their cause.

Trump inspires this confidence because in large measure he has not been shaped by Subjectivism. He was not raised in a feel-good environment. His father, who was a hard-nosed businessman, had a major influence on his life. In *The Art of the Deal* Trump reflects, "I learned a lot from him. I learned about toughness in a very tough business, I learned about motivating people, and I learned about competence and efficiency: get in, get it done, get it done right, and get out."[80] Beginning with eighth-grade, Trump's father sent him to New York Military Academy. Regarding that experience, Trump recalls, "I stayed through my senior year, and along the way I learned a lot about discipline, and about channeling my aggression into achievement. In my senior year I was appointed a captain of the cadets."[81] Therefore, Trump grew up in a very non-subjectivist environment in which he was confronted with reality, a world demanding the employment of discipline in the exercise of mind and will rather than floating downstream under the impetus of feelings. The demands of the business world have also required that he stay grounded in the realm of reality.

It is this orientation that he promised to bring to government, rather than the political correctness of the political class spawned by Subjectivism and Rogerianism that is ruining our nation. Though his supporters may not be able to identify the basis for their confidence as we have just defined it, they nonetheless sense that Trump's approach is rooted in reality as compared with the subjectivist agenda of the Left. They are drawn to this substance as a source of stability in the midst of the culture of quicksand that surrounds them.

Trump offers hope of restoring reality to the governmental scene with the prospect of addressing the illegal immigration problem, reduction of burdensome regulations, creating economic stability, returning strength to the military, quelling global unrest, and confronting other problems facing our nation.

The Missing Ingredient

Trump may win the presidency and achieve all those goals and more. However, neither he nor any president can restore the Christian culture essential to the rise of America to its former greatness. I asserted at the outset of this book that America's external problems are merely symptoms of its internal ones. Even if a Trump administration would achieve all of the objectives listed above, which would represent a vast array of accomplishments, without the restoration of America's moral underpinning through the reinstatement of our Christian culture, such achievements would be superficial and ephemeral.

Our Last Best Hope

The only solution to our societal decline resides in the evangelical church in America engaging in the culture war, defeating the Left, and reestablishing spiritual and moral substance within our culture. Since the ultimate objective must be the reestablishment of Christian culture, the evangelical church constitutes the only entity in our society capable of achieving that objective.

A concern of this books is that the belief system of the evangelical church in America has been infiltrated by secular culture, which has weakened it to the extent that it is incapable of engaging effectively in the culture war. This is the reason it is currently losing the culture war and the reason that it will fail in the future. Only as it purges itself of secular cultural influence can it be restored to health and possess the vitality to do battle effectively with the Left.

The sections ahead identify how the American evangelical church has been infiltrated, provide a prescription for restoring its strength, and offer a strategy for a counteroffensive that will defeat the Left and make America great again.

SECTION FOUR

EVANGELICAL INFILTRATION

Chapter 1

Symptoms of Infiltration

America can be saved from disaster and restored to its former greatness only through replacement of its current destructive culture just described with its previous Christian culture. This task can be accomplished only by those who are committed to Christ and actively seeking to follow His Word. In the United States today those who meet that description are found not exclusively but predominantly in the evangelical church, those denominations and churches committed to the authority of Scripture and salvation through Christ by faith. In the chapters ahead, references to the church will have the evangelical church in view unless otherwise noted.

The Contemporary Evangelical Church

Not only has secular society changed since the 1960s, but so also has the evangelical church. I refer to this version of American evangelicalism that emerged beginning in the 1960s simply as the contemporary evangelical church.

We can observe this evangelical culture shift in external changes that manifest themselves in most evangelical churches. Guitars and drums have replaced the organ and piano. The music portion of the service, now called worship, is for the most part grouped into one segment of the service during which worshippers stand. Hymns have been replaced by praise music, hymnals by lyrics projected on a screen, and chairs have replaced pews.

It is challenging to speak of trends within the evangelical community because it is comprised of a largely disconnected and variegated group of individuals, churches, and other organizations. Even many evangelical churches belonging to denominations assert their independence, some eliminating the name of the denomination from their church designation. Therefore, the trends described above do not manifest themselves uniformly across the contemporary evangelical church. A very small contingent of evangelicals has resisted these inclinations altogether, others blend the more traditional and contemporary, while most fully embrace these developments.

These external manifestations of the contemporary evangelical church are not the concern of this book except to note that the timing of their appearance and various of their characteristics reveal the influence of Subjectivism. This influence can be seen, for example, in trends such as a more casual atmosphere and the music style, which can be traced to the influence of the Jesus People, a movement that grew out of the hippie culture.

Less obvious but more significant are changes in attitudes, values, and beliefs of contemporary evangelicals. Above I noted the evident connection between external evangelical changes and Subjectivism merely to make the point that just as secular trends influenced the externals of the contemporary evangelical church, they also left their mark on the internal aspects of contemporary evangelical culture.

In response to my mention of changes in evangelical beliefs, some might contend, accurately, that the doctrinal statements of evangelical churches have not changed. Doctrinal statements, however, only address a handful of beliefs. Many important biblical concepts are not included in doctrinal statements, ones that can exercise a vast impact on the life and well-being of the church and its people.

It is the assertion of this book that although for the most part evangelical churches have not altered their doctrinal statements, crucial elements of the belief system of the contemporary evangelical church in America have changed significantly across the past half-century, reflecting the influence of Subjectivism and Rogerianism. The chapters ahead identify and evaluate this secular influence.

Just as the external influences of Subjectivism and Rogerianism manifest themselves in varying degrees among contemporary evangelicals, the same is true of its influences on evangelical beliefs. A small contingent of evangelicals have resisted these influences and others have adopted them in varying degrees. However, the mainstream has embraced them fully. Therefore, it is valid to speak of distinct trends related to the beliefs of contemporary evangelicals. My use of the term "contemporary evangelical" throughout this book refers to that overwhelming majority of evangelicals that have embraced this influence of Subjectivism and Rogerianism, which is described in the pages ahead.

Losing the Culture War

The American Left is currently beating the contemporary evangelical church badly in the culture war. The factors listed below represent just some of the indications.

Manifestations of External Defeat

A Gallup Poll reveals that while in 1970 40% of Americans believed that the Bible should be taken literally, today only 28% maintain that conviction. This represents a serious decline in the American commitment to Scripture.[82] Many other statistics could be marshaled revealing similar movement away from a Christian worldview toward a post-Christian belief system.

The battle over sexual morality comprises a major front in the culture war. The Left is seeking to replace biblical sexual standards with its own. Although Christians have won a few skirmishes, such as the battle waged by a group of pastors against the mayor of Houston over transgender bathrooms, evangelicals are clearly losing the war.

One glaring example of the dominance of the Left is found in the recently passed Oregon state law allowing 15-year-olds to get sex change operations financed by the government without parental consent.[83] Perhaps the most telling aspect of this story resides in the scant attention it received, making headlines only in a few conservative outlets for a few days before dying. The fact that such a flagrant assault on reasonable sexual standards does not make headlines vividly illustrates the dominance of the Left in the culture war. Many such developments could be cited to demonstrate that secular forces are rapidly eradicating our previous Christian culture.

Evangelicals can no longer take the position that we will allow secular culture to do its thing while we do ours. The Left is closing in on us and will not be satisfied until it has forced evangelicals to conform to its immoral agenda. Most Christians are aware that Christian bakers and photographers are being forced against their Christian convictions to provide services for gay weddings and when failing to comply are being severely fined and even driven out of business. Almost daily we are confronted with evidence that this cultural noose is being yanked increasingly tighter around the evangelical neck.

Manifesting Internal Defeat

The contemporary evangelical church is not only lacking sufficient strength to prevent the Left from transforming secular society, but it is even too weak to defend itself against the incursion of liberal advances into the church.

Brandon Robertson in his blog Revangelicalism reports:

> According to a survey released by the Pew Research Institute, only 58% of millennial evangelicals regularly attend a church service. According to Dave Kinnaman of Barna, there is a 43% drop in Christian church attendance between the teen and early adult years. And in a separate Pew Research Institute poll from 2011, 43% of millennial evangelicals support same-sex marriage.[84]

These statistics reveal that Millennials and those in Generation Z are not only opting out of church but also abandoning biblical values.

Another glaring manifestation of American evangelical pathology lies in its disregard for persecuted Christians. Thousands of Christians in Muslim, Hindu, Buddhist, and communist nations are being slaughtered, sold as sex slaves, or enduring other horrific persecution. A prominent leader in the Chaldean community reports that in Iraq ISIS is systematically beheading children along with the commission of other horrendous crimes.[85] In Nigeria, since 2000 it is estimated that Boko Haram has murdered between 9,500 and 11,000 Christians, and this estimate is considered conservative.[86] Many other such atrocities against Christian brothers and sisters are occurring on an ongoing basis. Yet on a given Sunday morning few American evangelical churches will even express concern for or pray regarding this horrendous widespread persecution of Christians around the globe.

Even many in secular society find this lack of evangelical response to the plight of our persecuted brothers and sisters scandalous. Imagine a brother seeing a sister raped without making a substantive effort to help or even expressing concern. Just as leprosy destroys feeling in limbs, it seems that American evangelicals have contracted a spiritual leprosy that prevents it from feeling the pain of body members around the world.

Occasionally the American church takes notice when an American Christian is persecuted, but it pays little attention when their foreign brothers and sisters are persecuted. Persecuted Christians in foreign lands often feel abandoned because of the American church's apparent lack of concern, and for the most part they are.

Though this is just one example among many demonstrating that the American evangelical church has contracted a serious spiritual disease, it is a glaring one. Failure to be stirred to action or even prayer by the rape and bloodshed of sisters and brothers signals a code blue condition, the absence of a pulse.

One of the more troubling indicators of evangelical sickness is found in its passivity in the culture war. In most evangelical churches on any given Sunday morning, the secular cultural assault against Christianity receives not even a mention in prayer, reflecting the lack of evangelical church engagement in the battle.

Many individual evangelicals, parachurch organizations, and some churches are making valiant efforts. For example, many evangelicals have fought hard on the abortion front, and many Christian lawyers have worked diligently to help Christians maintain freedom of speech and other rights. But the church as an entity has displayed meager interest regarding engagement in the culture war, especially in comparison to its significant resources and in light of the seriousness of the situation.

THE RESOURCES TO WIN

These evangelical losses in the culture war do not result from the incapacity of the church to win. The church in America possesses the resources to counterattack, defeat the Left, and take back America. Consider the list of resources available to the American evangelical church below.

SPIRITUAL RESOURCES

Spiritual resources possess real power that transformed societies in the past and that made America great previously.

God has given His people the Holy Spirit. Think about what that means. We have the God of the universe living within us. Colossians 1:11 says literally that we are "empowered with all power," the word *power* being used twice, once in the verb form and once in the noun form. That power overpowered the Roman Empire, the greatest earthly force of its time, and ultimately shaped Western civilization.

David Bentley Hart in his book *Atheist Delusions: The Christian Revolution and Its Fashionable Enemies* asserts:

> ... Among all the many great transitions that have

marked the evolution of Western civilization, whether convulsive or gradual, political or philosophical, social or scientific, material or spiritual, there has been only one—the triumph of Christianity—that can be called in the full sense a "revolution": a truly massive and ethical revision of humanity's prevailing vision of reality, so pervasive in its influence and so vast in its consequences as actually to have created a new conception of the world, of history, of human nature, of time, and of the moral good. To my mind, I should add, it was an event immeasurably more impressive in its cultural creativity and more ennobling in its moral power than any other movement of spirit, will, imagination, aspiration, or accomplishment in the history of the West.[87]

The Holy Spirit possesses the capacity to achieve that same transformation in America today through the evangelical church.

We also have the power contained in Scripture. Jesus said, "The words that I speak to you, they are spirit and they are life" (John 6:63 NKJV). The Word of God possesses the power to transform individuals, societies, and nations. When Martin Luther unleashed the Word of God in Germany and Tyndale in England, it transformed those societies.

Both Scripture and history provide assurance that prayer releases the power of God. Many revivals have been initiated through the power of prayer.

Jesus used the terms salt and light to teach that His church would possess sufficient spiritual capacities to influence society.

Salt can serve as a preservative that permeates surrounding substances and prevents decay. The church has the capacity to do the same, exerting a positive effect on culture by its presence and influence. Christian parents, teachers, judges, businessmen, politicians, journalists, and believers in every other walk of life can encourage morality, responsibility, decency, and other Christian virtues.

Only a small portion of salt is needed for it to function as a preservative. A U. S. Department of Agriculture publication reports: "Fortunately the growth of many undesirable organisms normally found in cured meat and poultry products is inhibited at relatively low concentrations of salt."[88] Likewise, even where Christians constitute a small minority, they can prevent the spread of moral decay and maintain basic societal health. Just as germs exist in every human body but are kept under control in the healthy person, likewise all societies manifest some level of corruption, but the church by exuding sufficient salt influence can prevent unrighteousness from running rampant and instead maintain a healthy society through the production of agape.

Just as the church can serve as salt by promoting morality within society, it also can function as light by disseminating truth, that is, a Christian worldview that embodies the knowledge essential to support human wellbeing. This light includes the gospel message, which not only has the capacity to transmit knowledge but also to transform lives.

Though estimates differ widely on the distance at which the human eye can see a candle, the most conservative calculation seems to place it at 1.6 miles.[89] It does not require large numbers of Christians lighting a candle to spread the light of Christian truth.

The church exercising its capacities as salt and light will never bring heaven on earth. However, as the church brings godly influence and biblical truth to bear on society it has the capacity to produce a generally moral and enlightened culture that engenders sufficient agape to sustain individual and societal health.

Collateral Resources

The capacity of the American evangelical church to fulfill its function as salt and light is significantly enhanced by a great storehouse of collateral resources, beyond those possessed by any church in all of history. Here is just a sampling.

- Freedom: Despite the current erosion of our freedoms, American Christians still possess significant latitude to function as salt and light.

- A cultural presence: Though our nation is becoming increasingly secular, with a growing segment of our population having no Christian roots, a 2012 Gallup poll determined that 77% of Americans continue to identify themselves as Christian,[90] embracing at least some basic Christian proclivities. Therefore, the church in its ministry as salt and light does not have to start from scratch.

- A substantial segment of the population: Some estimate that 23–24% of Americans affiliate with an evangelical church or denomination.[91] About 34% of Americans speak of having a "born-again" experience.[92] Those Christians seriously committed to evangelical doctrine and lifestyle might comprise around 8% of the population.[93] All of these representations of some sort of evangelical connection contribute salt and light to some extent. The homosexual community in the United States, comprising less than 3% of the population, has imposed its agenda on our nation. How much greater is the potential of the church, consisting of a substantially larger segment of the American population, to influence society, armed with the power of the Holy Spirit, Scripture, and prayer and possessing the other resources on this list?

- Human capital: The evangelical church in America includes trained pastors, teachers, a wide variety of other church workers, and also those skilled in supporting fields such as radio, television, Internet, and education.

- A vast infrastructure: Evangelicals in America own billions of dollars' worth of real estate, operate many colleges, seminaries, and other training institutions, and run publishing houses, book stores, and radio and television facilities.

This vast storehouse of resources and the freedom to employ them positions American evangelicals to wield enormous influence in shaping our national culture. Of Christians in all nations on earth, American believers are best situated to succeed in their roles as salt and light. Consequently, we can have confidence that the American church possesses the potential to win the culture war.

The Cause of Contemporary Evangelical Defeat

Why, then, are we losing?

A major contention of this book is that evangelicals are losing the culture war because we have become infiltrated by elements of the secular culture that have sapped us of our spiritual health and the related vitality essential to fight the culture war effectively.

This was the case with mainline denominations, which allowed the ideology of Materialism to infiltrate its seminaries, leading to the corruption of its theology and the reduction of these denominations to a shell of their former size and influence.

Evangelical Christianity has similarly lost its power through the infiltration of the perspectives of Subjectivism and Rogerianism. In his last book, *The Great Evangelical Disaster*, Frances Schaeffer recognized this trend and warned evangelicals:

> We can say the Bible is without mistake and still destroy it if we bend the Scripture by our lives to fit this culture instead of judging the culture by Scripture.... What is the use of evangelicalism seeming to get larger and larger if sufficient numbers of those under the name evangelical no longer hold to that which makes evangelicalism evangelical? ... (I)f we acquiesce, we will no longer be the redeeming salt for our culture.... It makes little difference in the end if Scripture is compromised by theological infiltration or by infiltration from the surrounding culture.... God's Word has many times been allowed to be bent, to conform to the surrounding, passing, changing culture of that moment rather than to stand as the inerrant Word of God judging the form of the world spirit and the surrounding culture of that moment. In the name of the Lord Jesus Christ, may our children and grandchildren not say that such can be said about us.[94]

Unfortunately, Schaeffer's concerns have materialized.

Instead of the church constituting a force fighting against the post-Christian worldview, it has been infiltrated by this cultural orientation, consequently contributing to the problem rather than providing the solution.

CHAPTER 2

AVENUES of INFILTRATION

This chapter identifies three primary channels through which post-Christian culture has infiltrated the evangelical church.

JESUS PEOPLE

The hippie movement spawned the Jesus People, hippies who had responded to the gospel and incorporated elements of the hippie culture into their approach to Christianity. An excellent comprehensive study of that movement is found in Larry Eskridge's book *God's Forever Family: The Jesus People Movement in America*.[95]

Though the Jesus People movement was splintered and diverse, resisting generalizations, it did manifest some common trends. Jesus People tended to embrace many of the external symbols of the hippie movement such as dress and other aspects of appearance. Many also gravitated toward hippie behaviors. Eskridge quotes Jim Doop, a Jesus People leader, who reflected years later: "They never considered that there was anything wrong with smoking [pot]."[96]

The Jesus People also maintained the hippie mode of music, adapting it for their worship and ultimately elevating it to its own genre, which became a major element of the music industry. A July 1971 *Time* magazine cover story reported: "'Music, the lingua franca of the young,' was the 'special medium of the Jesus movement.'"[97]

Different groups of Jesus People had varying degrees of relationships with traditional churches. Chuck Smith of Calvary Chapel in Costa Mesa seized the opportunity to minister to Jesus People and tailored his church program to accommodate them. Though initially many Jesus People groups had little connection with traditional Christianity, Eskridge reports that undesirable cult-like traits that developed within the Children of God, a major Jesus People group, spawned within the movement the sense that they needed the stability provided by traditional church connection.[98]

This attraction toward the traditional church was enhanced by the continued existence of the Jesus People movement after the hippie movement died out. As mentioned earlier, the hippie movement lasted only about five years, with the Jesus People outlasting it. This left the Jesus People culturally stranded, prompting their gravitation toward their spiritual family in the established evangelical church.

Another bond between the Jesus People and the evangelical church developed through the attraction of non-hippie evangelical young people to the Jesus People movement. These church kids were drawn to Jesus People by their music, their overt Christian commitment and enthusiasm, and no doubt because they viewed them to be cool. Jesus People represented the culture of these church young people even though they may not have personally adopted its lifestyle, and therefore for them Jesus People provided the best of both worlds: Christian commitment packaged in relevant culture.

As noted above, the Jesus People integrated their commitment to Christ with attitudes and practices of the hippie culture characterized by Subjectivism. Therefore, this connection of the Jesus People movement with the evangelical church resulted in the infiltration of the influence of Subjectivism into evangelical culture. This is not to suggest that they brought a full-blown hippie worldview into the church, but they did carry with them some of the hippie cultural orientation with related values and attitudes, which became an influence within the evangelical church.

BABY BOOMER INFLUENCE

The Baby Boomer generation in general identified with Subjectivism and Rogerianism through the influence of music, movies, and television, consequently absorbing its ideas, attitudes, and values. Earlier we describe the capacity of these media to bypass rational processing and implant concepts directly into the worldview of the listener and viewer. They were also influenced by educational institutions that propagated subjectivist and Rogerian concepts and values.

The technologies discussed earlier exerted significant influence over the Baby Boomer generation as a whole. As a result, not only did

Baby Boomers entering the church from secular society carry that cultural orientation into the church, but through these technological channels even Baby Boomers raised in the church came under the influence of secular ideology. Most had significant exposure to movie content, television programming, secular music, and other elements of secular culture, which to some degree shaped their worldview, attitudes, and values.

They carried this orientation into the church with them, where it was reflected in evangelical trends such as contemporary music, more relaxed dress, aversion to structure and authority, and greater emphasis on feelings. As evangelical Baby Boomers moved into positions of leadership, they brought these influences of Subjectivism and Rogerianism with them.

Many have observed the disproportionate influence Baby Boomers have exercised over American society. The generation prior to them has been referred to as the "do-nothing generation," and perhaps for good reason. For example, it never sent one of its number to the White House. It seems as if Baby Boomers filled this vacuum by imposing their will early, aggressively, and disproportionately on American society, its larger size adding to its impact.

Baby Boomers also exercised this disproportionate influence within the evangelical church, resulting in the infiltration of subjectivist and Rogerian concepts and values into the evangelical belief system.

The Emergence of Evangelical Psychology

During the 1960s evangelical psychology began to take root and become a dominant force within the evangelical community. Its growth and influence were prompted by two factors.

First, during that era American society, including evangelicals, became extremely enamored by psychology. Evangelicals, however, initially expressed concerns that because psychology grew out of a secular worldview many of its concepts were unbiblical. Therefore, the advent of a number of Christian psychologists possessing both psychological credentials and evangelical beliefs received an enthusiastic welcome from evangelicals. They assumed that evangelical psychologists would filter out unbiblical concepts and thus provide evangelicals with psychological input that would be solidly biblical.

Evangelical psychology also received an enthusiastic welcome because pastors and other evangelical leaders prior to the 1960s had paid scant attention to the practical challenges of life such as emotional and relational problems. Evangelical psychologists filled this void and were welcomed heartily since they promised to provide professional help in practical areas.

As the field of Christian psychology gained prominence, it was widely accepted that evangelicals would talk to their pastors regarding theological issues and look to Christian psychologists to deal with their emotional, behavioral, and relational problems, the "real issues of life." Consequently, Christian psychologists soon gained tremendous visibility and influence within the evangelical community.

At the time that evangelical psychology was gaining traction, the theory of Carl Rogers was dominating secular psychology and consequently comprised a prominent part of the training received by most Christian psychologists, even those trained in Christian institutions. Therefore, evangelical psychologists were strongly influenced by Rogers' thinking.

Many concluded that Rogers' concepts were compatible with a biblical worldview, a connection we will describe shortly. Consequently, the enthusiastic embrace of evangelical psychology coupled with the belief that Rogers' concepts reflect biblical ideas provided a wide avenue for the infiltration of Rogers' concepts into evangelical thinking.

In an earlier chapter, we noted that Rogers' theory comprised a psychological expression of Subjectivism. Because Jesus People and Baby Boomers infused the evangelical church with subjectivist attitudes and values, contemporary evangelicals felt at home with and welcomed Rogerian concepts introduced by evangelical psychologists.

The secular influences that entered the evangelical church through the channels described above transformed the evangelical church from its traditional orientation to its contemporary one. The chapters ahead describes the contemporary evangelical belief system that resulted.

Chapter 3

The Core Contemporary Evangelical Concept

Adopting the Core Secular Concept

We have observed that unconditional acceptance comprises the core of Carl Rogers' theory. It also reflects the essence of Subjectivism, giving the individual the right to do his own thing. It has become a dominant influence in therapy, education, government policies, and other elements of our society. Of greatest importance, it has been established as the sole moral principle of secular society and adopted as a way of life.

Through the channels mentioned in the previous chapter, unconditional acceptance found its way into the contemporary evangelical belief system, influencing our understanding of the relationship between human beings and God, advising believers regarding our relationship with other human beings, and shaping our perspectives on salvation and Christian living.

In the section on Rogerianism I made the point that Rogers equated acceptance and love, and that under his influence our society sees these terms as essentially synonymous. Likewise with unconditional acceptance and unconditional love. Contemporary evangelicals have also adopted this understanding of these terms, viewing unconditional acceptance and unconditional love as synonymous and interchangeable. Seldom if ever will you find an evangelical speaker or writer asserting that God's unconditional acceptance is biblical but not his unconditional love, or vice versa. The term unconditional love is used more frequently because love is a major theme in Scripture and also in society, though evangelicals employ both terms.

Contemporary evangelicals assert that God loves and accepts people unconditionally and that consequently they should also love and accept themselves and others unconditionally. Steven Furtick, in his just-released book *(Un)Qualified: How God Uses Broken People to Do Big Things,* provides an overview in the first chapter in which he asserts that the first step in viewing ourselves as qualified is grasping "God's unconditional acceptance of you."[99] This foundational theme of God's unconditional acceptance is accentuated throughout the book. His second step entails "your acceptance of yourself, including your weaknesses,"[100] which in essence comprises unconditional self-acceptance.

David Jeremiah's book, *God Loves You: He Always Has—He Always Will,* embodies the theme of God's unconditional love and acceptance in the title. If God always has and always will love us, this assertion necessarily eliminates any conditions for that love. Therefore, this title, without using the term, asserts that God loves us unconditionally. This expression of the idea of unconditional love and acceptance without using the term demonstrates that this concept is far more prevalent and far-reaching than indicated by the frequency of the use of the terminology unconditional love and acceptance, though those terms seem almost omnipresent among contemporary evangelicals.

At one point Jeremiah expresses this unconditional love and acceptance of God, again without using the term, in this way:

> I have studied the love that God has for his children, following the rich pageant of His pursuit from the Old to New Testaments, and time after time I was moved to tears by the majesty, the grace, the staggering insistence of His abiding affection for every citizen on Planet Earth.[101]

Scripture and history record many acts of rebellion and wickedness by human beings against God and other people, yet Jeremiah's message is that these in no way influence God's love for and acceptance of them. Despite these behaviors God maintains "staggering insistence" on loving "every citizen on Planet Earth." He is claiming that no human being has ever done anything to affect that love. Therefore, God's love and acceptance of every human being must be unconditional. He conveys the same message in these terms:

> I have a burden to tell you that God is love, and that He

deeply, stubbornly, and eternally insists on loving every individual on the face of the planet. It doesn't matter who you are or what you have done. As speaker and author Max Lucado has said, "You can't fall beyond His love."[102]

And He doesn't merely like you when you do well. He is personally and passionately committed to your good, even when you fail.[103]

Jeremiah in identifying every human being as an object of God's love and asserting that His love extends throughout all of time in effect is saying that at no point in all of history has God not loved every human being. This represents yet another formula for asserting that God's love is unconditional.

Jeremiah at another point expresses similar sentiments as follows:

His love remains intact and perfect. If you could somehow chart the love of God, it would show as a straight line across the top of the graph, never dipping, never plunging, but remaining constant, with a value of infinity. Any variance is simply imaginary, the result of our ignorance or inability to feel His love.

Therefore, in essence the message of his book is that God loves people unconditionally and that this perspective forms the core concept in the relationships of human beings with Him. Notice from the quotes above that this unconditional love of God is both of the philia type, "His abiding affection," and the agape type, "He is personally and passionately committed to your good."

A Prevalent and Enduring Theme

Literally hundreds of other evangelical books could be cited that advocate the theme of God's unconditional love and acceptance. This concept shows itself in vast numbers of sermons, in Christian radio and television programming, and even in Christian music.

The prevalence of the theme of unconditional love and acceptance in both the writings of Steven Furtick, who is in his 30s, and those of David Jeremiah, who is in his 70s, reveals that this has constituted not only a central concept but also an enduring theme of contemporary evangelical Christianity, influencing evangelicals from the outset of Baby Boomer impact to the present. It has become a cornerstone of contemporary evangelical culture.

A significant indicator of the contemporary evangelical community's commitment to unconditional love and acceptance is found in the absence of opposition to this concept. One is hard-pressed to find any prominent evangelical who is opposed to this theme. Though some may exist, it is clear that their concerns have not gained traction. Instead, the concept that God loves and accepts us unconditionally is embraced almost universally among evangelicals as an established biblical truth. In most evangelical circles, questioning the veracity of this concept is viewed almost as heresy.

Evangelical Adoption of Unconditional Love and Acceptance

In discussing the American adoption of Subjectivism, I pointed out that different people adopt cultural concepts to differing degrees. Not all Europeans are avid socialists. Nonetheless, almost all of them are influenced by socialism to some extent, resulting in this being the dominant theme of European culture.

The same is true of contemporary evangelical beliefs. In this chapter and the ones to follow, in describing various elements of the contemporary evangelical belief system, I am not suggesting that every evangelical has fully embraced each of these concepts. Each evangelical has embraced these concepts at his own level, and sometimes holds contemporary and traditional evangelical views simultaneously. In fact, we find evangelical writers and preachers on occasion regressing to more traditional evangelical perspectives. Some hold conflicting positions, traditional and contemporary ones, without realizing that they contradict one another.

Nonetheless, the contemporary evangelical beliefs described in this section have gained widespread acceptance within the evangelical community, influencing almost every evangelical to some degree, with most having essentially adopted the contemporary evangelical package. The last two weekends I attended two different churches in two different states belonging to two distinctly different evangelical denominations. Yet both sermons included a major emphasis on God's unconditional love and acceptance. Though anecdotal, this experience conveys the prevalence of the reception of this teaching among evangelicals. The same is true with related concepts that we will discuss in the future.

Consequently, though not all evangelicals have embraced contemporary evangelical beliefs with the same level of awareness or enthusiasm, these concepts have sufficiently permeated the thinking and lifestyles of evangelicals to generate evangelical cultural tilt, i.e. to affect the nature, well-being, and impact of the contemporary evangelical church as a whole.

The Broad Implications of Unconditional Love and Acceptance

As mentioned in our discussion on unconditional acceptance related to Rogerianism, this concept possesses vast implications relating to morality, relationships, and other aspects of life. It wields no less significance in the evangelical context but rather is amplified because evangelicals teach that God extends unconditional love and acceptance, therefore vastly magnifying its consequences.

In addition, contemporary evangelicals believe that since God accepts us unconditionally, we should also accept one another unconditionally, which extends the application of this concept to the horizontal plane.

Beyond that, as in secular society, evangelicals view failure to experience unconditional love and acceptance as the cause of many emotional, behavioral, and relational problems, and they embrace the corresponding belief that extending unconditional acceptance to the hurting person brings healing and the resolution of problems. This therapeutic application lengthens the reach of this theme even further.

Consequently, the concept of unconditional love and acceptance does not comprise a minor theme that exercises minimal impact, but rather it possesses profound and far-reaching significance. As a result, its adoption as a core concept exercises vast influence on evangelical thinking and living.

The Source of the Concept of Unconditional Love and Acceptance

The terms unconditional love or unconditional acceptance are not found in Scripture, but as we have observed they do represent the foundational cultural concept of secular society. Whether or not these concepts are scriptural will be considered in the next chapter. However, there can be little doubt that evangelicals did not derive them from Scripture but that they originated in secular culture, making their way into the evangelical belief system through the channels described in the previous chapter.

An indication that the theme of unconditional love and acceptance was derived from our secular culture is found in the timing of the evangelical embrace of this concept. If this theme comprised a major scriptural concept, Christians would have adopted it centuries ago. The fact that it appeared in Christian thought and vocabulary shortly after its embrace by secular society supports the assertion that its source is secular. Likewise, its adoption by evangelicals at the time when evangelical psychologists trained in Rogerian theory appeared on the scene also links the theme of unconditional love and acceptance with secular roots.

The Linchpin

The linchpin linking Rogers' theory and the contemporary evangelical worldview is found in the tendency of evangelicals to equate grace with unconditional acceptance—grace comprising the core concept of the evangelical worldview and unconditional acceptance comprising the centerpiece of Rogers' theory. The Bible teaches that God's grace entails His acceptance of us apart from works, which has led to the belief that grace is synonymous with unconditional acceptance.

Previously we have noted that both the secular and evangelical communities have equated unconditional acceptance and unconditional love. Earlier in the book we observed that love consists of two components: morality, which entails giving others what we owe them, and grace, which consists of giving others what we do not owe them. God's unconditional acceptance specifically identifies with the grace component of love since He does not owe us acceptance, but He offers it to us based on the sacrifice of Christ on our behalf.

Philip Yancey in his book *What's So Amazing About Grace?* addresses this theme of grace by asserting, "Only Christianity dares to make God's love unconditional,"[104] thus linking grace and unconditional love. He includes a quote from counselor David Seamands that expresses the relationship between grace and unconditional love from the negative perspective as follows.

> Many years ago I was driven to the conclusion that the two major causes of most emotional problems among evangelical Christians are these: the failure to understand, receive, and live out God's unconditional grace and forgiveness; and the failure to give out that unconditional love, forgiveness, and grace to other people.[105]

This equating of grace with unconditional love and acceptance is often not expressed explicitly but instead conveyed using other terms. For example, Yancey says,

> Grace makes its appearance in so many forms that I have trouble defining it. I am ready, though, to attempt something like a definition of grace in relation to God. *Grace means there is nothing we can do to make God love us more*— no amount of spiritual calisthenics and renunciations, no amount of knowledge gained from seminaries and divinity schools, no amount of crusading on behalf of righteous causes. *And grace means there is nothing we can do to make God love us less*— no amount of racism or pride or pornography or adultery or even murder. Grace means that God already loves us as much as an infinite God can possibly love."[106]

In asserting that the grace of God connotes that no human behavior could possibly alter God's love for us Yancey is in effect expressing God's grace in terms of unconditional love and acceptance.

Yancey's equating of grace with unconditional love and acceptance represents a widely and fervently held position of the contemporary evangelical community. In fact, almost any extended contemporary evangelical discussion on grace will almost invariably incorporate the term unconditional acceptance or unconditional love. Consequently, the evangelical and Rogerian systems, though rooted in diametrically distinct worldviews, one theocentric and the other humanistic, appear to converge in the core concept of each, the evangelical belief in grace and the Rogerian commitment to unconditional acceptance.

A Critical Implication

This brings us to a crucial issue. Equating grace with unconditional love and acceptance does not merely provide us with another name for grace—a more contemporary term for expressing the same concept. Rather, using unconditional love and acceptance in referring to grace loads it with the vast implications of those terms. It asserts that grace is bestowed by God unconditionally and that believers should also bestow grace to one another without conditions. In our study of Rogers we explored the vast implications of unconditional acceptance. Evangelicals have now invested the concept of grace with that broad array of implications.

Since grace comprises a core concept in the evangelical belief system, altering its meaning has resulted in significant alterations to evangelical beliefs, attitudes, and values. Since salvation, Christian living, and other components of our Christian worldview are rooted in God's grace, equating grace with unconditional love and acceptance influences our understanding of these major concepts.

In the chapters ahead we will examine the impact of unconditional love and acceptance when applied to salvation and Christian living. However, our first concern must be determining whether this concept is biblical. Is David Jeremiah correct when he asserts that God "deeply, stubbornly, and eternally insists on loving every individual on the face of the planet"? The next chapter is devoted to answering that question.

Chapter 4

Does God Accept and Love Unconditionally?

Does God Accept Human Beings Unconditionally

The belief that God accepts people unconditionally necessarily leads to the conclusion that human beings would only experience God's consistent blessing and never His judgment since unconditional acceptance would eliminate any basis for withholding blessing or judging. Even a cursory reading of Scripture, however, reveals that God judges human beings often and severely, thus demonstrating that He accepts conditionally. Consider this sampling:

- In response to human wickedness, God brought a flood over all the earth that, with the exception of eight people, killed the entirety of Earth's population.
- Because of their wickedness God totally annihilated Sodom and Gomorrah with fire and brimstone. Only Lot and his family escaped.
- Because of the wickedness of the Canaanites, God commanded that they be wiped out.
- Because of the disobedience of Israel and Judah, God brought the Assyrians and Babylonians, who inflicted terrible devastation.
- Scripture teaches that God is going to bring extremely severe judgment on the earth in the future. "For then there will be great tribulation, such as has not been since the beginning of the world until this time, no, nor ever shall be" (Matthew 24:21 NKJV).

- The Bible also asserts that unbelievers will ultimately suffer in an eternal Hell.

Drowning almost the entire world population or consuming a couple of cities with fire and brimstone graphically conveys non-acceptance. If these actions do not communicate non-acceptance, what possibly could? The last two items on this list, perhaps the most severe, are still future, demonstrating that God continues to accept human beings conditionally and judge those failing to meet those conditions even after the cross.

God's judgment does not represent a minor theme occasionally encountered on the pages of the Bible but rather one that is both pronounced and frequent, taught from Genesis through Revelation. These judgments are seldom mentioned in contemporary preaching, probably because they do not fit the contemporary evangelical template, but Scripture is nonetheless replete with them.

The Bible comprises God's book about Himself. In it God portrays Himself as He wants us to see Him. He informs us unmistakably that along with being a God of profound grace, He is also a God of severe judgment. Therefore, teaching that God accepts unconditionally represents a gross distortion of God's portrayal of Himself.

Some may seek to make the case that although God's actions may not convey unconditional acceptance His underlying attitude does, suggesting that even in the midst of His judgment His heart is overflowing with acceptance. Scripture, however, reveals that in many if not most cases of judgment not only are God's actions toward the sinner hostile, but His attitude is also. Consider the following words of Jesus: "But these enemies of mine, who did not want me to reign over them, bring them here and slay them in my presence" (Luke 19:27 NASB). The fact that He not only wants His enemies slain but executed in His presence conveys an attitude of non-acceptance. Hebrews 3:10 tells us that God was provoked with the rebellious generations of Jews coming out of Egypt. Thayer's lexicon tells us that the Greek word for provoke can mean "to loathe" or "to be disgusted with."[107] Multitudes of other passages convey similar sentiments.

There can be no question regarding the conditional nature of God's acceptance of human beings. In fact, if you read through both the Old and New Testaments marking every passage expressing God's conditions of acceptance of human beings with a yellow highlighter, you will go through quite a few highlighters before reaching the end of the Book of Revelation.

Is God's Love for Human Beings Unconditional?

Contemporary evangelicals are more prone to speak in terms of God's unconditional love for human beings rather than unconditional acceptance, not differentiating between the two but rather choosing language that communicates the message in more culturally relevant terms. David Jeremiah teaches, "Most Christians are familiar with the word agape, which is a term used to describe God's unconditional love."[108]

Some may contend that even though the scriptural events catalogued above clearly demonstrate that God does not accept people unconditionally, God nonetheless loves them unconditionally.

Psalm 5:4-5 informs us, however, that God's love is conditional. "For You *are* not a God who takes pleasure in wickedness, nor shall evil dwell with You. The boastful shall not stand in Your sight; You hate all workers of iniquity." Evangelicals tend to explain away this last phrase, "You hate all workers of iniquity," by asserting that "hate" means to love less. The verse that follows, however, reveals that the common meaning of hate is precisely what David had in mind: "You destroy those who speak lies; the LORD abhors the bloodthirsty and deceitful man" (Psalm 5:6). God's hatred for the wicked described here includes both action and feeling types of hatred. "You shall destroy those who speak falsehood" describes God's hostile actions against the wicked. "The Lord abhors the bloodthirsty and deceitful man" describes God's negative emotions toward the wicked.

David records similar sentiments in Psalm 11:5-6: "The LORD tests the righteous, But the wicked and the one who loves violence His soul hates. Upon the wicked He will rain coals; Fire and brimstone and a burning wind shall be the portion of their cup" (NKJV). This passage, as with the previous one, expresses both God's hostile feelings toward the wicked and also the actions resulting from that hostility. It is clear that God's wrath is antithetical to both philia, feeling-type love, and agape, action-type love.

God's animosity toward sinners is reflected in the means of judgment He chooses. He could use lethal injection, but instead He employs a terribly painful means of judgment, "fire and brimstone and a burning wind." This displays God's intention to punish them.

One of the shocking features of these passages to the ears of contemporary evangelicals is that both passages assert that God not only hates sin but also sinners. Though not found in Scripture, contemporary evangelicals recite the mantra, "God hates the sin but loves the sinner," with authority as if they are quoting a verse from the Bible. God does display love for sinners, a topic I will address shortly. Nonetheless, we must recognize that both of these passages affirm that God's love is not unconditional, but instead under certain conditions God displays hatred both toward wicked deeds and the persons who commit those deeds.

We also find God's wrath toward the sinner taught in John 3:36, "He who believes in the Son has eternal life; but he who does not obey the Son will not see life, but the wrath of God abides on him" (NASB). The Greek word for wrath in this verse is used in Scripture both in regard to an attitude of hostility and the ensuing actions. Other New Testament passages also make reference to God's wrath, such as:

- Eph 2:3 ESV among whom we all once lived in the passions of our flesh, carrying out the desires of the body and the mind, and were by nature children of wrath, like the rest of mankind.
- Eph 5:6 ESV Let no one deceive you with empty words, for because of these things the wrath of God comes upon the sons of disobedience.

In response to the above, some may point to New Testament passages that seem to teach God's unconditional love.

- John 3:16 ESV "For God so loved the world, that he gave his only Son, that whoever believes in him should not perish but have eternal life.
- Rom 8:28 ESV And we know that for those who love God all things work together for good, for those who are called according to his purpose.
- 1Jn 4:10 ESV In this is love, not that we have loved God but that he loved us and sent his Son to be the propitiation for our sins.

These verses, indicating that God loved us even while we were living in sin, seem to support the view that God loves us unconditionally.

Both sets of passages above, those speaking of the wrath of God and those speaking of His love, are found in Scripture. Therefore, we must reconcile them rather than ignore one set and embrace the other. We can synthesize these passages by considering the specific expression of love the latter group of verses has in view.

Love in these verses in every case is agape, either in the noun or verb form. The two verb uses are in the aorist tense, which views an act as a whole or completed action as opposed to ongoing action. "He mowed the grass" as opposed to "he is mowing the grass." Therefore, these verses are not depicting God's love for human beings as His ongoing orientation toward them. Rather, these passages refer to God's display of love toward human beings in a certain act. All three passages explicitly identify the act of agape in view—God's sending Christ to die for our sins. Therefore, they are not teaching that God maintains an ongoing, unconditional love for human beings but rather that God performed an act of love in sending Christ to provide redemption for them. Consequently, these verses do not teach unconditional love.

The fact that the New Testament does not teach unconditional love is also underscored in passages such as Hebrews 10:28-31 that asserts:

> Anyone who has set aside the law of Moses dies without mercy on the evidence of two or three witnesses. How much worse punishment, do you think, will be deserved by the one who has trampled underfoot the Son of God, and has profaned the blood of the covenant by which he was sanctified, and has outraged the Spirit of grace? For we know him who said, "Vengeance is mine; I will repay." And again, "The Lord will judge his people." It is a fearful thing to fall into the hands of the living God.

God's Love for People

Let me stress that the discussion above is not asserting that God has no love for human beings. Scripture tells us that God shows profound love toward us in a number of ways. Let me list some.

- He sends rain and sunshine: Even while we are living in sin, the Lord showers His goodness on us. Poverty and squalor do not exist because God has not provided sufficient resources for people to enjoy plenty. He has. These tragedies result because humans squander the resources God has provided through greed, wars, and other practices that waste the more than ample resources He has graciously bestowed on us.
- He prefers blessing to judgment: In Ezekiel 18:32 we read, "For I have no pleasure in the death of anyone, declares the Lord GOD;

so turn, and live." God sent Jonah to Nineveh to warn them of impending judgment because His desire was to bless and not to judge.

- He desires to see people saved: God desires that all people escape ultimate judgment and instead enjoy ultimate blessing in Heaven. "The Lord is not slow to fulfill his promise as some count slowness, but is patient toward you, not wishing that any should perish, but that all should reach repentance" (2 Peter 3:9).

- He sent His Son to redeem human beings at great price: Salvation is not only God's desire for human beings, but much more it comprises an objective in which He has invested immensely by sending His Son to die for the sins of the world.

- He sends His Spirit to draw people to Himself: God having made provision for the redemption of human beings, an appropriate response is required on their part. God displays His love for us in sending His Spirit to encourage and enable us to respond to His offer of redemption.

- He gives time to repent: The Lord also displays His love for us in giving us time to respond to His offer of redemption. Though in the absence of a biblical response that offer ultimately expires, God nonetheless shows great patience in providing us with the opportunity to respond.

- God provides goodness to encourage people to repent: "Or do you presume on the riches of his kindness and forbearance and patience, not knowing that God's kindness is meant to lead you to repentance?" (Romans 2:4). Apparently, it is God's intention that as we witness His goodness, we will be drawn to Him.

- God provides a vast storehouse of other blessings to those who believe such as the provision of His Spirit, entrance into His family, the privilege of prayer, His Word, and future blessings in heaven.

The Conditional Nature of God's Love

The list above clearly demonstrates God's love. The question this chapter addresses, however, is not whether God loves people but whether He loves people unconditionally.

The passages cited earlier in this chapter related to God's wrath and judgment and many others make it undeniable that God's acceptance and love are conditional. The judgment and wrath described result from failure to meet God's conditions for acceptance and love. Therefore, the contemporary evangelical teaching that God loves and accepts human beings unconditionally is erroneous.

Some might insist that God's love must be unconditional because Scripture asserts twice that God is love (1 John 4:8 and 4:16). Those verses, however, must be understood in relation to verses describing other characteristics of the nature of God. For example, Exodus 34:14 states, "for you shall worship no other god, for the LORD, whose name is Jealous, is a jealous God." Likewise, when the Lord appeared to Isaiah, we do not find the Seraphim crying, "Love, love, love is the Lord of hosts," but "Holy, holy, holy." Therefore, it is not valid to take the position that our full understanding of God and the role that love plays in His nature is encompassed by these two verses in 1 John 4.

The Takeaways

The discussion above leads to two salient takeaways. First, God's relationship with human beings is conditional. Therefore, it is essential that we identify those conditions, seek to meet them, and help others to accurately understand those conditions. The examples above and many others in Scripture warn us that failing to do so leads to disaster. From the positive perspective, meeting those conditions leads to joy and blessing. The chapters ahead discuss the nature of those conditions for the seeker and for the believer. They also relate why it is of ultimate importance for individuals, the church, and our nation to meet them.

The discussion above also takes us back to Francis Schaeffer's warning previously mentioned. The buy-in of contemporary evangelicals to unconditional love and acceptance reflects that culture rather than Scripture has wielded a greater influence over our thinking and resulting behaviors. It is essential for evangelical Christianity to return to its scriptural roots, taking all of the Bible seriously, and allowing it and not culture to formulate every dimension of our belief system. Failure to do so will lead to the continued shrinkage of the American evangelical church and leave it incapable of engaging effectively in the culture war. Conversely, returning to the foundation of Scripture will infuse evangelicals with the spiritual health and vitality essential for functioning as good soldiers of Jesus Christ, empowering them to serve effectively as salt and light in our society.

Chapter 5

Unconditional Acceptance and the Gospel

The Contemporary Evangelical Gospel

The belief in God's unconditional acceptance has influenced contemporary evangelicals to minimize the conditions related to salvation. If God loves and accepts human beings unconditionally, then conditions related to salvation must be minimal.

The following description of the gospel from Josh McDowell and Brian Hostetler's book *Beyond Belief to Convictions* reflects this influence of unconditional acceptance on the gospel. In a section with the heading "God Accepts You Unconditionally," they assert regarding eternal life: "Yet the basis of receiving such life is nothing we can do; it is strictly a gift from God."[109]

These authors express a gospel of unconditional acceptance by restricting the necessary response of the seeker to receiving a gift, which for all practical purposes eliminates any substantive condition. Though Scripture refers to eternal life as the "gift of God," Scripture clearly indicates that God requires that the seeker meet conditions for receiving that gift. Those conditions are our next consideration.

The Condition for Receiving Salvation

Scripture presents repentance and faith as the conditions for receiving salvation. On the day of Pentecost Peter called on people to repent in order to be saved (Acts 2:28), not mentioning faith. John 3:16 teaches that we must believe to be saved, not mentioning repentance. The Reformation accentuated that we are saved by faith alone, i.e., that faith is the only condition for salvation. This assertion seems to omit repentance. Later I will explain how repentance and faith are actually describing the same condition for salvation, that there are not two conditions for salvation but one.

Robbing Repentance and Faith of Their Essence

The contemporary evangelical commitment to unconditional acceptance results in an inclination to strip the conditions of repentance and faith of their substance. In other words, since unconditional acceptance necessitates that no conditions exist for salvation, but since the Bible obviously teaches that repentance and faith are conditions, then repentance and faith must have no genuine substance. This perspective might be expressed in a algebraic formula as follows:

Conditions for salvation based on unconditional acceptance = 0
Condition for salvation based on Scripture = Faith & repentance
Therefore, faith and repentance = 0

Contemporary evangelicals cannot reduce faith and repentance to absolute zero since they are taught in Scripture. However, they have in effect achieved that result by gutting them of their volitional element, commitment, and in so doing reducing them to cognitive concepts, believing facts.

Repentance

Traditional Repentance

The traditional understanding of repentance entailed a commitment to turn from one's autonomous, sinful lifestyle, instead obligating oneself to live according to the teachings of Scripture. This view of repentance is not saying to the seeker, "Change and you will be saved," which would comprise works salvation and be impossible for him to do. Rather, it comprises a call for the seeker to *commit himself* to abandon his sinful, self-directed lifestyle and instead submit to the authority of Christ.

Scripture in various places likens the relationship of Christ with the church to marriage. In exchanging marriage vows we make such a commitment, i.e., to abandon a single lifestyle that revolved around self and enter into a new arrangement that requires a commitment to love the other person. Even though we cannot keep that commitment perfectly— who has a perfect record at loving?—we can be sincere in making that commitment, we can be diligent in pursuing it, and we can maintain it in pattern if not in perfection.

It is likewise in establishing a relationship with Christ. Repentance, a scriptural condition for salvation, consists of this type of commitment to abandon one's previous autonomous lifestyle.

Contemporary Evangelical Repentance

Contemporary evangelicals have adopted a different perspective on repentance. The Greek word for "repentance" is comprised of two components together meaning "to change one's mind." Consequently, contemporary evangelicals tend to believe that repentance refers to a person changing his mind regarding how to be saved, previously thinking that salvation was based on works but now adopting a new perspective that acknowledges that salvation is based totally on grace.

This view differs from the traditional understanding of repentance in that it excludes the volitional element. Repentance is reduced to adopting a new understanding about salvation, and therefore it is devoid of any commitment to change. Consequently, this perspective of repentance eliminates any connection between salvation and lifestyle. In other words, the person can be saved with the intention of continuing in sinful behavioral patterns.

Even if the person with a pornography habit knows that it is sinful, this understanding of repentance places him under no obligation to seek to abandon it. He can be assured of salvation and still plan to engage in pornography, though he is aware of its crushing effect on his wife, that he is supporting a wicked industry demeaning to women and debilitating to society, and that he is displeasing God.

In short, this perspective on repentance allows the seeker to enter into a relationship with Christ not governed by any conditions but based solely on unconditional love and acceptance. It is tantamount to a marriage relationship in which the marriage vows leave open to the bride the prerogative to have relationships with old boyfriends.

The Unscriptural Nature of Contemporary Evangelical Repentance

This reduced understanding of repentance is problematic because it bases its definition of repentance on the components of the Greek term, which constitutes an erroneous methodology. The definition of words must be determined not by the terms comprising them but by their usage. If we talked about a cheerleader turning a cartwheel, we all recognize that she is not grabbing hold of a wheel on a cart and turning it, even though the terms making up the word "cartwheel" indicate that. Likewise, we cannot assign a definition to repentance solely based on the words that comprise the term, "change" and "mind," but rather it must be based on its usage.

The scriptural uses of the Greek word for "repentance" support the traditional understanding of the term described above. It does not refer to an alteration of one's opinion related to salvation but rather deals with a commitment to change one's behavior. For example, when the followers of John the Baptist queried him regarding what they should do to express repentance, he responded:

> "Whoever has two tunics is to share with him who has none, and whoever has food is to do likewise." Tax collectors also came to be baptized and said to him, "Teacher, what shall we do?" And he said to them, "Collect no more than you are authorized to do." Soldiers also asked him, "And we, what shall we do?" And he said to them, "Do not extort money from anyone by threats or by false accusation, and be content with your wages." (Luke 3:10-14)

Repentance described by John did not consist merely of a change in thinking but a commitment to a change in lifestyle. Other passages in the New Testament support this same understanding of repentance. In an interview in 2013 with *Christianity Today*, Billy Graham asserted, "To those who say you can have Christ without giving anything up, Satan is deceiving you."[110]

Faith

Scripture teaches that faith has a cognitive element that includes believing that Christ died for one's sins and that only through His sacrifice we can be saved. Faith, however, also includes a volitional element, a commitment to live under the authority of Christ, which is excluded by contemporary evangelicals.

This volitional component is found in verses such as Romans 10:9, "(B)ecause, if you confess with your mouth that Jesus is Lord and believe in your heart that God raised him from the dead, you will be saved...." Here we find that salvation includes acknowledgment of Jesus as Lord.

Some contend that "Lord" in this passage does not refer to "Master" but "God." I struggle to understand how viewing Jesus as

God conveys less authority and makes me less obligated to obey Him than viewing Him as master. In either case salvation includes recognition of His authority and the corresponding commitment to submit to Him.

The view that faith includes commitment is supported by a quote from *A Manual Grammar of the Greek New Testament* by Dana and Mantey.

> Deissmann in *Light from the Ancient East* gives several convincing quotations from the papyri to prove that πιστευειν εις αυτον [to believe into him] meant *surrender* or *submission to....* G. Milligan agrees with Deissmann that the papyri usage of εις αυτον [into him], is also found regularly in the New Testament. Thus to believe on or to be baptized into the name of Jesus means to renounce self and to consider oneself the lifetime servant of Jesus.[111]

Much more support could be marshaled to demonstrate from Scripture that faith includes a volitional dimension, specifically submission to the authority of Christ.

As with repentance, contemporary evangelicals reduce faith to a merely cognitive entity. A person is saved by believing that Christ died for his sins. This understanding of faith excludes the volitional component. It includes no submission to the authority of Christ, no commitment to live for Him. Salvation includes no obligation to respond to Christ's call to agape, instead leaving the seeker free to perpetuate his selfishness as a believer. As with repentance, this view of faith includes no link to the future lifestyle of the seeker. Therefore, just as with repentance, it leaves the person responding to the gospel free to continue sinful behaviors.

Some may argue that the call for the seeker to receive salvation as a gift constitutes a volitional response. However, this volitional response is vacuous, including no substance, but instead excluding any substantial response.

The Gospel of John makes reference to this vacuous form of faith that lacks commitment and therefore fails to establish a saving relationship with Christ. John says of Jesus:

> Now when He was in Jerusalem at the Passover, during the feast, many believed in His name when they saw the signs which He did. But Jesus did not commit Himself to them, because He knew all *men*, and had no need that

> anyone should testify of man, for He knew what was in man. (John 2:23-25 NAS)

John tells us explicitly that these people believed in the name of Jesus, and yet the passage indicates that they were not true believers. Apparently their faith included a cognitive element. This passage records that they believed when they saw the signs, indicating that the miracles He performed convinced them regarding the facts related to Christ. However, their faith lacked a volitional component, i.e. commitment. The response of Jesus reveals that this abridged form of faith does not meet the necessary condition for salvation.

In the phrase, "Jesus did not commit Himself to them," the Greek word translated "commit" is the most common New Testament word translated "believe." The translators' selection of the word "commit" indicates that this word for "believe" can include the idea of commitment. The passage seems to be saying that Jesus did not commit Himself to them because He knew that they had not truly believed, that is, they had not committed themselves to Him.

This takes us back to the marriage analogy. Salvation constitutes entering into a relationship that, like marriage, requires mutual commitment. Jesus displayed His commitment to us in giving His life on the cross. He calls us to display our commitment to Him through genuine repentance and faith, which includes not only acknowledging that we are saved by His sacrifice but also our commitment to abandon our previous, autonomous lifestyle and submit to His authority.

As with repentance, in many ways saving faith parallels a marriage commitment. In fact, traditional wedding vows conclude with the phrase: "And thereto I pledge thee my faith." These vows call the bride and groom to leave their self-oriented life, instead committing themselves to an exclusive relationship with their new spouse characterized by agape. Likewise, biblical faith constitutes a commitment by the seeker to acknowledge the authority of Christ in this new relationship. Jesus desires a marriage relationship with us, but He requires that this relationship includes commitment to Him. Submission to the authority of Christ ultimately calls us to a life of agape. Therefore, faith lacking this commitment element leaves the new believer free to indulge in selfish living.

The contemporary evangelical gospel, devoid of commitment, comprises more of a dating relationship with Christ or cohabitation, a relationship without commitment. As indicated in the passage in

John cited above, Jesus will not enter into this type of relationship; it does not result in salvation and eternal life.

Integrating Repentance and Faith

1 Thessalonians 1:9 provides us with a good explanation of the relationship between repentance and faith. In this verse describing the salvation of the Thessalonians Paul reminds them of "...how you turned to God from idols to serve the living and true God." The Greek word for "turn" is used in other passages in reference to salvation. For example, in Acts 11:21 we read, "And the hand of the Lord was with them, and a great number who believed turned to the Lord." In 1 Thessalonians 1:9 Paul speaks of their turning their hearts to serve God, which reflects the essence of saving faith. His reference to their turning in their hearts from serving idols captures the idea of repentance. Both faith and repentance make reference to the same turn related to salvation, repentance describing what we turn from and faith identifying what we turn to.

Sometimes the condition related to the gospel is framed in terms of repentance and at other times in terms of faith, both referring to the same turn, i.e., a commitment to turn from the old life to the new life, from autonomy to submission to the authority of Christ. The Reformation taught that salvation is by faith alone. This perspective is valid. However, at times Scripture uses the term repentance instead of faith to describe the commitment related salvation. This turn away from an autonomous approach to life to one lived under the authority of Christ represents the volitional condition the seeker must meet to enter into a relationship with Christ and the condition governing that relationship once it is established. He must not only embrace the truths related to Christ, but in response to those truths he must make a commitment to Christ.

This dual expression of repentance and faith parallels marriage vows, which ask the groom (or bride): "and do you solemnly promise before God and these witnesses that you will love, honor, and cherish her, and that forsaking all others for her alone, you will perform unto her all the duties that a husband owes to his wife as long as life shall last?" "Forsaking all others" parallels repentance, and the commitment to "love, honor, and cherish" parallels faith.

These perspectives on repentance and faith as a commitment to turn from autonomy to a life under the authority of Christ are graphically symbolized in baptism, going down into the water depicting repentance, the commitment to abandon the old, self-directed life characterized by selfishness, and coming up out of the water signifying faith, a commitment to a new, Christ-directed life characterized by agape. Therefore, baptism symbolizes the condition on which the relationship between the new believer and Christ is based.

Conditions versus Works

Many contemporary evangelicals would object to this view that repentance and faith include a volitional component, charging that this comprises works salvation. This charge fails to recognize that meeting conditions does not necessarily comprise works.

In denouncing works salvation, Scripture is rejecting the position that we can earn Heaven, that we can live a sufficiently good life to deserve salvation with all its attendant blessings and privileges. The Pharisees exemplified this attitude, confident that they had earned sufficient merit to deserve eternal life. Those embracing this perspective sense no need for someone to pay for their sins because they have earned the right to enter heaven based on their own merit. In other words, God owes them Heaven.

This perspective of earning one's salvation differs categorically from meeting the condition of repentance and faith. Doing so does nothing to earn forgiveness and eternal life. It does not contribute one whit to paying for our sins or providing the glories of Heaven. It serves only as a condition for entering into God's gracious provision earned by Christ. Therefore, meeting these conditions in no way can be construed as earning one's salvation.

Imagine that a man with a drug habit has a rich uncle who desires to turn his entire estate over to this nephew. However, because he does not want to see his estate squandered or his reputation tarnished, he requires that the nephew commit himself to enter a drug rehabilitation program as a condition for receiving this estate.

This uncle had worked hard all of his life to amass this estate. The nephew in committing himself to enter a rehabilitation program in no way adds to its value. In no way does it make the nephew deserving of this estate. The uncle has no obligation whatever to give it to him. He is giving it to this nephew totally out of grace. Entering into the rehabilitation program merely comprises a condition the uncle requires him to meet.

Likewise, repentance and faith contribute nothing to our salvation and all the attendant blessings, but they merely constitute God's condition for our receiving them.

In addition, God in stipulating the condition of repentance and faith is not requiring that we give up something of value. Rather, He is calling us to shed the vast liability that comprises our previous lifestyle, instead replacing it with something of great value that produces a life of wonderful blessing.

In the illustration above, the nephew in committing himself to a rehab program is not doing the uncle a favor. Rather, the uncle is doing him a favor in diverting him from a path that will destroy his life and instead calling him to commit to a healthy, productive direction. It is likewise with the condition related to salvation.

Consequently, repentance and faith do not entail our doing something for God but rather God doing something for us. Therefore, since we are not giving up something of value but getting something of value it is impossible to equate repentance and faith with earning our salvation.

In this chapter we observed that contemporary evangelicals omit commitment, the volitional dimension, from repentance and faith, robbing them of their substance. The next chapter will reveal the negative impact of this deficient perspective on the gospel.

Chapter 6

Problems Produced by the Minimized Gospel

In the previous chapter we considered *the problems with* the minimized gospel of contemporary evangelicals that excludes commitment. In this chapter we will look at *the problems caused by* this gospel for the seeker and for the church.

The Impact on the Seeker

Because the contemporary evangelical gospel fails to include the scriptural condition for salvation, a commitment to abandon one's autonomy and to submit to the authority of Christ, the person responding to this gospel can be given assurance that he is headed for Heaven when he is not.

The Apostle Paul warned against this type of false hope in several passages:

> Or do you not know that the unrighteous will not inherit the kingdom of God? Do not be deceived: neither the sexually immoral, nor idolaters, nor adulterers, nor men who practice homosexuality, nor thieves, nor the greedy, nor drunkards, nor revilers, nor swindlers will inherit the kingdom of God (1 Corinthians 6:9-10 ESV)
>
> Now the works of the flesh are evident: sexual immorality, impurity, sensuality, idolatry, sorcery, enmity, strife, jealousy, fits of anger, rivalries, dissensions, divisions, envy, drunkenness, orgies, and things like these. I warn you, as I warned you before, that those who do such things will not inherit the kingdom of God (Galatians 5:19-21 ESV).

> For you may be sure of this, that everyone who is sexually immoral or impure, or who is covetous (that is, an idolater), has no inheritance in the kingdom of Christ and God. Let no one deceive you with empty words, for because of these things the wrath of God comes upon the sons of disobedience (Ephesians 5:5-6 ESV).

Notice that two of these passages include the warning not to be deceived, indicating that Christians tend to be vulnerable to deception in this area.

This seems to be a prevalent outcome in the contemporary evangelical church. Pastor David Platt made a presentation to a Pastors Conference of the Southern Baptist Convention in which he expressed concern over how many people in evangelical churches believe they are saved who are not.[112] In that regard he spoke of "rampant easy believism," which graphically describes the contemporary evangelical gospel devoid of commitment, which is producing this false assurance of salvation.

What might have been the outcome if the rich young ruler had encountered a contemporary evangelical rather than Jesus? It seems likely that he would have gladly received the free gift of salvation and gone away assured that he possessed eternal life.

In the *Christianity Today* interview with Billy Graham cited above, he lamented that unsaved people refuse to accept the gospel "because it calls for the confession of sin and the complete surrender of one's selfish ways. It calls for repentance of sin against God."[113] If his analysis is valid, that people refuse the gospel because of the commitment it requires, then people no doubt are far more responsive to the contemporary evangelical gospel because it does not require commitment. However, this desire for salvation without commitment has resulted in the prospect of leaving countless people believing they have eternal life when they do not.

This outcome is disastrous on several counts. The most terrifying consists of the possibility of thousands if not millions of human beings one day opening their eyes in Hell, consigned to that fate for all eternity, realizing that the contemporary evangelical gospel devoid of commitment presented to them was invalid.

The Impact on the Church

Another tragic outcome of the contemporary evangelical minimized gospel resides in the church being populated by large numbers of unbelievers. Though Jesus taught that there would be tares among the wheat, the contemporary evangelical gospel is planting these tares in disproportionate numbers, leaving the church numerically large but spiritually weak.

Some might contend that people who are not genuinely saved would not be interested in church involvement, but that is not the case. Human beings are social creatures who seek groups to which they can belong. They join country clubs and Rotary clubs, and they develop social networks in bars and on social media. In their quest for social connection, contemporary evangelical churches, especially larger ones, provide an ideal alternative. They are filled with caring people, offer a friendly, nonjudgmental environment, cost nothing, and provide professional music, children's programs, and a wide variety of other services. Sermons tend to be "needs oriented," providing practical help with the challenges of life without engendering conviction. Since the persons in view have been assured that they are believers, when the gospel is presented they do not see it as applying to them nor do they see themselves as outsiders. In an increasingly hostile and bizarre world, the contemporary evangelical church provides a great social option for them.

This contingent, however, lacking the Holy Spirit and genuine spiritual interests would not bring to the church edifying spiritual qualities. Instead, they would tend to promote secular perspectives and values. Being viewed as believers, they might be selected for leadership positions, especially those who are successful and personable.

Though the church should be welcoming to unbelievers, the presence of unbelievers who are convinced they are Christians, and are perceived as such, presents a weakening influence on the church.

Disadvantaged Start to the Christian Life

At times through the ministry of the Holy Spirit seekers will respond with genuine repentance and faith to the minimal contemporary gospel. Though these seekers are born-again, this deficient gospel results in their getting a bad start in their new relationship with the Lord.

Those enlisting in the United States military take the following oath:

> I, John American, do solemnly swear (or affirm) that I will support and defend the Constitution of the United States against all enemies, foreign and domestic; that I will bear true faith and allegiance to the same; and that I will obey the orders of the President of the United States and the orders of the officers appointed over me, according to regulations and the Uniform Code of Military Justice. So help me God.

The recognition by these recruits of their commitment to leave their autonomous lifestyle and submit to military authorities orients them for success in military training and subsequent duties.

Imagine if a military unit, eager to sign up soldiers, stopped administering this oath and instead conveyed to new recruits that they could continue to function autonomously, to make their own choices regarding training and even fighting. Given the option to go to boot camp or stay at home where they can play video games and date their girlfriends, chances are they would opt for the latter. In battle, if they consented to fight at all, this lack of training would leave them unprepared, endangering them personally. The unit taking this approach to recruitment and training would be decimated in short order.

This in essence is the situation with the seeker responding to a gospel that includes no commitment to the authority of Christ. Still exercising his autonomy this new believer is unlikely to adopt the behaviors and make the sacrifices related to Christian living.

The disadvantages of this arrangement become especially apparent as we consider the challenges it presents for any person attempting to do follow-up and discipleship. The one attempting discipleship has no authoritative basis for calling the new believer to be baptized, to develop practices of Bible reading, prayer, and church attendance, and to implement patterns of godly behavior. Instead, he is reduced to presenting the disciplines of the Christian life as suggestions.

The resulting lack of effective discipleship will make it likely that the new believer will not enjoy a transformed lifestyle but rather will be susceptible to spiritual weakness and sickness. Instead of developing spiritual maturity, he is likely to get stuck in spiritual adolescence. Rather than growing into a strong agape producer, he will be more inclined to remain a taker.

Transformation without Obligation

We just observed that the contemporary evangelical gospel, devoid of obligation to adopt a biblical lifestyle gets the new believer off to a disadvantaged beginning in his Christian life.

Some may contend, however, that this arrangement is not a liability but rather an asset because not obligation but desire should provide the motivation for change. They would contend that transformation motivated by obligation is legalistic. The New Testament believer should not be incentivized by an "ought to" but a "want to" motive.

I will address this issue later in relation to the contemporary evangelical approach to Christian living, which is our next topic.

Chapter 7

Unconditional Acceptance and Christian Living

Performance Not Required

The contemporary evangelical view that God accepts the believer unconditionally necessarily leads to the conclusion that he does not need to "perform" to please God. If God accepts him unconditionally, then how he lives, his "performance," will not alter God's acceptance.

In regard to the Christian life Philip Yancey reflects: "By instinct I feel I must *do something* in order to be accepted."[114] He then states his perspective on Christian living as follows:

> The world runs by ungrace. Everything depends on what I do....
> Jesus' kingdom calls us to another way, one that depends not on our performance but his own.[115]

Yancey views grace, unconditional acceptance, as freeing the believer from obligation to perform. Pleasing God is not dependent on anything he does, but only on what Christ has done for him.

Tim Keller explains the contemporary evangelical position as follows:

> God imputes Christ's perfect performance to us as if it were our own, and adopts us into His family. In other words, God can say to us just as He once said to Christ, 'You are my Son, whom I love; with you I am well pleased.'
> You see, the verdict is in. And now I perform on the basis of the verdict. Because He loves me and He accepts me, I do not have to do things just to build up my résumé. I do not

have to do things to make me look good. I can do things for the joy of doing them. I can help people to help people – not so I can feel better about myself, not so I can fill up the emptiness.[116]

Keller is asserting that because we are God's children, His ongoing verdict regardless of our lifestyle is, "You are my Son, whom I love; with you I am well pleased." Since we enjoy God's ongoing favor, we do not practice biblical behaviors out of necessity, but we now "perform," do loving deeds, just "for the joy of doing them."

The Enemy

This contemporary evangelical perspective finds its antagonist in legalism. Since God accepts us unconditionally, eliminating the necessity for "performance," contemporary evangelicals view the imposition of any conditions needed to please the Lord as legalism.

This legalistic, conditional, performance-based approach to Christian living is viewed as putting the believer into bondage to whatever conditions the legalist imposes rather than allowing the believer to experience the freedom that flows from grace, God's unconditional acceptance.

These conditions lead to judgmentalism since conditions provide a basis to judge others whereas unconditional acceptance eliminates any premise for judging.

Contemporary evangelicals assert that the experience of God's unconditional acceptance and unconditional acceptance received from one another brings health, peace, and growth while the legalist's demand for performance brings failure, guilt, and pathology. Manifesting grace, unconditional acceptance, is Christ-like; legalism is Pharisee-like. Therefore, maintaining a healthy church environment requires vigilance in identifying and removing any expression of legalism and the judgmentalism it produces.

Contemporary evangelicals conclude that traditional evangelicals failed to understand the true nature of grace, that it entails unconditional acceptance, and therefore they engaged in legalism, stipulating conditions the believer had to meet to please God. It seems that it took a secular psychologist, Carl Rogers, to open our eyes to a valid understanding of New Testament grace as consisting of unconditional acceptance, which eliminates the need for "performance." Or as an evangelical counselor friend shared with me, "It seems that Rogers stumbled across a foundational biblical truth," one we were too blinded by our own legalism to see.

Chuck Swindoll passionately expresses this view of legalism as the enemy. After reflecting on the desire for freedom possessed by all human beings, Swindoll asserts:

> And it is every bit as true for God's people who have existed too long in the suffocating grip of legalistic demands and expectations. Long enough have those who wish to control and intimidate others in the body of Christ been allowed to do so.
>
> I am pleased to announce that their grip is loosening as grace is awakening.[117]

This quote not only identifies legalism as the enemy but also shows it to be a hallmark of a previous, conditional evangelical perspective from which contemporary evangelicals are breaking free.

Identifying "Performance"

Contemporary evangelicals assert that God does not require us to perform to please Him. What is this "performance" to which we are not obligated? Performance can mean putting on an act. Of course God does not want us to do that. Rather, the performance God seeks is the production of agape.

Christ identified the two Great Commandments as loving God and our neighbor. The New Commandment given by Christ calls us to love one another. These foundational New Testament mandates prescribe the type of performance to which God calls the believer.

Agape also includes all of its subsidiary expressions, which in essence circumscribes every dimension of Christian living. As we have already noted, agape includes morality and grace. It encompasses displaying the Fruit of the Spirit and exercising the Gifts of the Spirit in ministry to others. It manifests itself in every virtue. It includes being good husbands, wives, parents, children, employers and employees, neighbors, and friends.

Therefore, the assertion that God does not require us to perform is actually asserting that God does not require us to show agape, to display the behaviors embodied in agape listed above.

Of course, contemporary evangelicals want believers to display agape. They insist, however, that we should do so not because we are obligated, as a condition for pleasing God. They teach that instead we should display agape out of gratitude, joy, and desire that spring from the realization that we are accepted unconditionally regardless of our performance.

The Obligation of the Believer to Display Agape

Does God accept the believer unconditionally, apart from performance, or does his lifestyle make any difference in God's attitude and actions toward the believer?

Answering this question includes two distinct but related issues. The first issue is whether God obligates believers to act in certain ways, to meet conditions, to perform. If so, that leads to the second issue of whether meeting those conditions affects God's attitude and actions toward the believer.

Regarding the first issue, the New Testament conveys in various ways that the believer is under obligation to God to perform. Several are listed below.

The Commandments of Scripture

The fact that Scripture commands us to display agape, that this comprises the First and Second Commandments and the New Commandment issued by Christ, clearly indicates that we are obligated to do so. The fact that these directives are specifically identified as "commandments" makes this evident.

In addition, the New Testament is filled with commands from one end to the other, each one mandating a different facet of agape. The latter part of many of Paul's epistles includes lists of instructions that obviously Paul intends to be taken as authoritative, with many of them in the imperative. For example, in 1 Thessalonians 5:15-22 Paul includes this series of directives, all imperatives:

> See that no one repays anyone evil for evil, but always seek to do good to one another and to everyone. Rejoice always, pray without ceasing, give thanks in all circumstances; for this is the will of God in Christ Jesus for you. Do not quench the Spirit. Do not despise prophecies, but test everything; hold fast what is good. Abstain from every form of evil.

Though the New Testament believer is under the singular command to love, at times it is difficult to know what that looks like. The wide array of New Testament directives helps to flesh out the nature of agape in life's situations. Taken together they form a mandate to produce agape.

"Ought to" Passages

Contemporary evangelicals specifically assert that we should not function out of an "ought to" but a "want to" motivation. The New Testament includes numerous passages that use the Greek word that explicitly conveys the idea of "ought to." Here are a few:

- If I then, your Lord and Teacher, have washed your feet, you also ought to wash one another's feet (John 13:14).
- Now we who are strong ought to bear the weaknesses of those without strength and not just please ourselves (Romans 15:1 NASB).
- So husbands ought also to love their own wives as their own bodies. He who loves his own wife loves himself (Ephesians 5:28 NASB).
- (W)hoever says he abides in him ought to walk in the same way in which he walked (1 John 2:6).
- By this we know love, that he laid down his life for us, and we ought to lay down our lives for the brothers (1 John 3:16).
- Beloved, if God so loved us, we also ought to love one another (1 John 4:11).

The "ought to" in these verses clearly conveys obligation.

In summary, the commands of Scripture make it evident that we are obligated to show agape as do the "ought to" passages just quoted. Performance is a requirement.

The Relationship between Obligation and Acceptance

We are seeking to determine whether God's acceptance of the believer requires performance. We have recognized that the answer to this question includes two components. First, does God obligate the believer to perform? We have just concluded that the answer is affirmative. This leads to the second question of whether God's accceptance of the believer is based on meeting that obligation. We are not dealing with a person losing his salvation but instead maintaining God's favor and blessing as His child and servant.

Maybe a person has an obligation to his boss to produce 200 widgets each week. The boss, however, is his rich uncle, and consequently he treats him with favor regardless of how many widgets he produces, or even if he produces none at all. In fact, his widget production does not in any way affect their relationship.

The passages below indicate that God does not operate on those terms. His acceptance of believers, His being pleased with them, blessing and rewarding them, is determined by their production of agape.

- For the kingdom of God is not a matter of eating and drinking but of righteousness and peace and joy in the Holy Spirit. Whoever thus serves Christ is acceptable to God and approved by men (Romans 14:17-18).
- Therefore we make it our aim, whether present or absent, to be well pleasing to Him (2 Corinthians 5:9 NKJV).
- (S)o as to walk in a manner worthy of the Lord, fully pleasing to him, bearing fruit in every good work and increasing in the knowledge of God (Colossians 1:10).

Paul even more graphically describes God's conditional acceptance of the believer, that His acceptance is related to "performance," in 1 Corinthians 10:1-11, where he recounts the experience of Israel in the wilderness.

> For I do not want you to be unaware, brothers, that our fathers were all under the cloud, and all passed through the sea, and all were baptized into Moses in the cloud and in the sea, and all ate the same spiritual food, and all drank the same spiritual drink. For they drank from the spiritual Rock that followed them, and the Rock was Christ. Nevertheless, with most of them God was not pleased, for they were overthrown in the wilderness. Now these things took place as examples for us, that we might not desire evil as they did. Do not be idolaters as some of them were; as it is written, "The people sat down to eat and drink and rose up to play." We must not indulge in sexual immorality as some of them did, and twenty-three thousand fell in a single day. We must not put Christ to the test, as some of them did and were destroyed by serpents, nor grumble, as some of them did and were destroyed by the Destroyer. Now these things happened to them as an example, but they were written down for our instruction, on whom the end of the ages has come.

Paul recounts that God took the lives of a large number of these Israelites, which provides a vivid display of non-acceptance. Paul explicitly identifies God's attitude of non-acceptance in stating that

God was not pleased with those who sinned. Paul twice in this passage states that this story serves as an example for us, thus making the case that this type of response by God is not restricted to the Old Testament or to unbelievers, but that God deals with New Testament believers in this way also. It is instructive that God not only took the lives of these Israelites for sins that we might consider egregious, but also for what we might assess to be misdemeanors, such as grumbling. Paul's observation that "with most of them God was not pleased" is also significant, warning that participating in the prevailing evangelical culture does not prove that a believer's position is biblical or safe.

New Testament examples of non-acceptance can be found in God's taking the lives of Ananias and Sapphira and of those acting in an unloving manner while engaging in the Lord's table, recorded in 1 Corinthians 11:30.

Therefore, Scripture teaches that we are obligated to perform, to produce agape, in order to please God, and that He is displeased with us, not accepting of us, when we do not, even to the point of dealing with us severely. Or to state the case differently, God's dealing with New Testament believers displays that we are obligated to perform, and that God responds to us positively or negatively based on our performance.

Let me reiterate that this response of acceptance or non-acceptance based on performance is not related to salvation, but rather refers to God's being pleased with us as His children and His servants. A boss may be displeased with an employee, reprimand or even demote him, without firing him. This idea is conveyed in passages such as 1 Corinthians 9:27 where Paul reflects, "But I discipline my body and keep it under control, lest after preaching to others I myself should be disqualified." Here Paul is teaching that failure to live a disciplined life would disqualify him for his ministry, an indicator of God's conditional acceptance regarding ministry and the related obligation to perform. Scripture also affirms the positive side of this equation, that pleasing God results in His blessing and reward, like a boss giving an employee who performs well a promotion or year-end bonus.

Some might contend that God accepts the believer but not his inappropriate behavior. We have seen earlier that this perspective, distinguishing between the person and his behavior, is not scriptural. In addition, notice that the passages above refer not only to behavior being pleasing to the Lord but persons, e.g. "Therefore we make it our aim, whether present or absent, to be well pleasing to Him." Beyond that, God in taking the life of a believer conveys non-acceptance of the person in the most unambiguous terms.

This conclusion is diametrically opposed to the teaching of contemporary evangelicals. It, nonetheless, is supported by substantial Scripture.

The Conditional Nature of God's Love for the Believer

Some may contend that though the believer may need to display agape to please God, that God's acceptance of the believer is conditional, we do not need to perform, meet some obligation, to be recipients of God's love.

David Jeremiah graphically expresses that God loves the believer unconditionally as follows:

> There is a good side and a better side to God's unchanging love. The good side is that God won't wake up in the morning and decide He's had enough of us. The better side is that even when we wake up in the morning and decide we've had enough of Him, He will still love us.[118]

In a previous chapter we considered many passages of Scripture revealing that God's love for human beings in general is conditional, but the broadly held belief by evangelicals that God loves the believer unconditionally requires that we determine whether this teaching is compatible with Scripture.

James 4:4, which is written to Christians, indicates that God's love for the believer is conditional. He asks: "You adulteresses, do you not know that friendship with the world is hostility toward God? Therefore whoever wishes to be a friend of the world makes himself an enemy of God" (NAS). James is making the point that if our behaviors display allegiance to the agenda of this world we are in effect adulteresses. Apparently James uses the feminine to reflect our role as the bride of Christ, which makes sinfulness tantamount to infidelity in regard to our relationship with Christ. James teaches that this adulterous behavior makes us enemies of God.

Likewise, God in taking the lives of believers as described in passages above clearly displays a lack of agape. If agape is defined as seeking the benefit of another, taking a person's life could hardly be construed as an expression of agape.

These passages demonstrate that the contemporary evangelical cliché "There is nothing you can do to make God love you more and nothing you can do to make God love you less" is diametrically opposed to Scripture. Rather, this mantra flows out of the infiltration of a culture dominated by Subjectivism and Rogerian psychology.

The conditional nature of God's love for the believer is perhaps most graphically demonstrated in statements by Christ regarding His Father's conditional love for Him: "For this reason the Father loves Me, because I lay down My life that I may take it again" (NAS John 10:17). In this verse Jesus is telling us that the Father's love for Him is conditional, predicated on His doing His Father's will. Jesus conveys the same message in John 15:10: "If you keep My commandments, you will abide in My love; just as I have kept My Father's commandments, and abide in His love." Jesus is indicating that His abiding in His Father's love is conditioned on His keeping His Father's commandments.

This conclusion may sound preposterous, especially to contemporary evangelical ears. However, these are statements of Jesus, and this seems to be the obvious interpretation of them. Though we know that it is impossible for Jesus to sin, imagine for a second that when He was offered the kingdoms of the world by Satan, to avoid the life of rejection before Him culminating in the cross Jesus had succumbed to this temptation, bowing down and worshiping Satan. In the passages just considered, Jesus is saying that doing so would have negatively altered the Father's love for Him.

Or stated in the positive, the fact that Jesus never would capitulate to sin elicits a profound response of love by the Father toward Him. God loves righteousness and grace, and therefore He possesses infinite love for a Son who displayed those qualities perfectly even when He was engulfed in the most horrific circumstances imaginable.

If the love of the Father for the Son is conditional, certainly the same is true of His love for us. In fact, the first part of John 15:10 above makes that assertion: "If you keep My commandments, you will abide in My love." The related note in the Ryrie Study Bible states: "Abiding in His love is conditioned on obedience." This same truth is found in John 14:21: "He who has My commandments and keeps them, he it is who loves Me; and he who loves Me shall be loved by My Father, and I will love him, and will disclose Myself to him" (NAS), and again in John 14:23: "Jesus answered and said to him, 'If anyone loves Me, he will keep My word; and My Father will love him, and We will come to him, and make Our abode with him'" (NAS).

Scripture teaches that God's love for the believer is even conditioned on our attitude in giving. "So let each one give as he purposes in his heart, not grudgingly or of necessity; for God loves a cheerful giver" (2 Corinthians 9:7 NKJV). The word for love in this passage is agape, indicating that God's intentions to benefit us and His related actions are influenced by our love for others displayed in our willingness to share generously with them. This assertion that God loves the generous giver suggests that God responds likewise regarding the full range of our expressions of agape toward others.

The discussion above demonstrates that not only is God's acceptance of the believer conditional, but God's agape love toward us is also conditional, predicated on our obedience to Him and love for others.

Some might argue that Romans 8:35-39 teaches that God's love for the believer is unconditional.

> Who shall separate us from the love of Christ? Shall tribulation, or distress, or persecution, or famine, or nakedness, or danger, or sword? As it is written, "For your sake we are being killed all the day long; we are regarded as sheep to be slaughtered." No, in all these things we are more than conquerors through him who loved us. For I am sure that neither death nor life, nor angels nor rulers, nor things present nor things to come, nor powers, nor height nor depth, nor anything else in all creation, will be able to separate us from the love of God in Christ Jesus our Lord.

Any understanding of this passage must be compatible with all of the verses above indicating the conditional nature of God's love toward the believer.

We can reconcile these passages by noting that sin is not included in the list of those forces incapable of separating us from God's love. Paul is making the point that no force assaulting us can separate us from God's love, but he leaves open the possibility that our own sinful choices can negatively influence God's love for us. This passage is written to those who are "for your sake being killed all the day long." Therefore, Paul's purpose is not to give assurance of God's love to those living in sin but to those being persecuted.

Some contemporary evangelicals seek to support the concept of God's unconditional love by referring to passages related to His steadfast love for Israel that ultimately prevails. It is important to recognize that while God loves Israel as a nation with an everlasting love, His love for individuals within that nation has been conditional. We find God condemning and bringing terrible judgments on countless Israelites, demonstrating that His love for them was not unconditional. It is not valid to draw a parallel between God's interaction with the Jewish nation as a whole and individual New Testament believers, but rather the parallel should be drawn between individual Israelites in the Old Testament and individual believers in the New Testament. This parallel supports a conditional perspective on God's love and acceptance.

The above discussion reveals that God shows love and acceptance toward believers conditioned on their displaying agape toward Him and toward others, i.e. their keeping the First and Second Great Commandments.

The Woman Taken in Adultery

Contemporary evangelicals frequently employ the story of the woman taken in adultery found in John 8:3-11 to support their belief that God accepts people regardless of performance—unconditionally. This woman was taken from the very act of adultery and brought into the presence of Jesus. The passage gives no indication of remorse or repentance on her part and yet Jesus states, "Neither do I condemn you; go, and from now on sin no more." Therefore, this incident fits the contemporary evangelical template: Jesus displaying unconditional acceptance, which it is assumed will result in her changing her behavior. For that reason, this story is referenced by many authors in support of the contemporary evangelical belief in unconditional acceptance.

A major problem with the use of this story is found in the fact that almost every modern translation indicates in one way or another that this passage (John 7:53-8:11) is not included in the best manuscripts, which means that it is unlikely that it comprises inspired Scripture. Without getting too far into the weeds on this topic, the basic issue is that though we believe the original manuscripts of Scripture are without error, to our knowledge we have none of the original manuscripts. The manuscripts that we do have do not all agree. Most of the differences are minor and do not affect the message of Scripture. This passage probably comprises the most significant difference found among the manuscripts.

Several different theories have emerged for determining which manuscripts contain the content of the original. The most widely accepted theory concludes that this story was not included in the original manuscript and therefore is not actually part of the Bible.

Different versions convey this conclusion in different ways. For example, the English Standard Version (ESV) places in upper case letters in brackets right in the column of text this message: "THE EARLIEST MANUSCRIPTS DO NOT INCLUDE JOHN 7:53-8:11." They then include that section but enclose it with double brackets. The NIV includes a similar message enclosed in brackets in the column of text: "THE EARLIEST AND MOST RELIABLE MANUSCRIPTS AND OTHER ANCIENT WITNESSES DO NOT HAVE JOHN 7:53-8:11," but they also include this passage in the text. The majority of other recent versions of the New Testament use various approaches to convey the same message.

It is unfortunate that even though these versions assert that this passage is not in the most reliable manuscripts, which means that they do not believe it is actually part of the Bible, they include it in the Bible. Doing so creates confusion for God's people.

Because practically every student of Scripture knows that this passage is questionable at best and very likely not part of the Bible, one would think that authors seeking to validate the contemporary evangelical teaching on unconditional acceptance would avoid this passage like the plague, not wanting to base their position on very shaky ground.

The fact that they instead glom onto this passage like a drowning man grabbing a life preserver reveals that even they recognize that valid passages of Scripture do not offer support for their position, and consequently they must resort to this questionable passage to prop it up. Therefore, when you encounter contemporary evangelicals supporting unconditional acceptance with the story of the woman taken in adultery, rather than viewing it as support for their position you will now recognize it as a testimony to the lack of support found in the genuine text of Scripture.

Within Our Reach

Some would contend that the conditional nature of God's love and acceptance place these benefits out of reach of the believer because even as believers we are sinful and thus our performance could never be pleasing to God. Yancey expresses this line of reasoning in saying:

> The Christian life, I believe, does not primarily center on ethics or rules, but rather involves a new way of seeing. I

214

escaped the force of spiritual "gravity" when I begin to see myself as a sinner who cannot please God by any method of self-improvement or self-enlargement.[119]

This inability to perform in a way that is pleasing to God must mean that He accepts the believer unconditionally, regardless of his performance, or otherwise no one could ever be acceptable to Him.

Scripture, however, shows this position to be erroneous by asserting that the behavior of some of God's people have been pleasing to Him. For example, in Luke 1:5-6 we read,

> In the days of Herod, king of Judea, there was a priest named Zechariah, of the division of Abijah. And he had a wife from the daughters of Aaron, and her name was Elizabeth. And they were both righteous before God, walking blamelessly in all the commandments and statutes of the Lord.

Notice that Luke specifically conveys that he is not referring to imputed righteousness but behavioral righteousness—a blameless walk. Obviously, they did not live perfect lives. Therefore, this verse tells us that for the believer pleasing the Lord does not require perfection but a pattern of godly living.

Scripture describes Job in similar terms: "There was a man in the land of Uz whose name was Job, and that man was blameless and upright, one who feared God and turned away from evil" (Job 1:1). Scripture refers to other persons as maintaining lives pleasing to the Lord.

Of course, we all fail many times, and for this reason God makes the provision for forgiveness as we confess and forsake our sins. Our objective should be to live with a clear conscience before God in the present moment. This we can do. In light of God's provision of the Holy Spirit and other resources, we will never find ourselves in a situation in which sin is inescapable. We never need to sin. Rather, sin is a choice, unfortunately one that all of us make many times. But when we do sin, God has provided a means of forgiveness and restored fellowship that is always accessible to us. Therefore, at any given moment our lives can be pleasing to God, and that should be our continuous objective.

Consequently, though God's love and acceptance and all the attendant blessings are conditional, God has placed meeting those conditions within our reach. We can live in such a way that we enjoy

God's approval, as did Zechariah, Elizabeth, and Job.

CHAPTER 8

MOTIVATION OF THE BELIEVER

What should motivate the believer? As we will see shortly, this is a vitally important question because motivation comprises a major factor in success.

Contemporary evangelicals assert that the believer should not be motivated by conditions of acceptance. We should not perform, display agape, so that God will be pleased with us. Doing so is legalistic, ensnaring us in the performance trap, a pharisaical approach to the Christian life. Rather, they teach that we should be motivated to maintain a biblical lifestyle in response to the experience of God's unconditional acceptance, which inspires subjective motivations such as desire, gratitude, or joy. That is, God already loves and accept us completely, and therefore how we perform will make no difference in his attitude and actions toward us. Therefore, nothing we can do will result in more or less acceptance and blessing. Instead, we should be motivated by what He has already done and is continuing to do for us as a Father who is well pleased with us.

In the previous chapter we recognize that the foundational aspect of this theory is unbiblical. The believer does have an obligation to God to produce agape, and doing so does comprise a condition of His acceptance, and God's attitude and actions toward us are influenced by our maintaining a lifestyle characterized by agape or our failure to do so.

Nonetheless, perhaps part of the contemporary evangelical belief system is correct. Even though Scripture shows that God accepts and is pleased with the believer based on our performance, maybe that should nonetheless not comprise our motivation. Maybe God intends that the Christian life should be driven by "want to" motivation flowing from what God has already done for us rather than the quest to escape chastening and get His blessing. Is that the case? That comprises the issue this chapter examines.

First we ask, How important is motivation? Does it matter what motivates us?

The Overwhelming Importance of Motivation

On paper, communism comprises the best possible economic system. It should work well to have the smartest people do central planning and to assign all workers to jobs compatible with their skills. Since only one company produces a given product, there is no need to invest in marketing, which would leave more money for workers. The wealth is spread fairly so that rather than having astronomically rich people while others live in abject poverty, everyone earns enough to have a decent life. In response, everyone should be content and motivated to work hard.

Even though it works on paper, communism does not work in real life. Virtually everywhere it is tried communism proves to be an abysmal failure. By way of contrast, in countries where capitalism is given a fair chance to function, it engenders success.

We can capture the reason why communism fails and capitalism succeeds in one word: motivation.

A guiding principle of communism is framed in the slogan, "From each according to his ability, to each according to his needs." In other words, this system theorizes that the worker will be motivated by satisfaction and gratitude for what he is already receiving. This arrangement, however, leaves the individual receiving the same amount, based on his needs, regardless of how hard he works or how much creativity he exercises. The system provides no motivation, no incentive, for the worker to use his abilities to their full extent since doing so does not benefit him.

By way of contrast, capitalism is all about motivation for working hard. The diligent worker using his ingenuity reaps the benefits of those efforts. Doing so will provide him with financial success and all the benefits that go with it. Because communism does not provide reward for effort and diligence and capitalism does, the former fails while the latter succeeds.

Therefore, while communism looks good on paper, it fails in real life because it misunderstands the significant role motivation plays in human functioning. Motivation makes all the difference. Whole systems of government succeed or fail because of motivation. Whole economies produce vast profit or go bankrupt because of motivation. Families enjoy plenty and stability or endure scarcity and chaos because of motivation. That is the way God created human nature.

Two Distinct Types of Motivation

What is that sound that seems to be coming from another world? It won't stop. It seems to be getting closer. Then it dawns on you. That otherworldly sound is your alarm. You didn't get to bed until 2am, and now, four short hours later, your alarm is reminding you that this is the very last minute you can get up and still make it to work on time.

Do you want to get up? Absolutely not. Do you get up? Yes. Well if you got up, then at some level you wanted to get up.

This seeming paradox is reconciled with the realization that we are dealing with two distinct types of motivation: subjective and objective. With subjective motivation your feelings "want to" take a certain course of action. With objective motivation your mind tells you that you "ought to" engage in certain behaviors and your will responds to that analysis. Your feelings, the subjective side of your being, tell you that getting out of bed is a terrible idea. Your mind, surveying the objective realities confronting you, tells you that staying in bed is a terrible idea with all sorts of negative consequences and that getting up, though eliciting a lot of short-term bad feelings, will bring long-term benefit.

By subjective motivation I am referring to motivation engendered by the full range of human subjective inclinations such as various types of feelings, emotions, premonitions, and instincts— inclination toward action not resulting from thoughtful analysis but some type of subjective impetus. The desire to turn off the alarm and go back to sleep represents this sort of motivation. It is not the result of intellectual deliberation but a subjective response to immediate experience.

By way of contrast, objective motivation results from identifying and processing relevant objective data that lead to conclusions regarding the impact of a decision and the corresponding action. Getting out of bed will enable you to keep your job, which in turn will provide money to buy food and pay the mortgage. Not doing so will lead to the corresponding negative results.

Objective motivation to a great extent is impelled by conditions of acceptance that the mind grasps and on which the will acts. In this case you would be confronted with the conditional acceptance of your boss. Failing to meet the condition established by the boss of showing up for work would in turn result in failing to earn money to pay the mortgage company and the supermarket, conditions for continuing to live in your home and eating.

One major difference between subjective and objective motivation is that subjective motivation leads to spontaneous behavior since we feel like doing the anticipated action. We need not be intentional to float downstream; it just happens. Going back to sleep when the alarm goes off will occur instinctively if we let it.

Objective motivation, however, usually requires intention and discipline. Getting out of bed and getting ready for work when every cell of our body craves more sleep demands the exercise of significant intention and discipline.

MOTIVATION AND HUMANISM

Previously we discussed the humanistic beliefs that human beings possess a subjective proclivity for wholesome living as do animals. Why then do human beings behave so badly so often? They explain this by theorizing that humans have developed a blockage preventing this positive subjective motivating force from exercising its unobstructed influence on our lives. Humanists are convinced that with the removal of this blockage, whatever it might be, our natural human goodness will flow out, shaping us into wholesome, fully functioning persons. Different humanist theories hold diverse perspectives on the nature of the blockage and how it might be removed.

It is essential to recognize that humanists view this motivational force to be subjective in nature. Just as squirrels do not employ their minds to calculate the benefits of getting out of their nests in the morning and gathering nuts, but instead are subjectively motivated to do so, likewise humanists take the position that the pent-up inclinations waiting to be released in humans are of this subjective type. They believe that their release will prompt the human being to spontaneously adopt wholesome behaviors based on instinctive desires as opposed to objective calculations and disciplined actions.

We tend not to think of communism as a humanistic system, but it nonetheless follows the humanistic pattern. As noted, it provides no objective motivation for the worker to produce more. Instead communists believe that the worker possesses a subjective inclination to produce, but that this predisposition is blocked by capitalist systems that prevent the worker from enjoying his fair share. Communism by providing the worker his fair share will remove the blockage created by capitalism, which in turn will release the worker's subjective motivation to produce at full capacity.

We saw the humanistic theory at work with Subjectivism. Mailer postulated that the blockage resided in authority imposed by society and theorized that if it were removed by granting the human being full autonomy he would be subjectively motivated to function as a wholesome human being.

The Rogerian perspective identifies the blockage as conditional acceptance and postulates that its removal through extending unconditional acceptance will free the individual's self-actualizing tendency, a subjective motivational force, to mold the individual into a fully functioning person. Recall that the Rogerian therapist intentionally excluded objective input from the counseling process because guidance and motivation are viewed as emanating from the individual's subjective inclinations.

None of these humanistic systems have worked. We have already discussed the failure of communism. Subjectivism produced the chaos of the Summer of Love and Woodstock, but nothing more. The ineffectiveness of Rogerianism was graphically displayed in his experiment but even more so in the adoption of unconditional acceptance by American society as its core cultural value.

These failures suggest that subjective motivation is not sufficient to impel the human being to consistently make productive choices. The humanistic model is flawed in its underlying evolutionary construct that views human beings as functioning based on subjective motivation as do animals.

Instead, as noted in Section 1, God designed human beings to produce agape by intentionally managing their lives through the employment of their mind and will. In other words, humans are designed to function through the exercise of objective motivation, analyzing objective realities with their mind and implementing the resulting plan through the exercise of their will.

In that section we noted that at times subjective motivation produces agape, especially during the honeymoon stage of a relationship. However, subjective motivations manifested two deficiencies. First, our subjective capacities do not possess the capability for good decision-making. Therefore, even when they are inclined to display agape, these attempts are frequently faulty. Also, our subjective inclinations frequently tend toward selfishness. These limitations render subjective motivation insufficient to consistently produce agape and consequently to engender the resulting human success. Instead it is essential that humans be driven by objective motivation.

I enjoy writing—at times, but if I wrote only when I felt like it, when I was motivated subjectively, this book would never get finished. Achieving that goal requires objective motivation.

Motivation and Contemporary Evangelical Christianity

Despite the failures of Rogerianism and other systems following the humanistic model based on subjective motivation, the contemporary evangelical belief system embraces subjective motivation as a core concept.

The insistence on subjective motivation is explicitly stated in the quotes from Keller and Swindoll above but can be found in countless other contemporary evangelical books and podcasts. We are not to be motivated by obligation, but rather from the desire, joy, and gratitude— subjective motivation—emanating from God's unconditional acceptance.

It is important to recognize that this position is rooted in the comprehensive perspective of the contemporary evangelical belief system. Its approach to salvation eliminates obligation, including no volitional dimension, no commitment. Its approach to the Christian life eliminates obligation, asserting that performance is not necessary. Instead, it asserts that God totally loves and accepts the believer just as he is, that God's continuous verdict regarding the believer regardless of his lifestyle is that he is His beloved son with whom He is well pleased. This position eliminates any basis for objective motivation. Since there is nothing he can do to make God love him more or less, regardless of his lifestyle the believer is living in the fullness of God's blessing already. Nothing we do will alter God's attitudes or actions toward us, and therefore no basis for objective motivation exists. I am perfectly accepted by this Boss whether I turn off the alarm and go back to sleep or discipline myself to go to work, and regardless of the number of widgets I produce.

Consequently, the only type of motivation left is subjective motivation, gratitude, joy, and desire to serve the Lord based on what he has already done for us. The theory is that we don't need the threat of getting reprimanded or demoted or the positive motivation of getting promoted or receiving a bonus to get us out of bed to serve this Boss, but our gratitude toward Him will be sufficient to motivate us to perform effectively as believers without being driven by obligation, i.e. conditions of acceptance.

As already observed, objective motivation is viewed negatively as legalism, as seeking to gain God's favor by certain behaviors. This type of motivation is considered illegitimate, a pharisaic approach to the Christian life, robbing us of the freedom supplied by grace to serve God because we want to rather than because we ought to.

For contemporary evangelicals, legalism is not merely restricted to rules against drinking alcoholic beverages or attending movies, it includes all restrictions and obligations that infringe on our freedom in Christ. They insists that the Christian life not be lived by compulsion but desire to live for Christ. Therefore, preaching about sin and God's chastening or service and God's reward is both unnecessary and misguided.

Mirroring the Humanistic Motivation Model

This position on motivation parallels the humanistic perspective that we described earlier, which asserts that within the human being resides the impetus toward wholesome living, but that this inclination is inhibited by some type of blockage. When that restraining obstruction is removed, his natural inclination toward goodness flows out, subjectively motivating the individual to become the person he was intended to be.

Contemporary evangelicals reflect Rogers' theory in their belief that the experience of God's grace, His unconditional acceptance, removes the blockage, releasing the subjective motivation of the believer to maintain a Christian lifestyle. Objective motivations such as obligation are not only unnecessary but counterproductive, comprising the original blockage—conditional acceptance. Therefore, effective Christian living results from the elimination of these obligation type, performance-based, legalistic motivations, which will allow us to live in the freedom of subjective motivations, wholesome "want to" motivations such as gratitude, joy, and desire instead of the old, legalistic "ought to" motivations.

Though the humanist and the contemporary evangelical perspectives differ regarding the source of this subjective motivation, humanists believing the source to be natural human goodness while contemporary evangelicals identify God as the source, the important parallels are found in the assertions of both perspectives that motivation is subjective and that removal of the blockage releases that subjective motivation, making objective motivation unnecessary and undesirable.

In effect, contemporary evangelicals postulate that believers possess a spiritual self-actualizing tendency, which when freed by the experience of God's unconditional acceptance produces sufficient subjective motivation for effective Christian living, thus superseding any need for motivation out of obligation.

Is the position expressed above biblical? Does Scripture teach that the believer does not need to function out of obligation but instead that the healthy believer will do so solely in response to subjective motivation? In light of the necessity of employing the right kind of motivation in order to enjoy success as we observed at the beginning of this chapter, this comprises a highly significant question. The chapter ahead suggests an answer.

Chapter 9

The Need for Objective Motivation

The question confronting us in this chapter is whether Scripture teaches us that Subjective motivation is enough to maintain a biblical lifestyle. We have observed the failure of subjective motivation in communism, Subjectivism, and Rogerianism. Apparently contemporary evangelicals believe this is not the case with Christianity. Perhaps upon experiencing God's unconditional acceptance, upon realizing His perpetual verdict that he is a beloved son with whom He is well pleased, the subjective motivation of the believer will be sufficiently strong and consistent to maximize agape.

We have observed that subjective motivation does produce agape at times, especially during the honeymoon stage, but this chapter seeks to determine whether being driven by subjective motivation to the exclusion of objective motivation is God's design for Christian living.

Biblical Reasons Supporting the Need for Objective Motivation

The Need for New Testament Mandates

In a previous chapter we noted that believers are obligated to produce agape, but the question here is whether Scripture intends for us to be motivated by that obligation. Scripture indicates that this is the case by including and accentuating mandates related to Christian living.

If God has designed us to be motivated subjectively, we would anticipate that passages related to Christian living would be limited to reminders of our unconditional acceptance, that God is unconditionally well pleased with us, which would in turn stoke our subjective motivation to produce agape. In other words, Scripture would read much like a Rogerian therapy session. Instead, we find in the New Testament repeated challenges based on conditions of acceptance and obligation to live biblically, a very non-Rogerian motif.

For example, in Galatians 6:7-10 Paul warns:

> Do not be deceived: God is not mocked, for whatever one sows, that will he also reap. For the one who sows to his own flesh will from the flesh reap corruption, but the one who sows to the Spirit will from the Spirit reap eternal life. And let us not grow weary of doing good, for in due season we will reap, if we do not give up. So then, as we have opportunity, let us do good to everyone, and especially to those who are of the household of faith (ESV).

In this very non-Rogerian passage, Paul is not seeking only to teach but to motivate. He is not merely listing commandments, but he is warning them that they must act in love rather than selfishly because God will ensure that they reap the corresponding harvest.

The New Testament contains virtually hundreds of passages indicating that subjective motivation is not sufficient by providing believers with mandates, exhortations, encouragement, and other forms of objective motivation.

The Mandate to Exercise Self-Control and Endurance

Another indication in the New Testament that the Christian life was not designed to be lived solely based on subjective motivation is found in the call to exercise self-control and endurance. We noted earlier that implementing subjective motivation requires no discipline because it carries us down steam with the tide of our desires.

By way of contrast, Paul refers to the Christian life in terms of an athletic contest:

> Every athlete exercises self-control in all things. They do it to receive a perishable wreath, but we an imperishable. So I do not run aimlessly; I do not box as one beating the air. But I discipline my body and keep it under control, lest after preaching to others I myself should be disqualified. (1 Corinthians 9:25-27).

In essence Paul is telling the Corinthians that when the "want to" motivation gives out, in order to win the race the "ought to" motivation needs to kick in. We must keep running even when we don't feel like it.

Paul admonished Timothy to "Fight the good fight of the faith" (1 Timothy 6:12). The word "fight" in this passage translates the Greek word from which we get our English word "agony," showing that Paul is admonishing Timothy not to function merely out of subjective motivation, but instead to discipline himself to live biblically even in the absence of desire.

The Example of Christ

Perhaps the most compelling indication that subjective desires are insufficient to motivate us to please God but that we are designed to be motivated by obligation is found in the scriptural account of Christ in the Garden of Gethsemane. In this situation we find Christ saying, "My Father, if it be possible, let this cup pass from me; nevertheless, not as I will, but as you will" (Matthew 26:39).

Fully aware of the awful suffering that would be inflicted by the cross and related events, Jesus is asserting that He had no subjective desire to bear that pain. He was willing, however, to endure that agony out of obligation to His Father's will. In effect, this passage reveals that the greatest expressions of agape come at those times when subjective desire runs out, when we must exercise discipline and courage to obey God's commands, to meet our obligation to Him, and to display agape toward others. Therefore, rather than motivation by obligation being antithetical to New Testament motivation, it constitutes its greatest expression.

Even believers grateful to Christ for salvation and a plethora of other blessings, even believers possessing the indwelling Holy Spirit (as did Christ), do not produce sufficient and consistent agape solely through subjective motivations. We must through our minds identify our obligations to God, the expressions of agape He calls us to display in every given situation, and then exercise our will to meet them. Scripture conveys in many ways that this is God's design.

I find myself challenged by Paul's description of his ministry in 2 Corinthians 6:4-5:

> (B)ut as servants of God we commend ourselves in every way: by great endurance, in afflictions, hardships, calamities, beatings, imprisonments, riots, labors, sleepless

nights, hunger....

We have good reason to believe that often during his ministry, he, like Christ, would have desired to be spared these sufferings, but he endured them because of objective motivation, because he grasped that these sufferings were part of God's plan for him, and he was committed to do God's will.

FAILURES of BELIEVERS

Another evidence from Scripture that subjective motivation is insufficient is found in the failures of believers. The book of 1 Corinthians provides an ongoing catalog of sinful behaviors performed by believers in that church. If subjective motivation were sufficient to produce godliness, it would have prevented these flagrant failures. Paul sought to motivate the Corinthians to stop their sinful practices and adopt biblical ones by reminding them of their obligation to the Lord to display agape, a reminder that reached its zenith in his description of agape in 1 Corinthians 13. After Paul's extraordinary description of agape in that chapter, he begins the next chapter with the command, "Pursue love." The Corinthians were not producing agape by means of subjective motivation, and therefore Paul commands them to be motivated by obligation.

We find many other examples of failure both in the New Testament and in the lives of contemporary believers, including our own. We are all quite aware that we fail many times. If subjective motivation were sufficient to produce agape consistently, we would all have a much better track record.

Contemporary evangelicals might contend that these sinful practices stem from the failure of believers to recognize that they have been accepted unconditionally, and therefore insufficient subjective motivation has been unleashed to adequately prompt them to produce agape.

A major problem with this position is that Scripture does not address spiritual failure from this perspective. Throughout 1 Corinthians or other passages dealing with the sins of believers we do not find Paul telling them, "You are struggling to produce agape because you have not fully grasped the grace of God that accepts you just as you are. The solution to your sinful behavior is not to acknowledge the authority of Christ and your obligation to Him and to discipline yourself to display agape, but rather you need to recognize that you are accepted unconditionally, even in the midst of your sinful behavior, and as you hear God saying to you that you are His beloved son with whom He is well pleased, you will spontaneously discontinue your sinful living and produce agape."

REWARDS AND PUNISHMENTS

The contemporary evangelical view of motivation is compatible with communism while a biblical perspective is more reflective of capitalism.

Contemporary evangelicals believe that we will be subjectively motivated to produce agape because our needs have been met. A biblical perspective related to Christian living is based on motivation by blessing and reward. For example, in 1 Corinthians 15:58, Paul challenges his readers, "Therefore, my beloved brothers, be steadfast, immovable, always abounding in the work of the Lord, knowing that in the Lord your labor is not in vain."

Conditions Related to God's Blessing

The Apostle Peter instructs:

> Finally, all of you, have unity of mind, sympathy, brotherly love, a tender heart, and a humble mind. Do not repay evil for evil or reviling for reviling, but on the contrary, bless, for to this you were called, that you may obtain a blessing. For "Whoever desires to love life and see good days, let him keep his tongue from evil and his lips from speaking deceit; let him turn away from evil and do good; let him seek peace and pursue it. For the eyes of the Lord are on the righteous, and his ears are open to their prayer.
> But the face of the Lord is against those who do evil." (1 Peter 3:8-12)

In this passage Peter seeks to motivate his readers by assuring them that righteous living will result in God's blessings.

Conversely, this passage warns us that, "The face of the Lord is against those who do evil," cautioning that God will not even hear their prayers. A similar thought is expressed in Psalm 66:18 (NAS): "If I regard wickedness in my heart, The Lord will not hear." This constitutes a serious consequence considering the importance of communication in a relationship.

Likewise, in Jesus' performance review of the seven churches in Revelation 2-3, He extends both positive and negative motivation in order to encourage them to produce agape.

Conditions Related to Reward

In 2 Corinthians 5:10 Paul teaches, "For we must all appear before the judgment seat of Christ, that each one may receive the things done in the body, according to what he has done, whether good or bad." This and other passages clearly teach that eternal rewards are conditioned on "performance," our use of the gifts God has given us to accomplish His purposes. Paul shares this same perspective in 1 Corinthians 3:12-15:

> Now if anyone builds on the foundation with gold, silver, precious stones, wood, hay, straw—each one's work will become manifest, for the Day will disclose it, because it will be revealed by fire, and the fire will test what sort of work each one has done. If the work that anyone has built on the foundation survives, he will receive a reward. If anyone's work is burned up, he will suffer loss, though he himself will be saved, but only as through fire.

Some might contend that we should be motivated by love rather than blessing and reward. However, Scripture frequently holds out God's blessings and rewards as valid motivations. The Apostle Paul in various passages conveys that reward motivated him.

Apparently God expects believers to be motivated not solely by subjective inclinations, but He also intends for them to be incentivized by the prospect of blessing and reward.

The Quandary When Feelings Fail

The findings above indicate that just as communism, Subjectivism, and Rogerianism, all based on subjective motivation, do not work, neither did God design the life of the believer to function solely on subjective motivation, based totally on a "want to" basis. Rather, he intends believers to be motivated by obligations, chastening, blessings, and rewards.

Many times each day, perhaps hundreds of times, subjective motivation fails to incline me toward producing agape. To the extent that I control my diet, I do so in response to "ought to" motivation and not "want to." I know that I am obligated to God to eat responsibly. Sometimes I am motivated subjectively to work, I feel like being productive, but many times when I should be working I feel like doing other things. I work because God commands me to be a good steward of my time and gifts. Though I enjoy church with its great music and preaching, some Sundays I feel like staying home. I attend church anyway because Scripture instructs me to go. In many situations I don't feel like being nice, but I seek to display love because I am responsible to God to do so. I mow my grass every week, not because I want to, but because God wants to me to be a responsible part of my community.

Any honest person must admit to finding himself in many situations in which his desires stray from biblical aspirations, and instead he wants to engage in the contrary behaviors.

Contemporary evangelicals who assert that we should live for the Lord not out of obligation but incentivized by subjective motivation fail to tell us what to do in those situations just described, when we lack the desire to live biblically, when our desires are pulling us toward unloving behaviors, e.g. the Christian tempted by pornography.

Those situations leave us with two options: to follow our desires toward sinful behavior or to be motivated by obligation to live biblically. Contemporary evangelicals reject both of those options. They would not advocate sinful living, but they view motivation by obligation, "ought to" living, as a return to legalism. This quandary leaves many contemporary evangelicals confused. Even worse, the easier of the two options listed above is to follow our subjective feelings toward selfish behaviors. Statistics related to the lifestyle of contemporary evangelicals indicate that this latter option is often chosen.

The Ultimate Need for Objective Motivation

The discussion above highlights the limitation of subjective, "want to" motivation and the corresponding necessity of objective, "ought to" motivation.

In the end, the problem with subjective motivation resides in its inability to function at a moral level. Our subjective component knows nothing of promises and commitments and obligations. The theory that subjective motivation somehow spontaneously produces responsible behavior and moral people has never been shown to work. In fact, it has always been shown not to work. Nor does it work in the Christian life. Though this is God's design for animals, He has made humans to function differently.

Only objective motivation can identify and keep promises and commitments and obligations. As a result, subjective motivation cannot provide stability to life in general and relationships in particular. Stability in the human realm requires the objective motivation produced by acknowledgment of obligations and responsibilities and the accompanying intentional actions to meet them.

A profoundly beautiful wedding song, "I Will Be Here" by Steven Curtis Chapman, depicts a groom telling his bride that regardless of future circumstances she can count on him to be true to the promise he is making to her and to God. Subjective motivation can provide no such assurance. It is only obligation to commitment that can make this promise and keep it. Feelings are ephemeral. Couples engage in altercations that can send emotions into a tailspin. A man can encounter a woman at work who may have greater appeal at the moment. Relationships based on commitment, and people with the character and discipline to maintain that commitment, provide stability to families, business, governments, and society as a whole. Objective motivation provides the foundation for maintaining moral behavior and a moral society.

Ultimately, only objective motivation that recognizes and responds to the authority and mandates of Christ will produce sufficient agape to engender fulfillment and success.

Chapter 10

Contemporary Evangelical Outcomes

We are left to wonder how much harm is being inflicted on the contemporary evangelicals by abandonment of Scripture authority and obligations and instead following subjective motivations. This chapter seeks to assess the damages.

Condoning the Viewing of Nudity

One practical area in which the contemporary evangelical message of unconditional acceptance displays its influence is in the acceptance of viewing movies that include nudity.

On December 26, 2013, Alissa Wilkinson wrote a review for *Christianity Today* on the movie *The Wolf of Wall Street*.[120] This movie contains the full spectrum of ungodly behavior, but the review especially indicates that it contains substantial nudity. Wilkinson nonetheless gave the movie 3 ½ stars out of four for factors such as artistic value. She indicated that most of her readers will not feel comfortable watching this movie but left the door open for those who might.

This review elicited a response from Trevin Wax of *The Gospel Coalition* entitled Evangelicals and Hollywood Muck[121] in which he pondered, "My question is this: at what point do we consider a film irredeemable, or at least unwatchable? At what point do we say it is wrong to participate in certain forms of entertainment?" At least part of his concern was prompted by the fact that by some counts *The Wolf of Wall Street* contains 22 sex scenes.

Wax's article led to a response from Wilkinson ("Why We Review R-Rated Films: You're a neighbor before you're a consumer"),[122] which prompted a second response from Wax ("Christians and

Movies: Are We Contextualizing or Compromising?").[123]

I found it informative that Wilkinson apparently has no problem with nudity in movies as long as it is not gratuitous but instead conveys art, enables us to understand who we are, portrays real life (as the Bible does), faithfully conveys the intended message, or enables us to minister to our neighbor by entering into his culture.

Trevin Wax expressed concern that the eroticism of movies such as *The Wolf of Wall Street* may be so blatant as to override any artistry and redeeming message. In response he questions where to draw the lines but can find no answer, seeming at least in part restrained by fear of regressing toward his legalistic childhood. As observed earlier, legalism for contemporary evangelicals includes any restriction, any obligation to live in a certain way. Therefore, they view the rejection of any practice as legalism. This perspective eliminates the establishment of any standards.

In his search for some standard, he was not able to identify viewing nudity in movies as a place to draw the line. Though I found Wax's search for a place to draw a line commendable, his inability to identify one, even related to an issue as obviously troublesome as nudity, was disappointing. Yet the contemporary evangelical perspective on legalism allows for no other outcome.

We have good reason to believe that this discussion between two highly visible contemporary evangelical sources represents the position of a rather large segment of contemporary evangelical Christianity. The contemporary evangelical belief system with its emphasis on God's unconditional acceptance and related concern over legalism has brought us to the point where viewing nude women in movies is legitimate, and even a means of ministry to others by acquaintance with their culture.

Another indicator of the broad evangelical acceptance of nudity in movies is found in the minimal objections to this trend. Since it is endorsed by very visible evangelical sources, if strong beliefs did exist to the contrary, we would expect that open challenges to these endorsements would be quick and vehement in their appearance. Though, as I will mention, some responses to this trend have been forthcoming, they are hardly sufficient to counteract the general evangelical cultural perception that except for blatant voyeurism viewing nudity in movies is okay.

The acceptance of this practice leads us to ask whether the rationales given above for engaging in it are substantive.

- Does labeling something as art justify a practice? No doubt many strippers would view what they do as art, and perhaps rightly so. After all, if dancing is art, why would doing it undressed not be? Is it okay, then, to go to strip clubs as long as I am there to enjoy the art? Legitimizing practices by identifying them as art does not serve as a valid criterion.
- Does the fact that movies portray real life as we find it in the Bible legitimize it? Can we really believe that the Bible's mention that David and Bathsheba committed adultery is morally equivalent to the depiction of adultery in a movie? I do not believe that anyone can make that case in sincerity and honesty.
- Does loving my neighbor by relating to him culturally require my viewing films with nudity? Of the full spectrum of contemporary culture, must I include that piece in my repertoire in order to understand and relate to him? I do not believe anyone can honestly make that case either.
- How do we know if a believer should engage in a particular practice? Throughout this book we have emphasized that God calls us to produce maximum agape: love for God and neighbor. Therefore, we should assess viewing nudity in movies based on that criterion.

Let's begin our assessment by first considering the impact on the viewer.

- How many males can assert with honesty that they have the capacity to view a nude actress, who in most cases would be an extremely attractive woman, without lusting, especially when, as is usually the case, she is depicted in a sensuous context? I believe that almost all honest males would confess their inability to do so. The reality is that almost every male will lust when viewing nudity in movies. Though some might accuse me of being judgmental, I am only judging human nature and contend that any other view of human nature on this count is naïve in the extreme. This conclusion leads us to ask whether watching such movies shows love toward Christ who commanded men not to look at a woman with lust.
- God had a good reason for giving men the command not to lust. Doing so is not healthy emotionally, relationally, or behaviorally but instead promotes problems in all three of

these areas. Therefore, watching nudity in films is not loving both because of the negative impact on the viewer and also because of the harm to others resulting from the impact on him.

- I suspect that most wives whose husbands are viewing a nude woman in a movie, especially an attractive one in a sensuous setting, at some level would feel jealous and betrayed. Though many may not want to admit it, I have had them share these feelings with me in counseling sessions. Therefore, in many cases this practice is unloving to wives.

- Since in this area practically all men might be considered "weaker brothers," not being able to view nudity in movies exclusively as art appreciation, it seems that legitimizing this practice and participating in it is unloving toward those other 99% of males out there incapable of focusing exclusively on the art, who might be influenced by our participation to engage in this practice.

- The impact on the behaviors of unmarried people, perhaps especially unmarried couples, resulting from this practice seems to be self-evident. In most cases doing so would erode morals, the foundational element of agape. Critics may contend that if the movie portrays a negative outcome to promiscuous sex, viewing it may actually enhance their morality. This position exposes naivety regarding human nature. Certainly, the high levels of emotional arousal created by nudity would make a far stronger impression than some underlying moral message.

Another consideration related to whether viewing nudity in movies maximizes agape has to do with the women who expose themselves in this form of entertainment.

- Phillip Holmes in a *Desiring God* article summarizes John Piper's critique of the issue of viewing movies with nudity in seven points, many of which I believe are quite compelling.[124] From my perspective, the most incontrovertible one is related to concern for the women who expose themselves. Regarding this behavior, Piper observes that you cannot fake nudity. A movie can portray a robbery or murder that is not an actual robbery or murder, but the nudity is real. A human being is degrading herself by exposing her body to every man who chooses to look. Whether she realizes that this is what she is doing makes no difference; she is degrading herself, and viewing a movie in which she does so implicates the viewer in her self-degradation. For that reason, it seems evident that watching a movie with nudity is more selfish than loving.

- Piper also asks how many men would want their wife to appear nude in a movie or how many parents would want their daughter exposed for the whole world to see? Therefore, viewing someone else's wife or daughter who is exposing herself is unloving toward those related to her.

We must also ask whether this practice maximizes agape in the societal sense.

- When women expose themselves to millions of men, regardless of justifications, what effect is that having on our cultural fiber as a whole? How does it impact the sexual development of children who are exposed to it—who no doubt have more access to it than we would like to think? How is it affecting the morals of teenagers in their attitudes toward sex and morality? What influence does it have on moral behaviors of dating couples? How is it affecting marriages? What does it do to societal morals in general? What does it do to individual and national character? Any reasonable assessment must conclude that this practice is having a negative effect in these areas. Or to state it differently, it seems to be a reasonable conclusion that our cultural decline in these areas is encouraged at least in part by nudity in movies. Therefore, viewing movies with nudity does not comprise an expression of agape but selfishness toward society in general.

- How does it affect the spiritual life of believers? Does it present a spiritual environment in which the Holy Spirit is free to do His work? Scripture and experience seem to indicate that this is not the case. It seems likely that the individual is less inclined to spend time in Scripture or prayer after watching a movie containing nudity. If this practice has a negative impact on our spiritual life, it is detracting from our capacity to show agape to God and others, and therefore it does not constitute a loving practice.

I have devoted substantial space to this narrow slice of contemporary evangelical culture for several reasons. (1) I believe it is more helpful to consider in detail a specific issue rather than paint with a broad brush; (2) This does not entail an area where evangelicals are trying but failing, but a practice being broadly accepted as legitimate.

Yet another reason for highlighting acceptance of viewing nudity in movies is the likelihood of this practice encouraging other negative trends within evangelical society.

We know that pornography runs rampant in the church at epidemic proportions. Here are some 2014 statistics for Christian men between 18-30 years old: (1) 77% look at pornography at least monthly; (2) 36% view pornography at least daily; (3) 32% admit being addicted to pornography (and another 12% think they may be). The statistics for middle age men are not much better.[125] I wonder if the acceptance of viewing nudity in movies is not serving as a "gateway drug" to pornography. It is easy to see how it could. First, it could whet the appetite of many males for more. Also, it would make it easy for a person to rationalize that if evangelicals believe that watching nudity in movies is okay, why is it worse to watch it on the Internet?

Evangelical women are also at risk. An article dealing with the attraction of evangelical women to *Fifty Shades of Grey* by E.L. James exposes this danger. It reports:

> Indeed, Christians, usually resolute on the dangers of porn, are big fans of James' explicit and allegedly profane sexual tales, as Barna Group researchers discovered in a survey last year. The evangelical Christian research group reported that "there is no difference between the percentage of Christians who have read Fifty Shades of Grey and the percentage of all Americans who have read the book."[126]

One wonders whether viewing nudity in movies has not also served as a "gateway drug" that has made women more vulnerable to pornography and other forms of erotic input. Can we believe that it is loving to God or to these women to participate in drawing them into a moral black hole?

Likewise, one wonders whether the burgeoning tendency among girls and young women toward sexting, taking and sending nude selfies, is not motivated at least in part by nudity in movies. If female nudity is legitimate in that context, why not for them? Taking down these cultural guardrails and consequently increasing the vulnerability of these girls does not display agape, especially when we realize that they may be engaging in a practice that could embarrass and hurt them for the rest of their lives. Imagine if future neighbors or children discovered those pictures.

The sum total of the analysis above revealing that viewing of nudity in movies does not maximize agape but instead produces selfishness brings me to my ultimate concern regarding this issue. The embrace of unconditional acceptance and the consequent war against legalism seem to have nurtured a quest to explore the farthest reaches of what is acceptable rather than pursue the farthest reaches of what will produce maximum agape. We have become absorbed with whether viewing nudity is acceptable as opposed to whether it is productive, that is, whether it produces godliness and agape, whether it makes us more pleasing to God, whether it will lift our society out of its current slide toward degradation.

If that were the question, if we were pursuing holiness and agape, it would become immediately evident that viewing nudity in movies does not comprise the most promising means of reaching that objective. The discussion above reveals the contemporary evangelical pursuit of that which is most gratifying as opposed to that which is most edifying—how much selfishness I can enjoy as a believer versus how much agape I can produce. Contemporary evangelical culture with its hallmark of unconditional acceptance encourages us to pursue the former instead of the latter, while Scripture calls us to pursue the latter and *not* the former. We have adopted an orientation diametrically opposed to the one to which God has called us.

Consequently, we find that instead of functioning as a restraining force against the full menu of seduction being served by the sexual revolution in secular society, evangelicals are participating at high levels in consuming promiscuous entertainment as well as cohabitation, infidelity, divorce, and other manifestations of sexual promiscuity. We will consistently be on the losing side of the culture war as long as our orientation and objectives are self-centered rather than God-centered and other-centered.

Sexual Promiscuity as a Marker of Societal Collapse

Why is national and evangelical decline in the sexual arena so significant. An article by Ed Vitagliano entitled "The morally heroic and the rescue of culture" provides an answer. He cites two secular studies, a 1934 book entitled *Sex and Culture*, by British anthropologist J. D. Unwin and a 1956 study by Pitirim A. Sorokin,

239

founder of the sociology department at Harvard University, entitled *The American Sex Revolution*. These studies indicate that the sexual wellness of societies determines their success as a whole.[127] Vitagliano summarizes:

> Both Unwin and Sorokin saw a common factor in every such decaying society: changing attitudes and actions regarding monogamy in marriage.
>
> Strong cultures always upheld monogamy in marriage and resisted a loosening of mores regarding sex outside it. However, when the people turned away from this view of sex and marriage, they always began the process of decline.
>
> In effect, cultures always experienced something akin to our own sexual revolution as a catalyst to the decay process....
>
> Unwin said the culture "that tolerates sexual anarchy is slowly but surely debilitating itself, impairing its collective health and endangering its very survival."

The discussion above reveals that sexual anarchy is prevalent not only in secular society but also among evangelicals, indicating that secular society is headed for the disastrous outcomes predicted in the studies cited above, and that the contemporary evangelical church rather than providing the solution is contributing to the problem.

Another finding of these studies cited by Vitagliano is that sexual promiscuity in a society signals the existence of wider spread societal chaos:

> Sexual laxness becomes a manifestation of a broader and deeper problem—a growing love of pleasure and self-indulgence. In order to enjoy life's pleasures, self-discipline is cast aside and decay sets in, much like a once strong and fast athlete who has retired to a luxurious but sedentary lifestyle loses the "edge" that once resulted in excellence.

Likewise, the sexual chaos in the evangelical community described above signals broader evangelical cultural decay. One article reveals:

> The findings in numerous national polls conducted by highly respected pollsters like The Gallup Organization and The Barna Group are simply shocking. "Gallup and Barna," laments evangelical theologian Michael Horton, "hand us survey after survey demonstrating that evangelical

Christians are as likely to embrace lifestyles every bit as hedonistic, materialistic, self-centered, and sexually immoral as the world in general." Divorce is more common among "born-again" Christians than in the general American population. Only 6 percent of evangelicals tithe. White evangelicals are the most likely people to object to neighbors of another race. Josh McDowell has pointed out that the sexual promiscuity of evangelical youth is only a little less outrageous than that of their nonevangelical peers.[128]

This extensive article cites many statistics over a broad range of societal issues, and virtually all show evangelicals trending with secular decline. Moreover, the trend is moving in the wrong direction. George Barna concludes: "Every day, the church is becoming more like the world it allegedly seeks to change."[129]

Though it is difficult to establish cause-and-effect in studies in general, and especially those related to cultural trends, one can identify a rational correspondence between the teaching of unconditional acceptance and its corollaries and these trends. This concept conveys to evangelicals the message that God loves and accepts them just the same regardless of their behaviors. It is easy to see how this belief system would make it easier for evangelicals to yield to immense pressures created by the natural human inclination toward selfishness, especially when the secular tide is flowing strongly in the same direction.

This article also contains some good news, suggesting a path to recovery from our current cultural slide. That is the focus of the next chapter.

Chapter 11

Road to Recovery

The Good News

Ed Vitagliano's article cited above includes an encouraging finding. He reports:

> Historically, there were always some within a culture that resisted the initiation of sexual revolution, and these people hindered the corruption process.
>
> While neither Unwin nor Sorokin was religious, both argued from their research that a decaying society might be saved—but only if there remained within it a stratum of citizens who were willing to hold to the culture's moral traditions.
>
> Sorokin explained that, as the ideas and consequences of a sexual revolution become evident, the members of this moral resistance "become more religious, morally heroic and sexually continent in the periods of disorders and great calamities."
>
> If they remained committed to sexual restraint and monogamous marriage; and if these counter-revolutionaries did not themselves succumb to the rising tide of immorality; "the process of decline may be halted," Sorokin said, and the society "may regain its mental and moral sanity; may halt the dangerous drift through complete deterioration."

This conclusion provides encouragement that only a minority is required to save a society. These findings correspond to the teaching of Jesus regarding the capacity of the church to function as salt and light.

The evangelical church in America could comprise that minority if it would purge itself of the secular beliefs described in this section and recommit itself to a biblical orientation. Specifically what would this reorientation entail?

Production of Agape

This question returns us to the beginning of the book and God's ultimate purpose for our existence, which is the production of agape. We are designed to be agape producing organisms. We have observed that the contemporary evangelical belief system, especially unconditional acceptance and its implications, undermines the production of agape. For the church to regain its own spiritual vitality and become that minority that restrains the corruption in our society and restores decency and godliness will require significant alterations. It will necessitate restoration of those elements of the Christian life undermined by unconditional acceptance that will again enable it to maximize agape production.

Recommitment to God's Authority

Unconditional acceptance taken at face value eradicates authority. Therefore, the road back to biblical Christianity requires the reinstatement of God's authority.

The foundation stone for the Christian life is found in a gospel that includes submission to the authority of Christ. Believers must be reminded that this salvation commitment leads to the truth of 1 Corinthians 6:19-20, "Or do you not know that your body is a temple of the Holy Spirit within you, whom you have from God? You are not your own, for you were bought with a price. So glorify God in your body" and 2 Corinthians 5:15, "and He died for all, that those who live should live no longer for themselves, but for Him who died for them and rose again" (NKJV).

Commitment to the authority of Christ also requires the recommitment to the authority of Scripture to which Frances Schaeffer called us. Many contemporary evangelical beliefs cited in this book are easily exposed as unbiblical by numerous passages. This trend reveals that contemporary evangelicals are not taking the authority of Scripture seriously. They allow culture to trump Scripture in the formulation of their perspective on the Christian life. That order must be reversed. Scripture must trump culture. Becoming a minority that stands against the culture will require taking Scripture seriously in the formulation of every belief and the examination of every behavior.

It is only as the church embraces and applies all of Scripture that it will possess both the guidance and impetus to maximize agape.

Emphasis on Performance

The evangelical church must help the believer understand the necessity to perform, to produce agape, in order to please God and to receive His blessing and reward. What does this performance, this pursuit of agape entail?

A Personality Characterized by Agape

Shortly we will discuss ministry, which focuses on what we do. Displaying agape, however, begins with who we are, the type of personality we present. The central element of a godly personality is morality— righteousness. It is imperative that the evangelical community teach believers to discipline themselves to resist sinful behavior and to pursue godly practices.

Evangelical embrace of unconditional acceptance has resulted in a dearth of preaching and teaching against sinful behaviors and the need for believers to strive to live morally. This failure has resulted in large measure from the fear of being legalistic and judgmental that has been engendered by the belief in God's unconditional acceptance. An emphasis on preaching and teaching that promotes godly living must be reinstated. Of course, churches can erroneously focus on external issues rather than biblical righteousness, which leads to superficial godliness. Contemporary evangelicals, however, have taken the pendulum to the opposite extreme, failing to teach and maintain biblical standards of righteousness.

Maintaining godliness also requires that Christians block out the immoral input the Left imposes on our society. Most movies, secular music, and television programming include ungodly content. If we willfully expose ourselves to the spiritual Ebola virus contained in the preponderance of secular entertainment, we will create an environment in our hearts and homes in which the Holy Spirit will not work. I am not suggesting a problem with these media per se but rather with the content channeled through them in most cases. Music and other forms of relaxation comprise important aspects of life, but we must find pure and edifying sources.

Managing Our Resources for Maximum Agape Production

Effective management of our resources for the production of maximum agape represents a major component of Christian living, a condition for receiving God's blessing and reward, and a means of influencing our society.

Peter instructed: "As each has received a gift, use it to serve one another, as good stewards of 'God's varied grace...'" (1 Peter 4:10). A steward in biblical times in many ways parallels a contemporary CEO. He was called to manage the resources of another in order to earn maximum profit. Likewise, God holds us responsible for managing the resources with which He has entrusted us to produce maximum agape.

A manager of a company must ensure that every aspect of the operation is functioning effectively. Therefore, his management strategy must assign the necessary resources to every component of the operation. He must allocate sufficient company financial resources to facilities, equipment, personnel, research and development, maintenance, sales and marketing, and various other components of the operation in order to produce maximum profit. If he fails to pay enough in order to get good employees, production will tank. If he puts all of his money in sales, the product he is selling will be inferior. If he fails to maintain the facilities and equipment, sooner or later the operation will break down.

Likewise, producing maximum agape requires that we manage all of our resources in order to keep all dimensions of life functioning effectively. A biblical perspective on priorities in management for maximum agape might be depicted by this diagram.

It could include many other aspects of the life of the believer. If our family falls apart, if we lose our job, if we allow our health to deteriorate, or if some other component of our life fails, production of agape will decline sharply or even totally cease. As a result, we will probably become agape-consumers.

Therefore, effective management for maximum agape requires substantial knowledge, wisdom, skill, and discipline. The evangelical community must teach and train believers in this type of biblical management and provide motivation for doing so. Effective management of our lives to achieve profit for God must become part of the evangelical culture.

Success in management invariably requires minimizing overhead in order to maximize profit. The goal is not merely to balance resources in order to maintain an effective operation, though as already noted, that comprises a major objective of management. Any owner also requires minimizing the expenditure of resources in all categories as much as possible without detracting from the operation in order to maximize profit. Likewise, producing maximum profit for God requires reducing overhead to the greatest reasonable extent.

Scripture says much about profit. In the Gospels Jesus praised those who used His resources to earn profit and condemned those who did not. In John 15 Jesus teaches that God removes the branch that does not bear fruit and prunes branches bearing fruit so that they might yield more. The apostle Paul in 1 Corinthians 6:12 and also in 1 Corinthians 10:23 states, "All things are lawful for me, but not all things are profitable" (NASB). Paul was committed to doing that which would generate maximum profit.

In contemporary terms, we should not be pursuing the largest house or most expensive cars our income can support, but rather we should be seeking to determine how those funds can be invested most profitably for the Lord. We should not be assigning maximum expendable time to entertainment, but instead we should seek to use our time to produce the maximum agape that it will allow. Of course we need an adequate home and transportation, and continued productivity requires recreation, but these should be means to the end of maximizing the production of agape and not ends in themselves.

The same is true at the church level. Rather than developing facilities, hiring staff, and producing programs that will best cater to constituents, churches will need to make choices that will most expeditiously advance the Lord's agenda— that of agape production. If the church models biblical management, it will help to establish a management culture that will encourage the congregation in that direction.

Development of Discipline and Character

Discipline and character comprise essential qualities for the production of agape. We might have good intentions regarding the production of agape, but without the discipline and character to bring those intentions to reality our intentions will not be productive.

History reveals many cases in which a smaller but stronger-willed minority dominated a larger population. Currently in Great Britain and France we find relatively small Muslim populations successfully imposing their agenda on larger general populations. Likewise, the gay community in the United States, which consists by some calculations of less than 3% of the population, has successfully imposed its agenda on the general population, especially overpowering a much larger evangelical segment of our society.

Why do evangelicals display such weakness?

The application of unconditional acceptance in the home and by the church has discouraged believers from instilling the discipline necessary to develop strength of character. This problem is exacerbated by the secular message to the same effect.

Scripture is clear that character is developed by responding with discipline to challenging circumstances.

> Not only that, but we rejoice in our sufferings, knowing
> that suffering produces endurance, and endurance produces
> character, and character produces hope. (Romans 5:3-4)

This internal strength will only be developed in the broader sense by a Christian culture in which discipline and character become prominent values.

The contemporary evangelical promotion of unconditional acceptance has undermined that value. The weakness resulting from this lack of discipline incapacitates believers in their fight to overcome temptations within and enemies without. The resulting lack of discipline and strength of character is responsible to a great degree for our being run over by the Left.

Historically in our nation, character development was emphasized by parents, schools, and the church. This emphasis currently is missing in all three venues. Many good Christian schools and homeschools provide welcome and encouraging exceptions.

It is essential that Christian parents teach their children scriptural mandates of morality and grace and train them in the application of these virtues in their daily lives. This requires intentional, systematic input. Pastors and other evangelical leaders need to consistently challenge their flock with the need for discipline, character development, and endurance. Parents must do everything possible to place their children in an educational environment in which discipline is encouraged. Where that is not possible, special emphasis must be placed on character development in the home.

Though teaching the content and principles of Scripture provides the necessary foundation for character development, teaching is not sufficient. Parents and others must also engage in the *application* of these principles, thus enabling young people and young Christians to develop discipline and strength of character. Knowing about physical fitness is important. Going to the gym is essential.

Agape against the Darkness

The nonfiction Christian classic, *Hiding Place*, by Corrie Ten Boom records the events related to a Dutch family seeking to help Jewish people escape Nazi capture and extermination. Ultimately the Nazis caught and imprisoned this family for their efforts to hide and otherwise help Jews. It is challenging to observe the agape displayed and strength exhibited by this family in the midst of some of the most difficult circumstances imaginable.

Corey's father, Casper Ten Boom, was a godly, wise, and humble man who owned a watch repair shop. He was now in his 80s and feeble. When the family was apprehended and taken for interrogation to determine their fate, the chief interrogator, spotting this elderly and feeble man, displaying an unusual moment of compassion said to those who had arrested him, "That old man!.... Did he have to be arrested?" He called Casper up to his desk and said, "I'd like to send you home, old fellow.... I'll take your word that you won't cause any more trouble."[130] Corrie recounts:

> I could not see Father's face, only the erect carriage of his shoulders and the halo of white hair above them. But I heard his answer. "If I go home today," he said evenly and clearly, "tomorrow I will open my door again to any man in need who knocks." The amiability drained from the other man's face. "Get back in line!" he shouted. "Schnell! This court will tolerate no more delays!"[131]

Though in so stating, Corrie's father pronounced his own death sentence, dying in prison not many days later, his proclamation of dignity and strength, this glorious expression of agape, pierced the walls of that dark and evil Nazi court and comes down to us today as an example of the courage and power God calls us to display as the darkness and evil of the Left press in on us.

That power to stand against the darkness, however, did not come merely as an inspiration of the moment. It emanated out of deep roots. The story reveals that Casper Ten Boom drank deeply, regularly, and often from Scripture. He acknowledged its authority and applied it to every dimension of his life. This served to form within him a godly personality and a wise stewardship of his resources in God's service, secured by a disciplined character. When confronted by the forces of evil he stood like a tree planted by the rivers of water, and he brought forth his fruit in its season

Even though evangelicals represent a minority of the American population, we also, armed with the Word of God and prayer and empowered by the Holy Spirit can comprise a formidable force capable of winning the culture war and retaking America. Francis Schaeffer implores regarding capitulation to the culture, "In the name of the Lord Jesus Christ, may our children and grandchildren not say that such can be said about us." To this I would add, may history instead record that following the example of Casper Ten Boom we displayed the strength of agape to stand against, counterattack, and defeat the culture of evil confronting us. May it be said of us that *this* was the greatest generation.

SECTION FIVE

MOBILIZATION OF THE CHURCH

Chapter 1

A Third Great Awakening

Evangelistic Decline

A 2015 report on the Southern Baptist Denomination reveals: "Churches recorded 5,067 fewer baptisms, a decrease of 1.63 percent to 305,301. Reported baptisms have fallen eight of the last 10 years, with last year's the lowest total since 1947."[132]

An even greater concern is the failure of evangelicals to reach those outside the church. Attendance at a typical large evangelical church, a good one, would reveal that most of those being baptized are children of church members. If you were attending a church of 1,000 people, the odds are that converts coming from outside church families would probably not number substantially more than 10 annually. There are exceptions, of course, but the reality is that the American evangelical church is not reaching our society.

Why are evangelicals not seeing more people come to the Lord? How can they reverse that trend so that America can experience a Third Great Awakening?

The Eradication of the Fear of the Lord

Belief in God's unconditional acceptance leads to the assertion that we should not fear God. If God accepts us unconditionally, then we have no need to fear Him.

Contemporary evangelicals, however, must somehow explain the many scriptural passages asserting that we should fear the Lord. They do so by redefining fear to mean "reverential awe" or some synonymous term. Eradication of the traditional view of fear is viewed as good riddance by contemporary evangelicals, a move away from the old fire-and-brimstone Christianity they consider an embarrassment.

The plethora of Bible passages that clearly indicate that we should genuinely fear God in the commonly accepted meaning of the term show that this redefinition is erroneous. Genuine fear is obviously what Jesus intended in Matthew 10:28 when He said, "And do not fear those who kill the body but cannot kill the soul. But rather fear Him who is able to destroy both soul and body in hell." It is obvious that Jesus is not talking merely about reverential awe since the thought of one's soul and body being cast into hell elicits the highest level of genuine terror. Many other passages require this same understanding of fear.

Some passages do not immediately yield this definition of fear such as the scriptural assertions that the fear of the Lord is the beginning of wisdom and knowledge, but further consideration shows otherwise.

Regarding wisdom, I recently heard of a youth pastor who abandoned his wife of many years for a woman in the congregation. On many counts this decision was not wise. The fear of the Lord, genuine terror of being chastened by the Lord, would have prevented him from choosing this path. Most unwise decisions would be avoided if the guard rails of genuine fear of God were in place.

Genuine fear of the Lord also serves as the beginning of knowledge. Our present society, having abandoned the fear of the Lord, has fallen prey to blatant foolishness. Peter Singer, Professor of Bioethics at Princeton University, is making court appearances on behalf of chimpanzees for whom he is seeking the same rights as human beings. In his article "Chimpanzees Are People Too," he wrote:

> Tommy is 26 years old. He is being held in solitary confinement in a wire cage. He has never been convicted of any crime, or even accused of one. He is not in Guantanamo, but in upstate Gloversville.
> How is this possible? Because Tommy is a chimpanzee.

One wonders if Singer in his efforts to secure the same rights for chimpanzees as humans will be demanding that they be issued driver's licenses. Does he think they should pay taxes?

Even more bizarre, and more dangerous, "Singer argues that newborns lack the essential characteristics of personhood—'rationality, autonomy, and self-consciousness'[24]—and therefore 'killing a newborn baby is never equivalent to killing a person, that is, a being who wants to go on living.'"[133]

Thus, Singer assigns the rights of humans to chimpanzees but deprives those same rights to human babies.

Malfunction of the human mind is manifested not only by Singer but by those school officials who employ him and those who take his classes.[134] If these people were gripped by sufficient fear of the Lord to motivate them to study Scripture and take it seriously, they could avoid decisions based on ignorance and instead embrace knowledge. How many Supreme Court decisions would have been reversed if justices had feared the Lord?

There is good reason to believe that in most cases in which the Bible refers to the fear of the Lord it has in view the common meaning of the term fear, even in passages where this definition is not immediately obvious.

The Argument That God Does Not Want Us to Live in Fear

Some argue that we should not experience genuine fear toward God by setting up the straw man that God does not want us to spend our lives cringing in fear of Him.

Of course He doesn't. I had a wonderful father, and I had a great relationship with him. With just a high school diploma he managed to become senior vice president of a large Philadelphia bank. He was also on five school boards, and as I recall he became chairman of them all. His success at least in part can be attributed to a keen mind and a very engaging personality. Also contributing to his success, however, were his piercing blue eyes that could freeze practically anyone on the spot.

Despite that cryogenic stare, I did not spend my growing up years cringing whenever I was in the presence of my father. Rather, we had a warm and loving relationship. There were those times when I did cringe, however, and those happened to be the times when I needed to be cringing. Many times those piercing blue eyes, or the prospect of being frozen by them, kept me out of trouble.

Likewise, when we are seeking to live as our Heavenly Father directs, we have nothing to fear. When we take a divergent path, however, or contemplate doing so, we should fear the Lord, and if we do, that fear will be extremely beneficial to us. Therefore, the fear of the Lord does not comprise a negative teaching of Scripture but a positive one.

Or, to simplify the argument, we don't refrain from teaching a child to fear a red-hot burner out of concern that he will spend his life obsessed by fear of stoves. The same logic applies to the fear of the Lord.

Thε Aʀɢυмεɴτ Thᴀτ Wε Shoυlᴅ Fυɴcτioɴ oυτ oꜰ Loᴠε ᴀɴᴅ Noτ Fεᴀʀ

Some raise the argument we previously considered that we should function out of love for the Lord instead of fear of Him. The operative word is "should." I concur that love represents the ideal motivation. Fear is the motivation of immaturity, whereas those who are more mature are prompted to obedience and action out of love. I must confess, however, that I have not outgrown the need to fear the Lord at least some of the time—and those times tend to be critical ones. I sense this is true for other people as well.

Fεᴀʀ oꜰ τhε Loʀᴅ ᴀɴᴅ Rεᴠiᴠᴀl

Unbelievers even more so need to be motivated by the fear of the Lord. The negation of the fear of the Lord by contemporary evangelicals is in large measure responsible for the church's failure at evangelism. History reveals that reformation and revival only occur in the context of the fear of the Lord. One reason Martin Luther was effective in bringing about reformation was the dominating attitude of the fear of the Lord among the society of his day. Luther himself exhibited an overpowering fear of the Lord.

The First Great Awakening in America was precipitated by Jonathan Edwards' sermon "Sinners in the Hands of an Angry God," a sermon that included numerous passages such as the following, in which he describes the plight of the unconverted:

> They are now the objects of that very same anger & wrath of God that is expressed in the torments of Hell: and the reason why they don't go down to Hell at each moment, is not because God, in whose power they are, is not then very angry with them; as angry as he is with many of those miserable creatures that he is now tormenting in Hell, and do there feel and bear the fierceness of his wrath. Yea God is a great deal more angry with great numbers that are now on Earth, yea doubtless with many that are now in this congregation, who it may be are at ease and quiet, than he is with many of those that are now in the flames of Hell.—So that it is not because God is unmindful of their wickedness, and does not resent it, that he does not let loose his hand and cut them off. God is not altogether such an one as themselves, though they may imagine him to be so. The wrath of God burns against them, their damnation does not

slumber; the pit is prepared, the fire is made ready, the furnace is now hot, ready to receive them; the flames do now rage and glow. The glittering sword is whet, and held over them, and the pit hath opened its mouth under them.[135]

The Second Great Awakening was accompanied by a similar focus on the fear of the Lord.

It is easy to understand why the fear of the Lord comprises a requisite to revival in our society. The reality is that selfish living can offer substantial gratification, and Americans find a high degree of such pleasure within their reach. Most Americans live at a rather high level of affluence compared to world standards. This life is good, and in the absence of the fear of the Lord they enjoy a vague confidence that they will be okay in the next life also—*if* one exists. Consequently, they pursue the gratifications of their current existence without much concern for anything beyond it.

Even those not able to experience the good life in reality can easily access it vicariously. With hundreds of television channels, the Internet, video games, almost limitless movies, and other sources of entertainment, a significant amount of vicarious pleasure is well within the reach of almost everyone with the push of a button.

Why then should people be interested in the gospel when they already have a life providing a considerable amount of pleasure? And beyond that, they have been assured by secular society that they are okay just as they are, and thus if there is a God He should be okay with them as well. They have nothing to fear.

One might contend that people can and should be reached by a gospel confined to the love of God and not fear. Though a gospel focused only on the love of God prompts some people to respond, especially those encountering difficult times, most people will not pay attention to a gospel of love until after they are confronted with God's wrath.

Even though the contemporary evangelical gospel message presented in terms such as "God loves you and wants to have a relationship with you" excludes mention of lifestyle change, thus providing easy access to salvation, most Americans still lack interest. A genuine interest in the gospel will be produced only by warning them of their desperate need for it because they are under God's judgment in this life and the next. Though this warning may sound harsh and cruel, failure to warn people of the reality of God's wrath represents the ultimate cruelty whereas warning them represents a profound expression of agape.

Although some would object to the use of negative motivation related to the gospel, Jesus used it, conveying that it is both appropriate and necessary. In our society we find negative motivation being used all the time to sell products. You need to buy identity protection because millions of people have had their identity stolen, resulting in the total disruption of their lives. The stock market could crash at any time, so it is essential that you own a hard asset such as gold. When the power grid goes down the food supply will collapse, so you need to buy at least a three-month supply of emergency food for your family.

If negative motivation works in sales, and apparently it does, then certainly we should employ it if it will prompt people to listen to and consider the gospel message. This is especially true since the negative message presented to unbelievers embodies valid and vastly significant concerns. The fact is that millions of people have responded to the gospel because they had been confronted with the dreadful consequences of not doing so.

Evangelicals wring their hands over why they are losing Millennials and what they must do to reach them. Some suggest that they must provide an auditorium with chairs instead of pews, or this week is it pews instead of chairs? They want a liturgical service but a casual atmosphere or some other nuance that the church has missed and needs to get right. Maybe then they might come to church and listen to what we have to say.

If we would help these people fully understand that eternal retribution is their present destiny and only Christ can save them from that fate, they would be willing to come and sit on dirt floors. I am not suggesting that we should be culturally insensitive but rather that until we help people grasp the reality of the fear of the Lord we will forever be playing cultural trivia that will reach very few people.

Of course, the gospel message consists of good news. It contains God's offer of redemption. It speaks of God's inviting us into His family, of His provision of power to untangle the threads of our chaotic lives caused by sin, of a life of peace and joy, and of eternity in Heaven. Therefore, the total package encompasses a very positive message. Nonetheless, until we first lay the foundation of God's judgment, people in contemporary society for the most part will not pay attention to the rest of the message.

Because of the countercultural nature of this message many will react adversely to it, perhaps even labeling it as hate speech, regardless of the compassion with which it is presented.

I believe, however, that many would respond with the opposite reaction. Many people in our society are realizing that the culture of the Left is both vacuous and harmful. They are tired of super-sensitive political correctness that denies people the right to speak truths that are obvious to any rational person. They are also frustrated that they are not allowed to tell the king he has no clothes just because doing so might make him feel unsafe. Many Americans are tired of playing make-believe and are longing for reality.

I believe many people are seeking not the unconditionally accepting, politically correct God of contemporary evangelicals but rather a God who offers both grace and truth, a God who hates sin and brings judgment on the perpetrator but who also extends grace to the repentant heart. They are seeking reality, something solid on which to plant their feet, and something that will sustain them in the real world.

In other words, I believe America is prepared for a Third Great Awakening.

CHAPTER 2

THE NEED TO ENGAGE
IN THE CULTURE WAR

We might assume, "Well, that takes care of it. Purge the church of secular cultural concepts, especially unconditional acceptance, replace them with a biblical gospel that leads to a Third Great Awakening, emphasize the believer's obligation to 'perform,' to produce maximum agape, stressing an effective approach to management, and this should lead to a healthy church that by its very existence will restore Christian culture to America."

However, that is not enough. Taking back America from the Left requires that the church function not only as light, propagating the truth of the gospel, but also as salt, acting as a preservative in our society, preventing the bacteria of evil from producing societal putrefaction. Doing so requires engaging in and winning the current culture war.

Though winning a war, even a cultural war, may not seem to be an expression of agape, nothing could be further from the truth. The Left is rapidly carrying us toward national destruction. Just as the service of our soldiers who protect our nation from external enemies constitutes a profound expression agape, the same is true of combatants in the culture war who are fighting to save our nation from internal enemies.

Why is engaging in the culture war essential? We find compelling reasons in the evil nature of our enemies, their tactics, the success they have achieved, and the ultimate outcome if they win.

The Evil Nature of the Left

We must be clear about the nature of the agenda of the Left. It is evil. This reality is well documented in David Kupelian's compelling book *Marketing Evil: How Radicals, Elitists, and Pseudo-Experts Sell Us Corruption Disguised as Freedom*. I would urge every American with the slightest reservation regarding the evil nature and agenda of the Left to read that book.

Those who have advocated the killing of 58 million unborn babies, including late-term abortions that employ brutal procedures that inflict excruciating pain on viable, innocent children, are evil. Even after videos exposing the macabre work of Planned Parenthood have made undeniable the brutality of these deadly assaults on innocent children, the Left continues to circle the wagons in defense of that organization and its evil work.

The evil of the Left is also exposed in its advocating, promoting, and forcing upon American society every form of sexual perversion, popularizing and propagating it in movies, television programming, and through other means of communication. They have not only dominated American university classrooms, aggressively propagandizing students, but even worse, they impose their Leftist culture on campus life. They have become thought police, making any position other than their own politically incorrect, smoking out those who embrace different ideas, especially Christian ones, and displaying hostility toward them. Beyond that, they are aggressively working to impose the same agenda on American society as a whole.

Evil Tactics of the Left

Not only is the Left promoting evil and seeking to force it on America, the tactics they use to impose that agenda are also evil. They employ every means available to achieve total domination of our culture and place themselves in absolute power. Because they reject Christian culture they are not restrained by Christian morality, or any other form of morality for that matter, which frees them to employ every unethical means to advance their cause, whether it involves lying, cheating, or other tactics they find useful.

The Left advocates and practices immorality as a matter of strategy and policy. Saul Alinsky's book *Rules for Radicals: A Practical Primer for Realistic Radicals* in essence delineates the principles of war employed by the Left. In a chapter entitled "Of

Means and Ends," he essentially argues that any means employed to advance the cause of the Left are legitimate. He asserts:

> The man of action views the issue of means and ends in pragmatic and strategic terms. He has no other problem; he thinks only of his actual resources and the possibilities of various choices of action. He asks of ends only whether they are achievable and worth the cost; of means, only whether they will work.[136]

This lack of concern for morality flagrantly manifests itself in every aspect of the functioning of the Left. The shameless lies of President Obama represent perhaps the most obvious example. As a devotee of
Alinsky, it seems that lying is merely a principle of governing for Obama. Although his dishonesty regarding ObamaCare provides the most infamous example, it is just one among countless others. His blatant disregard for the Constitution that he has sworn to uphold offers another glaring example of his disdain for ethics, which apparently is for him defined as that which will advance his agenda. It is common knowledge that his insistence on open borders coupled with his administration's opposition to the use of photo identification for voters constitute a tactic for expanding the Democrat Party voting bloc. His interest is not in pursuing the welfare of the American people but only in increasing his own power and that of the Left, and he is willing to use any means to achieve that end.

Obama would not be able to employ such unethical tactics so blatantly without the support of the mainstream media, which also operate with total disregard for honesty, using every means available to hide the unethical behavior of Obama and the Left and to promote their agenda. Their widespread implementation of propaganda techniques to distort truth and promote lies is on display in virtually every newscast.

In light of the evil nature of the Left, its evil tactics, its evil objectives, and its success in advancing its evil cause, defeating this movement represents a profound expression of agape.

The Ultimate Evil Objective of the Left

The ultimate objective of the Left and the evidence of its ultimate evil nature is exposed by the Left's embrace of homosexuality and feminism on the one hand and militant Islam, which displays utter brutality toward homosexuals and horrendous mistreatment of women, on the other hand.

What do these diametrically opposite entities have in common? Only one thing—hostility toward the God of the Bible, the Judeo-Christian worldview, and those who represent it. Like the friendship of Pilate and Herod in their hostility toward Christ, these archenemies join hands in their hostility toward Israel and Christianity. That hostility comprises their only point of agreement, their only mutual objective. Both the Left and militant Islam, which contrary to the Left's propaganda encompasses a large segment of Islam, hold a mutual perverse animus toward any entity representing the God of the Bible.

This unlikely coalition has been especially empowered by an American president committed to both the American Left and Islam. He has used and abused the power of the White House to pursue the destruction of Israel, the church, and America Christian culture.

This reality exposes the foundational evil nature of the Left and its core objective, which is to destroy every vestige of a Judeo-Christian presence in the world. This unified objective can be clearly observed in the Iran nuclear deal, which is designed to strengthen Islam, destroy Israel, and put the United States in grave jeopardy. The commitment of the Left to crush Christian culture can be witnessed in its promotion of the Supreme Court decisions to ban prayer and Bible reading from public schools, to implement legalization of abortion, and to force our nation to recognize gay marriage. They inject anti-Christian sentiments and immorality into American society through movies, television programming, and music. They demand that any expression of Christianity be scrubbed from public buildings. They insist on the prohibition of prayer or any mention of God at public high school football games, Christmas celebrations, and graduations. The expulsion of the God of the Bible from our society, the eradication of any vestige of Christianity from our culture, constitutes the ultimate objective of the Left.

The Shallow Left and the Deep Left

Subjectivism, the ideology of the Left, extends to people the right to do their own thing—whatever feels good. Rogerianism, the psychological expression of that ideology, asserts that people should be accepted unconditionally. The culture that embodies these concepts is propagated by the Left, especially by people in academia and news and entertainment media. Many of those who advance these concepts are sincere, having been indoctrinated to genuinely believe them. They comprise the shallow Left.

At a deeper level of the Left, however, reside those who, despite having shaped and imposed this nefarious culture on America, are not genuine believers. They do not believe the cultural concepts inherent in Subjectivism and Rogerianism at all. They have no intention of letting people do their own thing. They have no interest in unconditionally accepting anybody. This conclusion is easily supported by analysis of their policies and practices, which only allow those on the Left to do their thing, which extend acceptance only when it advances their objectives. As already observed, their sole purpose resides in assaulting the God of the Bible and His representatives on Earth.

They have implanted Subjectivism and Rogerianism into our society to function as an opiate to weaken our nation, thus allowing them to take control of it in order to use its vast power and resources to make war on God and His people, a tactic they have used with great success.

In *Amusing Ourselves to Death*, published in 1985, Neil Postman made the case that while America dodged the totalitarian fate prognosticated by George Orwell's *1984*, we have instead willingly been taken captive by the pleasure-oriented culture predicted by Aldous Huxley in *Brave New World*.[137] The Left has achieved enslavement of the American public to pleasure through the imposition of Subjectivism and Rogerianism.

Postman could not have seen at that time the strategy of the deep Left to use that enslavement to pleasure as a platform for imposing Orwell's totalitarian *1984* on us. Today, however, we can witness this advance of Orwell's totalitarian state by the deep Left in the discarding of constitutional protections, the growth of central government, the exponential increase in the power of the executive branch, the imposition of ObamaCare, intentional escalation of dependence on the state, information gathering by the NSA, and many other tactics.

The Left anesthetized us with its post-Christian culture of Subjectivism and Rogerianism so that in our unresponsive condition it could enslave us. It is succeeding.

The Horrific Prospects

The culture the Left has imposed on us is leading to collapse from within and vulnerability to destruction from without.

It is essential that we fully grasp the outcome that awaits America if the Left continues to weaken our nation by winning the culture war. I sense that most Americans have not come to grips with the awfulness of the realities coming closer with each passing day.

Our economy is a house of cards, confronting Americans with the internal threat of an economic meltdown that could be far worse than the Great Depression. Externally, we face the threats of Chinese and Russian nuclear buildup and the pursuit of nuclear capability by Iran accompanied by promises that it will destroy Israel and America. In recent months all these nations have displayed increased signs of aggression.

While Israel has invested in its "Iron Dome" to protect its citizenry from incoming missiles, our government has made no such provision for our protection, leaving us vulnerable. We are also confronted by the prospects of an electromagnetic pulse bomb that could take out our power grid and inflict other catastrophic damage, which by some estimates could leave 90% of Americans dead in two years.

For many decades Americans have placed confidence in our military to protect us. We can no longer do so, however, because, despite the commitment of many brave men and women in our military, our Armed Forces have been reduced in size by about a third, are being drastically underfunded, and are being used by our administration for demoralizing social experiments.

When confronted with danger, Americans tend to look to government for help. Yet, all of the above challenges are exacerbated by American governmental selfishness and incompetence. Many have concluded that Barack Obama is either incapable of governing effectively or intentionally seeking to take down America and that Congress is allowing if not assisting him in advancing his agenda. He has produced chaos in both domestic and global affairs, placing our nation at a serious disadvantage in both arenas. Therefore, Americans cannot depend on this government for help in times of crisis.

The combination of these weaknesses and dangers leaves us highly vulnerable to an array of catastrophic outcomes. Although the horrors of such prospects are unthinkable, we must nonetheless think about them because history is replete with examples of the extreme inhumanities inflicted on conquered nations that include murder, rape, and enslavement.

We need only to consider the atrocities of ISIS to envision an inkling of the fate that might befall us should America be conquered. Americans tend to assume that the same sensibilities our nation displays in warfare, such as stipulating rules of engagement and treating those conquered with kindness, would be extended to us. This mistaken assumption makes most Americans oblivious to the cruelties they would suffer at the hands of conquerors such as the Chinese, the Russians, or an Islamic nation.

We are not merely facing the prospect of having to downsize the number of family cars or selling the boat or taking less elaborate vacations. We are facing the prospect of the collapse of life as we know it and entering into a totally different existence of unspeakable suffering.

Recently I watched a video of a husband and wife in Syria weeping in utter despair as she was being led off by ISIS soldiers to a site just a few yards away to be sold as a sex slave. We live in a world in which we could also be confronted by such profound atrocities and the prospect of suffering them ourselves.

In 1932 and 1933, Stalin placed quotas on Ukrainian farms that resulted in practically all of the Ukrainian wheat being shipped to Russia. He then sealed off the country, leaving Ukrainians to starve. Some estimate that this resulted in 7 million deaths.[138] Many people around the globe, jealous of the abundance Americans have enjoyed, those who danced in the streets after 9/11, would like nothing more than to see this sort of fate exacted on our nation. In drastically reducing our defenses, Obama is leaving us vulnerable to such atrocities.

Though protection from such awful prospects requires the restoration of our economy and rebuilding our military, substantive, lasting recovery will require ridding America of its irrational and destructive Leftist culture and restoring Christian culture. Therefore, the road back must begin by clearly acknowledging the evil and devastation of Leftist culture and clearly grasping the need to rid America of it. We must recognize that it comprises a cancer in our societal body that is killing us, and therefore dealing with the symptoms without removing the cancer will ultimately not spare us from the catastrophe that is fast approaching.

We must also acknowledge that this cancer has metastasized to the evangelical church, manifesting itself in the symptoms described in previous chapters, and that recovery must begin there. The evangelical church must take the initiative to have surgery and face the chemo treatments that follow, confronting squarely the reality that our national survival depends on it. Only then will it possess the vitality necessary to function as salt and light in our society, and in so doing restore the American capacity to resist internal collapse and external assault.

However, an even more ominous threat confronts America, making the need to restore its Christian culture even more urgent. We will examine that danger next.

Chapter 3

His Terrible Swift Sword

The previous chapter dealt with the *natural* outcome of failing to engage in the culture war—the disasters toward which the culture and policies of the Left are carrying us. Still more ominous than these natural consequences, however, is the *supernatural* one, the terrible, swift sword of God being loosed on our nation.

Is America an object of God's wrath?

To answer that question, we must first recognize the extent to which God has been good to America. He has blessed us in virtually every area of our national existence not only above every other nation on earth but also above every nation that has ever existed. He has given us a rich and beautiful country bounded by seas on either side. He has provided for us a stable and just form of government. He has showered unspeakable wealth on our country, providing us with homes, cars, and other possessions that most other people on earth can only dream of. He has protected us from invasion and given us military victories. The list of God's blessings on America could go on virtually endlessly.

How has America expressed its gratitude? We have banned praying to Him and reading His Word from our schools. We evicted Him from the public square. We have murdered 58 million unborn children on the altar of sexual promiscuity. We have abandoned His principles of righteousness, indulging in and propagating every kind of lewdness in our nation and around the globe. We have rejected His design for the family. We use His name for a curse word as part of common discourse. We fund universities that mock and deny God and teach our young people to do the same. The catalogue of our national sins could go on almost indefinitely.

How do we think God might respond to such blatant rebellion after He has blessed us so abundantly?

When Israel, God's people, rejected God's laws, reflecting attitudes and actions similar to those currently displayed in America, God brought severe judgments on them, which are recorded in many places in Scripture such as Ezekiel 7. It is essential that we give close attention to this description of God's judgment because we have every reason to believe that such divine retribution will soon fall on America. If God did not spare His chosen nation, we have no reason to believe that He will spare us. God through the prophet Ezekiel warned:

> Now I will soon pour out my wrath upon you, and spend my anger against you, and judge you according to your ways, and I will punish you for all your abominations. And my eye will not spare, nor will I have pity. I will punish you according to your ways, while your abominations are in your midst. Then you will know that I am the LORD, who strikes.... For the vision concerns all their multitude; it shall not turn back; and because of his iniquity, none can maintain his life.... The sword is without; pestilence and famine are within. He who is in the field dies by the sword, and him who is in the city famine and pestilence devour. And if any survivors escape, they will be on the mountains, like doves of the valleys, all of them moaning, each one over his iniquity. All hands are feeble, and all knees turn to water. They put on sackcloth, and horror covers them. Shame is on all faces, and baldness on all their heads. They cast their silver into the streets, and their gold is like an unclean thing.... Forge a chain! For the land is full of bloody crimes and the city is full of violence. I will bring the worst of the nations to take possession of their houses. I will put an end to the pride of the strong, and their holy places shall be profaned. When anguish comes, they will seek peace, but there shall be none. Disaster comes upon disaster; rumor follows rumor. They seek a vision from the prophet, while the law perishes from the priest and counsel from the elders. The king mourns, the prince is wrapped in despair, and the hands of the people of the land are paralyzed by terror. According to their way I will do to them, and according to their judgments I will judge them, and they shall know that I am the LORD. (Ezekiel 7)

This passage contains some critical lessons for us. It is imperative that we take them to heart.

- It speaks of God pouring out His wrath, refusing to spare them or have pity. Unfortunately, the evangelical church in America has misrepresented God in describing Him almost exclusively as a God of love, assiduously omitting scriptural truth regarding God's wrath and judgment.

- This passage warns that our nation's judgment will be commensurate with our evil. With the blood of 58 million babies on our hands and our other blatant rebellion against God's laws, we can anticipate that God's judgment will be severe.

- This passage informs us that when God pours out His judgment, we will come to the realization that He is God, that the university professors who mocked belief in His existence were wrong, that sources of American entertainment that thought they could mock and curse Him with impunity were deceived. But it also informs us that this acknowledgment will come too late, that the judgment in progress will continue until it is fully completed.

- This passage assures us that God will use "the worst of the nations" as His instrument of judgment. This conjures up images of cruel enemies such as ISIS or North Korea. We cannot even conceive of the cruelties to which they would subject men, women, and children.

- God warns, "When anguish comes, they will seek peace, but there shall be none." Attempts at any type of treaty or conditions of surrender will fail, leaving us to feel the full weight of the cruelty of these enemies.

- This warning asserted that this enemy would "take possession of their houses." American homes are the nicest in the world. There is nothing more an enemy would enjoy than moving into our homes and either killing us, using us as household slaves for all sorts of purposes, or sending us off as slave laborers.

- This passage notes that the king and princes will be in despair. We tend to look to the government for help in times of crisis, but they themselves will be overcome by the enemy. We will be on our own to face the atrocities inflicted by a cruel conqueror.

Scripture gives special emphasis regarding God's judging Judah because of the innocent blood that Manasseh shed.

> And the LORD sent against him bands of the Chaldeans and bands of the Syrians and bands of the Moabites and bands of the Ammonites, and sent them against Judah to destroy it, according to the word of the LORD that he spoke by his servants the prophets. Surely this came upon Judah at the command of the LORD, to remove them out of his sight, for the sins of Manasseh, according to all that he had done, and also for the innocent blood that he had shed. For he filled Jerusalem with innocent blood, and the LORD would not pardon. (2 Kings 24:2-4)

This passage asserts that God would not pardon Judah because of the innocent blood Manasseh had shed. How great must be the wrath of God against the United States for the shedding of the blood of 58 million innocent unborn children? And while it is true that guilt lies on the heads of those Supreme Court Justices who legalized this procedure, a large portion of the guilt must also be assigned to presidents and congressmen who have sanctioned and funded these atrocities, and millions of mothers who made this choice to kill their children, and no doubt a majority of the fathers who condoned and even encouraged it. Beyond that many American citizens have promoted this wicked cause, and many rich and influential businessmen have thrown their substantial support behind it. Nor can the rest of us claim innocence, because had we risen up en masse to stop this mass murder, doing whatever it took, we could have saved those innocent lives. I am grateful for those who have worked hard and suffered much to fight this wickedness, but the limited and timid response by most of the American people, including the evangelical church, also implicates us in the guilt.

Therefore, unlike Judah where innocent blood could be laid at the feet of a king, the much larger shedding of American blood by a much broader contingent of our population, either by support or acquiescence, leaves us far guiltier before God. Thus, we are certain objects of His impending wrath.

Surely as America continues in its present course, the wrath of God will not be long in coming. When it does come it will be severe, and God will not pity or relent until His wrath against America is spent. As we consider America's thankless response to God's blessing, as we consider America's wickedness, as we consider the many teachings of Scripture regarding God's holiness and His corresponding wrath against unrighteousness, Americans have every reason to be very afraid that God is about to unleash His anger on the United States.

God has miraculously protected this country in many ways and at many times in history past. We have every reason to believe, however, that God's protective shield has been removed, that New York City could be the next Hiroshima and Los Angeles the next Nagasaki.

Please understand what I am saying. The natural consequences of our current culture include decline and weakness that are inevitably carrying us to our destruction. Beyond these natural consequences, however, God will ensure that this destruction falls on us because of our wickedness. Billy Graham wrote:

> Some years ago, my wife, Ruth, was reading the draft of a book I was writing. When she finished a section describing the terrible downward spiral of our nation's moral standards and the idolatry of worshiping false gods such as technology and sex, she startled me by exclaiming, "If God doesn't punish America, He'll have to apologize to Sodom and Gomorrah."[139]

America's wickedness is now profoundly worse than when she expressed that concern. Unless America quickly changes course, repents of its wickedness, and again becomes a righteous nation, God will surely loose the fateful lightening of His terrible swift sword, He will not delay much longer, and when His sword falls He will not return it to its sheath until He has completed His awful work of judgment.

Chapter 4

The Need to Go on the Offensive

Previous chapters have exposed the urgent need for the church in America to go on the offensive. They also have displayed the power of the enemy, which makes that task seem overwhelming.

How can the church take on such a formidable enemy? The answer begins with the reality that we must start by doing *something*. To be passive—to do nothing in our current situation—would be disastrous on two counts. First, it would leave us and our nation to suffer the disasters described above. In addition, it would make us culpable for America's evils because we did not stand against them. Consequently, action at this hour is of the essence.

A major principle of war is *the offensive*. It is impossible to win a war or even a single battle on the defensive. A Dunkirk represents a victory of sorts, but only a D-Day can win a war.

AWOL

The evangelical church in America, however, is failing to take the offensive. In fact, it has for the most part refrained from engaging in the culture war at all. Some individual Christians are fighting the culture war as are some parachurch organizations, but the church as the church, as an organized entity, has done little.

One can attend almost any evangelical church on any given Sunday morning and receive the impression that he has entered into an alternative universe in which the devastation being inflicted on our nation by the Left does not exist. Despite the fact that our nation is being overrun by an evil enemy from within that is out to destroy our Christian culture and every institution that represents it, and despite the fact that this enemy is achieving great success, in all likelihood this Sunday the church you attend will make no mention of this conflict in announcements, prayer, or the sermon. And chances are slim to none that any plan for engaging in the culture war will be presented. At best they will fill baby bottles with change so that brave soldiers in parachurch organization can do the fighting for them. Ostrich-like, the church deals with our impending disaster primarily by pretending it does not exist.

Accepting others unconditionally precludes engaging in war. Imagine if during World War II the United States accepted Germany and Japan unconditionally. We would have had no basis for fighting them. Likewise, unconditional acceptance has left the evangelical church AWOL in the culture war. I am not suggesting that the American evangelical church overtly and explicitly accepts unconditionally the various forms of evil in our nation. I am, however, asserting that the attitudes, the frame of mind, engendered by unconditional acceptance elicits a reticence to do battle with those assaulting Christian culture.

This evangelical non-involvement is devastating because the evangelical church comprises the only rallying point for genuine Christians in the war. This culture war is ultimately a religious war, and the only viable religious entity in our nation is failing to engage in it. Therefore, its absence has left a leadership vacuum. The individual can do little without the leadership the church provides. Its inaction is leaving lonely Christian cultural warriors to be picked off one by one as the church stands by and watches. Only if the church as the church takes a leadership role do we stand a chance of winning the culture war.

It is also imperative that the church engage in the culture war because only the church possesses the capacity to reinstate Christian culture. No Tea Party is equipped to do that. Therefore, the culture war can only be won by the engagement of the evangelical church as a church.

The Church and Politics

The evangelical church often justifies opting out of the culture war by asserting that the church should not involve itself in politics. It asserts that its responsibility in the culture war is restricted to leading people to Christ and discipling them.

Certainly evangelism and discipleship comprise major responsibilities of the church. The church has no biblical basis, however, for claiming exemption from the culture war—for assuming the status of conscientious objector, nor does such a position work in the real world.

Evangelicals assert that abortion is murder. What if a daycare next to the church were invaded by a group of militant jihadists that was killing the children one by one—one every hour, and the church was the only means of stopping them? Would the church assert that intervention would be political and therefore it was not its responsibility to do what it could to save those children? Would it reduce its responsibility to sharing the gospel with those jihadists? Yet in abortion clinics close to churches across our nation babies are being slaughtered almost daily. Does drawing a circle around the abortion issue and labeling it "political" absolve us of our responsibility to save those babies? Are we not obligated before God to actively and aggressively do all we can to spare them from being murdered, from having a scissors rammed into the base of their skulls to bring about their painful demise? Does not the scriptural command to love drive us to engage in saving them? I believe that someday God will ask the church in America those questions. When they stand before Him their "not called to get involved in politics" mantra will melt in the blaze of God's eyes.

Though other issues related to the culture war may not be that dramatic and clear-cut, they are nonetheless condemning. Do we not have a responsibility to formulate an effective response when the Left expels the teaching of Christian concepts and character from schools that we support with our tax money and instead indoctrinates the minds of children and young people with ungodly concepts that encourage immoral behaviors? Does merely identifying that issue as political absolve the church of responsibility for engaging in that battle?

In discussing with evangelicals these and other concerns related to the decline of America and the resulting disaster that confronts us, I am often greeted with a cheerful, "Well, it is good to know that God is in control," the subtext being, "We just need to trust God to take care of these issues." To this I reply, "Yes, God is in control, and He was also in control when Nebuchadnezzar conquered Jerusalem, killing the men, raping the women, and carrying the children off into slavery." The fact that God is in control does not absolve the evangelical church of its responsibility to confront the wickedness in our society nor does it assure that Christians will escape the looming disaster.

I am thankful for the lonely evangelical warriors who are fighting abortion, and the few lone voices such as Franklin Graham, who have often stood alone and paid a price to take on the enemy, and for bakers and photographers who like Shadrach, Meshach, and Abednego have opted to be thrown into the fiery furnace of government oppression rather than bow the knee to the Supreme Court's idol of homosexual rights. I am glad for the owners of Hobby Lobby and other businesses who have done battle rather than cave to the ungodly demands placed on them by ObamaCare. Sadly, though, for the most part the evangelical church as the church has let them stand alone.

Agape and the Culture War

Yet another excuse the evangelical church gives for not engaging in the culture war is that we are bound by Christ's command to love our enemies. Somehow evangelical leaders have concluded that Christ's command to love our enemies trumps His command to love our neighbors.

Though Christ has assigned us the responsibility to love our enemies, when that enemy is destroying our society, our neighbors and children, we are not left with the option of loving everybody in the agape sense of acting for their benefit. Think of the horrendous outcome if during World War II America had decided we should love the Nazis and Chamberlain-like had shrunk from the battle until it was too late.

As the Left triumphs in the culture war, think of what they are doing to our children. Think of the ugly, selfish society into which they are plunging our neighbors and friends. Allowing the Left to exact these atrocities in the name of love is a travesty.

We have reduced the Gospels to the Jesus who blesses the children, conveniently ignoring the Jesus who made a whip and drove the moneychangers out of the temple—twice. In being forced to choose between love for moneychangers and love for worshipers, Jesus displayed love toward the worshipers. The non-engagement in the culture war by the evangelical church in America is tantamount to opting for the moneychangers. Ultimately, this does not comprise a biblical expression of agape but its antithesis.

It is also highly unloving and unconscionable for evangelical church leaders to abandon individual believers such as those mentioned above to fight this battle on their own. This approach is tantamount to the priest and Levite in the Lord's parable of the Good Samaritan walking on the other side of the road, bypassing the man beaten and bloodied by robbers and left for dead. The church as a church must rise up and as a collective Good Samaritan stand with and help those who are being beaten and bloodied by the Left. Doing so does not just include paying their fines, which merely allows the Left to take our money to advance its cause, but must include going to battle with the Left over stealing our religious rights, over giving homosexual rights priority over the right to freedom of religion.

Time is Running Out

Many in our society and elsewhere have been amazed by the passivity of American Christians in the face of such assaults. If doing so reflects the church's desire to be like Christ, it is seeking to be like a Christ of its own making, an unconditionally accepting Christ unlike the one found in Scripture. Supreme Court Justices are willing to make decisions against Christians because they know that the church will do nothing in response. The forces of the Left are closing in on us with the intent to destroy Christian culture and all entities that represent it. As we are confronted with the disaster that they are inflicting on our society, it is imperative that the evangelical church in America wake up to the desperateness of the hour, shakes off its inertia, divest itself of unbiblical excuses for failing to engage in the conflict, and go on the offensive. Time is running out.

But what can evangelicals do?

Let me be blunt in saying that the perspective that there is nothing we can do, that the Left is too strong, that we must passively wait for it to totally dominate us, is a lie. The chapters ahead lists strategies that will enable evangelicals to counterattack, to win the culture war, to reinstate Christian culture, that is, *if* evangelicals are willing to implement them. Launching an effective strategy and winning the culture war comprises one of the greatest expressions of agape that the church in America can perform.

Years ago I had occasion to visit the office of a successful Chicago architect. On his wall was a poster that read, "Not to decide is to decide." All that evangelical Christians need to do to seal their fate is . . . nothing. The window of opportunity is closing. The next few months and years will reveal whether evangelicals were willing for the Lord's sake, their children's sake, America's sake, and their own sake to engage in the culture war.

The most significant question of our time is this: Will evangelicals be willing to go on the offensive, take the initiative? Only time will tell.

Chapter 5

The First Step toward Winning the Culture War

Since the present evangelical church culture is failing to prevent our demise, winning will require basic changes in that culture—and change comes hard.

In previous chapters we discussed cultural changes the evangelical church must make to rid itself of secular cultural infiltration and to be restored to health. In addition to those changes, the strategy below requires that the church make other alterations in current evangelical culture so that it will be able to function effectively as an army in fighting the culture of the Left.

The Absence of Prayer

Some may think that prayer comprises a strange and ineffective strategy for launching a counterattack in the culture war. However, if we believe our own rhetoric, prayer comprises the foundational element. Prayer in fact is the greatest resource the church possesses.

We profess belief in the existence of an unseen spiritual world in which dwells a God who hears and answers the prayers of the righteous. God's people are being assaulted by a powerful and evil enemy, and we are on the brink of defeat. In similar circumstances Jehoshaphat called on God, God heard his prayer, and brought about the enemy's defeat. Either that is true or it is not. If it is not, let's just put a lock on the church door and join the Left. But if it is true, then the only rational first response to our present crisis is to initiate the fight with the Left by employing the weapon of prayer.

In light of this spiritual reality, in these days when the enemy is coming up over the church walls, attacking bakers and photographers and other Christian businesses, it is perplexing and frustrating that during most Sunday morning services in most churches no mention is even made of these assaults in the morning prayer. Likewise, prayer is seldom made for our brothers and sisters in other countries who are being beheaded, raped, and enslaved.

One reason for this omission stems from the short shrift prayer in general receives in Sunday morning services in the overwhelming majority of evangelical churches. This omission is especially egregious since the morning worship service comprises the main gathering of the church. We leave ample time for worship (singing), the sermon, announcements, and of course the offering, but little time—perhaps no more than a minute or two—is allotted for prayer. And most of that time is consumed with concern for our own church body to the exclusion of prayer regarding the decline of our nation and for fellow Christians around the globe. The Apostle Paul gave these instructions:

> First of all, then, I urge that supplications, prayers, intercessions, and thanksgivings be made for all people, for kings and all who are in high positions, that we may lead a peaceful and quiet life, godly and dignified in every way. (1 Timothy 2:1-2)

Most commentators agree that Paul is referring to prayer during the worship service. He is asserting that this should be given first priority— not last—in our primary gathering of the week.

Despite this unequivocal exhortation to pray, beginning with the pressing words "First of all," seldom if ever is this glaring, prevailing, ubiquitous deficiency acknowledged. I have heard fine pastors give an urgent call for prayer to the congregation while they are unwilling to devote substantive time to prayer in the morning worship service.

Unwillingness to assign time for prayer during the major church gathering communicates vividly to the congregation that the church leadership does not genuinely believe in its significance and power. Their actions speak louder than their words. It also robs God's people of a model for prayer, as the current minimal model most churches provide is rather plastic and lacking in the heartfelt fervency of which James spoke.

Giving Priority to Prayer

Given this glaring blind spot—neglecting the powerful resource of prayer, a church strategy must necessarily begin by rearranging the morning worship service to devote a significant portion of time such as half an hour to prayer.

It is ironic that most prayer meetings, which even in most large churches are attended by only a handful of people, consist primarily of Bible studies and prayer requests, with minimal time dedicated to actual prayer. These factors indicate that we do not actually believe our own teaching about prayer. Since prayer is our greatest resource, is it any wonder that we are losing the culture war?

It is also ironic how foreign the approach described above seems to us while Scripture conveys that it was the norm for the early church. We find a further irony in the fact that the American church persists in its prayerlessness despite the fact that the church is growing in other countries where Christians are praying fervently whereas the church is shrinking in America where we are neglecting prayer.

Th**e** Powe**r of** Pr**aye**r

On the positive side, a purified church that engages in the culture war through prayer and then follows God's direction for fighting the war should and can expect victory. God is still answering prayer, still unleashing His power on behalf of believers. The same God who conquered cultures with His truth in the past is still at work today. We have every reason to believe that if the evangelical church in America returns to its biblical roots and from that platform engages in the culture war beginning with prayer, then God will empower it to triumph.

Prayer is especially essential for engendering the spiritual health and strength of the evangelical community needed to engage in the battle confronting us. It is essential as a means of discerning God's guidance. It is also critical for moving the hand of God on our behalf. Without it the rest of our strategy will lack spiritual guidance and power, resulting in defeat.

In light of the necessary initiatives described below, currently foreign to the American evangelical church, prayer will be especially critical to move us to make the required changes. None of these initiatives are out of our reach. In fact, all of them are accessible, though they will take work. The challenge will be getting the evangelical church in America to overcome its inertia, to take initiative, to rise above its current cultural, to push against resistance.

Overcoming ourselves will be the hard part. That will require the greatest prayer effort. If the evangelical church can achieve that, it can with the help of God win the culture war and save America.

Chapter 6

Church on God's Terms

Most evangelical churches today offer church on your terms. You can come and go as you please, join or not join, participate or not participate, serve or not serve, and pretty much live how you want. This approach to church represents an outgrowth of unconditional acceptance, which views the individual as okay regardless of how he chooses to do church.

This model of church on your terms, however, differs from church on God's terms, and failure to do it His way is not working. Rather, it leaves the church with an inadequate foundation for developing strong Christians who can produce agape and fight effectively in the culture war.

Who's In and Who's Not

One symptom of church on your terms is an unidentified church body. That is, no one knows for sure who's in and who's not. Joe, Sally, and their children have been attending for years but have never joined. Because they are fairly regular attenders, the church lists them in the church directory. Is this family part of the church body or not? Who knows? This is the way the system is currently set up, and no one seems to have a problem with it. It seems that no one is asking whether this is God's design.

Scripture holds church leadership accountable for its constituents.

> Obey your leaders and submit to them, for they are keeping watch over your souls, as those who will have to give an account. Let them do this with joy and not with groaning, for that would be of no advantage to you. (Hebrews 13:17)

This passage asserts that Christian leaders will give an account to God for those under their charge. The approach to church taken by the leadership of most churches does not reflect that God has assigned them this responsibility. I say that because they can meet this biblical responsibility only by identifying specifically who belongs, and most churches lack a management mechanism for doing that.

They can meet this God-ordained responsibility only by developing a process for identifying those who belong. This would require stipulating conditions for belonging and determining who has met those conditions. The process would also entail meeting with attenders who have had sufficient opportunity to decide whether or not this will be their church home and confronting them with their scriptural responsibility either to join or to find another church that they are willing to join.

Though obviously no one is going to place guards at the door to keep out those who want to attend but not join, the church can implement a number of measures to keep this responsibility before the congregation. The goal must be to develop a church with a clearly defined membership— individuals for whom the leadership has the responsibility before God to give an account. Visitors are welcome, but the identity of the flock should remain clear to leadership and the congregation.

STRUCTURE

It should not surprise us that God has established conditions for the relationship between the church and its members. We have noted that every relationship requires conditions for meaning, structure, and functioning. The same holds true for the church. The failure of contemporary evangelical churches to identify and enforce these conditions has left the church lacking biblical meaning, biblical structure, and a biblical basis for functioning. Establishing biblical conditions will provide the basis for the organization, supervision, care, and training of those in the church body.

Many churches have a small group ministry, but in practically every case belonging and participation are voluntary. Imagine if each church, with its constituency now clearly defined, would assign members to groups that reflected where they were on their spiritual journey. New believers would be placed in discipleship groups whereas those who had been discipled might be placed in groups that would help them identify their spiritual gifts and develop those capacities. Other groups would have more specialized functions such as in-depth Bible study, helping those with drug or alcohol problems, preparation for marriage, parenting, or dealing with personal finances.

These groups would all meet at a designated time, perhaps on Wednesday night, and all members would be required to attend except for those with compelling conflicts, who would be assigned a different time to meet. In other words, the entire church body would be present. Children and youth would have their own specialized small groups, perhaps focused on systematic development of biblical knowledge and character building. Group leaders would be well trained and well prepared. A brief plenary session might be used to address issues pertinent to the entire church body.

Small group leaders would not only teach but would have oversight responsibility for those in their groups, caring for the well-being of each individual and family and providing a resource for those facing challenges. In turn, these small group leaders would report to an overseer, providing a structure that would give account to the church leadership for every individual belonging to the body regardless of the size of the church.

Imagine how much healthier church members would be and how much stronger the church as a whole would be as a result of utilizing this organizational structure. This structure would lend itself to maximum production of agape within the lives of individuals, families, and the church body. It would also provide structure and training for engagement in the culture war.

The Response

Perhaps the immediate reaction to the idea of structuring the church as described above might be: "You've got to be kidding. That will never happen." It is interesting that every other major institution—government, business, education—mandates structure. Why? Because that's how things get done. So why then should the church not do likewise? One obvious answer is: "That's not how we've always done it."

It might be argued that a systematic approach to church organization, teaching, and training is not doable in our current society. I have a friend who is a director of an educational program for Mormon public high school students that they refer to as "seminary." It includes a four-year cycle for those in ninth through twelfth grade of topics including Old Testament, New Testament, church history, and the Book of Mormon. Monday through Friday the teachers gather at the Mormon educational site for a devotional at 6:10 AM, with the students arriving for classes that are taught from 6:30 to 7:20 AM, after which time they are transported to their public high schools for the school day. I am not suggesting that evangelicals adopt this particular model. I mention it to underscore that conducting an organized and disciplined approach to training is possible even in 21st century America.

Every Church an Outpost in the Culture War

The structure and training described above would enable every church to function as an outpost in the culture war, with strong defenses, well-equipped soldiers, and the organization necessary to mobilize them. The structured local church would provide the basic building block for the evangelical army.

Only military units that are well organized are capable of doing the necessary training and fighting required for victory. Only as the individual church develops a definitive organizational structure and training program will it become an effective fighting unit in the culture war.

CHAPTER 7

THE CHURCH AS A FORMIDABLE FIGHTING FORCE

UNITY

One of the great travesties of our time can be observed in the unity that the Left is able to engender, creating Rainbow Coalitions and bringing together elements as diverse as homosexuals, feminists, and Muslims, while Christians, whom Christ called to unity, cannot join together in fighting the Left—or for doing much else for that matter. From a scriptural perspective something is seriously wrong with that picture.

This lack of unity is leading to our demise since we can effectively engage in the culture war and save America only through unified action. This point cannot be emphasized enough. Many Christians are desperately seeking how they can effectively engage in the culture war, but as individuals they can only do so much. From time to time individuals and small groups of believers find some effective means of inflicting some blows. The war can only be won, however, through *evangelical unity*.

Prior to the Revolutionary war the colonists began to establish Committees of Correspondence, which initiated the unification of the colonies. It was this unification that ultimately led to the birth of our nation. Those involved in these committees recognized that as long as the colonies were separated they would be at the mercy of England. The unity they initiated made our freedom possible.

Likewise today, evangelical denominations, churches, parachurch organizations, and other evangelical entities need to establish Committees of Correspondence that work toward unification among evangelicals of the nature that will enable us to fight for freedom from the tyranny of the Left being imposed on us through our government and especially through an unelected judiciary. I believe that the Left's greatest secret fear is a unified evangelical opponent. They know that if we were united we could win the culture war, but as long as we remain fragmented they can dominate us.

The capacity of unified evangelicals was demonstrated by the "Moral Majority," which was instrumental in bringing in the Reagan years, even though that movement did not enjoy total evangelical participation. The power of evangelical unity is also displayed from a negative perspective in the loss of the 2012 presidential election because a large segment of evangelical voters—some estimate half—stayed home. A unified and engaged evangelical church would have spared American society the terrible disaster President Obama is inflicting during his second term.

In referring to unity I am not suggesting that all churches in a given town drop their individual identities and join together as a united church. Though that might be ideal, at this point in history it is not practical. I am suggesting the establishment of a non-tax-exempt organization free from government control that would serve as a social action center, providing leadership and coordination for all evangelical denominations and churches in fighting the culture war. It is essential to stress that this entity would not in any way exercise authority over churches. Rather, all participation would be voluntary. That said, however, effectiveness would require a high degree of participation and responsiveness.

The creation of such an entity would require initiative by major denominations, independent churches, parachurch organizations, and other evangelical bodies. They would need to join together in its formation and support. This social action center would serve as the centerpiece of the strategy for the battle against the Left. Without such a unifying entity, evangelicals have little hope of prevailing in the culture war. United, they have a high prospect of winning.

Figures vary widely regarding the percentage of Americans who are committed evangelicals. Some of the variance results from differing definitions of the term "evangelical." But 10% seems to be a good estimate. Rounding off the population of America to 300 million, that would indicate that there are 30 million committed evangelicals, which would probably translate into more than 20 million adults.

I am convinced, however, that the figure would be somewhat higher for several reasons. First, as noted above, I believe that a biblical gospel message would initiate a Third Great Awakening, which would expand the roles of the evangelical church.

In addition, I am convinced that many believers who currently are hanging around the fringes, discouraged because of the evangelical church's oblivion to our current crisis and the resulting lack of initiative, would reengage upon seeing meaningful activity and thus become active participants in the culture war.

Millennials would be among those ready to engage, many of whom are looking for a cause worth living and dying for, which the contemporary evangelical church is currently not providing. I am convinced that if these Millennials saw evangelicals actively and meaningfully engaging in the culture war, instead of dropping out they would be at the forefront of the battle.

The number of evangelicals would also expand because of renewed participation by men. Contemporary evangelicals wonder why they are losing men. They fail to realize that the church's feelings-oriented, unconditionally-accepting message and modus operandi is a turnoff for men. An evangelical church that replaces the message of unconditional acceptance with an approach conveying reality and strength would again attract men. Likewise, as the church engaged in the culture war with an effective strategy, a substantial contingent of men would show up ready to participate in the fight.

With the additions anticipated above, the number of evangelicals committed to the culture war could expand substantially.

The need for unified action underscores the importance of the structure within the local church described above, which would enable churches to function as army units with trained soldiers responsive to the leadership of the social action center. The 20-million-plus adult evangelicals referenced above would not be loosely connected and somewhat engaged people but rather members who belong to a tight-knit organization, structured from top to bottom, and thus capable of being responsive to leadership in the employment of various strategies. This structure would enable the evangelical church in America to function as a mighty army, fighting effectively, and taking strategic objectives in the culture war.

Leadership

The development of a social action center as described above would require a qualified person willing to take leadership. Those forming the social action center would need to prayerfully identify and recruit a person with the necessary qualification.

If a person with visibility and leadership skills such as Franklin Graham would be approached and willing to take leadership in such an organization, I believe most evangelical churches would be responsive. A less visible but sufficiently motivated and gifted person could also serve in this role. God has designed us to follow leaders as opposed to organizations and committees.

Though perhaps enthusiasm for following such a leader might not have emerged a few years ago, people are sensing the desperateness of the hour and eagerly seeking an effective way to engage in the culture war. I believe they would respond if an effective leader emerged. One of the objectives of the prayer initiative cited above would be to ask God to identify and provide that leader.

Evangelicals need not wait for the emergence of this leader. Instead, they can pray for God's guidance and then take action to draft one. For example, if a person in the pew created a Facebook page seeking to draft Franklin Graham to take leadership, and it received 100,000 likes, or if a group of denominational leaders would visit him and ask him to prayerfully consider assuming this role, I believe he would think and pray seriously regarding this possibility.

One caution is in order, however. The wrong leader, especially one stuck in the contemporary evangelical unconditional acceptance mode or one who is not sufficiently aggressive, would make the whole concept of a social action center a liability rather than an asset. The result would be the squandering of resources without gaining victories, while giving evangelicals a sense that they were achieving something when they were not. At the outset of the Civil War, the North was losing because its generals would not fight, a source of consternation for President Lincoln. Similarly, evangelicals do not merely need a leader. Rather, it is essential that we discover God's selection—one willing to engage aggressively in the culture war.

The teaching of unconditional acceptance has prevented Christians from displaying initiative and strength in fighting the culture war. The Apostle Paul's confrontation with Elymas provides us with a model for taking on the fight with evil.

> But Elymas the sorcerer (for so his name is translated) withstood them, seeking to turn the proconsul away from the faith. Then Saul, who also is called Paul, filled with the Holy

Spirit, looked intently at him and said, "O full of all deceit and all fraud, you son of the devil, you enemy of all righteousness, will you not cease perverting the straight ways of the Lord? And now, indeed, the hand of the Lord is upon you, and you shall be blind, not seeing the sun for a time." And immediately a dark mist fell on him, and he went around seeking someone to lead him by the hand. (Acts 13:8-11 NKJV)

This verbal assault did not comprise a fleshly outburst, but rather this passage tells us that Paul spoke these words in response to being filled with the Holy Spirit. Contemporary evangelicals would condemn this type of response. I believe, though, that a need exists for a display of this type of conviction and strength in presenting our position.

President Obama shows far greater strength in advancing his agenda than do most contemporary evangelicals. Unless God gives the evangelical church a leader with strength and willingness to confront God's enemies as did Jesus in the Temple and Paul in the passage above, we will be ineffective in fighting the culture war.

HUMAN CAPITAL

Waging war successfully requires planning and strategy, which requires a high level of expertise. The social action center would need to identify and utilize personnel for its staff with a great deal of savvy in areas such as politics, marketing, communications, use of social media, management, finances, public relations, etc. God has blessed the church with these skilled people, and with unity and proper leadership they will be eager to employ their skills in fighting the culture war.

The homosexual community has successfully advanced its agenda based on a strategy presented in the book *After the Ball – How America will conquer its fear and hatred of Gays in the 90s*, by Marshall Kirk and Hunter Madsen.[140] Kirk was a researcher in neuropsychiatry and Madsen earned a doctorate in politics from Harvard and worked in advertising on Madison Avenue.[141] Their effectiveness demonstrates the benefit of high levels of expertise in developing and implementing a strategy.

Christians must find and utilize the same level of skill in order to succeed.

Monetary Capital

For the social action center to function and implement various strategies it would require substantial financial resources.

The willingness of churches and individuals to give would be predicated on the social action center being run efficiently and effectively, more like a business and less like the government. If the social action center was efficient and effective, most Christians would be so enthused by the fact that evangelicals were engaging in the culture war effectively that they would willingly increase their personal giving for this purpose. I do not believe the availability of sufficient finances would present a problem.

Social Media

One special gift from God to the church in contemporary times resides in social media. Communications comprise a critical element for every army. The Internet and social media could serve as a means of coordinating initiatives in the culture war. These tools will be especially effective in the hands of those with technical, organizational, and marketing skills. An evangelical army coordinated through this medium would be able to exercise significant power in launching a counterattack.

Social media has been used around the globe to enable smaller revolutionary entities to defeat larger, more established ones. It served as a dominant force in the Egyptian revolution that resulted in the resignation of President Hosni Mubarak and the dissolution of the ruling National Democratic Party. Unfortunately, these developments led to the Muslim Brotherhood's takeover. Nonetheless, this revolution demonstrates the capacity of social media to empower a smaller revolutionary group to get out its message and coordinate its efforts.

Facebook, Twitter, and other elements of social media and Internet capability or other social media that the church might create for itself would provide powerful tools for waging culture war in the hands of a knowledgeable and skilled social action center.

Chapter 8

Strategies for Winning

If evangelicals developed the configuration described above, they would comprise a formidable fighting force. With the local church well organized and trained, with a unifying social action center, with an effective leader and a staff possessing expertise in a wide variety of areas, with a communication network set up through social media, and through the power of Holy Spirit and prayer, the evangelical church in America would be sufficiently well equipped, organized, and empowered to win the culture war.

The one remaining necessity would be the formulation of an effective strategy, which would be well within the capacities of the social action center enabled by the Holy Spirit, guided by Scripture, seeking God's direction in prayer, organized by an effective leader, and advised by a staff possessing high levels of expertise.

Though such a social action center with the expertise available to it would be capable of developing a strategy far beyond anything I could devise, I mention the following ideas just to give some inkling of the possibilities.

Evangelistic Engagement

The organization and capabilities described above could serve as a potent instrument for evangelism. For example, I mentioned earlier that a major hindrance to evangelism in America resides in the absence of the fear of the Lord. The social action center could coordinate a national
campaign to create awareness among Americans of biblical truth in that regard or some other facet of the gospel message.

For example, for a month it could communicate the message

through radio and television advertising, social media, billboards, etc., that someday everyone has an appointment with death, raising the question of their destination beyond that. This message would be very carefully crafted, using the best marketing techniques both in terms of the framing of the message and designating the outlets through which the message would be communicated.

That month might be followed by a coordinated series of evangelistic campaigns throughout the nation that would help people deal with the issue of their eternal destiny.

This type of coordination would enhance evangelism by flooding the nation as a whole with a singular message, one that people might even begin to look for in various places. This sort of coordinated campaign would give both motivation and opportunity for Christians to engage friends in conversations related to the emphasis of the month. It could be used to shape our culture so as to make it more amenable to the gospel. It would arouse sufficient interest that by the end of the month people would be more inclined to attend an evangelistic rally or watch it on television or on the Internet.

Political Engagement

The social action center could wield substantial influence in national, regional, and local elections, in many cases determining the outcome. The power of such an organization becomes evident when we consider that most elections are decided by just a few percentage points.

We find the Left exercising its influence over the voting process through organizations such as labor unions. Therefore, it is essential that those committed to a Christian culture also become active and unified in supporting good candidates.

Of course, I am not suggesting that churches require that its people vote for a certain candidate, but the social action center could influence its constituency by providing information that would help them make informed choices. Knowing that a candidate was the choice of the social action center probably would be a deciding factor for most believers.

Perhaps the greatest impact on elections would result from encouraging all constituents to vote, which would make a huge difference in outcomes. In addition, the social action center could mobilize people to encourage friends and neighbors to vote in a certain direction, to put out yard signs, and to be politically active in other ways, multiplying their influence.

Imagine the political power the use of social media could unleash in mobilizing evangelicals as active participants in local, state, and national elections. Think also of the influence unleashed by the outcomes of such elections, for example, evangelicals serving on local school boards. An added benefit would be that the political power engendered by this mechanism would encourage more good candidates to run for office.

This political influence would also give the social action center leverage with elected officials, allowing it to influence legislation. This would provide evangelicals with a powerful weapon in fighting the culture war. For example, the political influence the social action center exercised could wrest control of our educational system from liberals.

The social action center could also use its political influence to help persecuted brothers and sisters around the globe. This could be achieved through putting pressure on the American government to assist those being persecuted by using the billions of dollars America gives in aid to other countries as leverage to ensure the rights of Christians. The social action center could also coordinate letter writing campaigns, which are helpful in achieving good treatment and release of prisoners. Many other strategies could be used to alleviate the suffering of persecuted Christians.

Cultural Engagement

This unifying organization could also exercise influence by boycotting certain organizations or products. In this area also social media would be especially effective, providing a channel for announcing boycotts, explaining the reason for them, and updating constituents on progress. The American Family Association has done effective work in this area as evidenced by its recent boycott of Target, but the unifying organization in view would possess a far greater capacity to exercise such influence.

Boycotting could influence advertisers to drop support of television shows with immoral content or dissuade companies from establishing anti-Christian policies. As such, it could serve as a preservative, blocking the encroachment of ungodly influences.

This strategy could be used to counter similar ones the Left uses to punish those supporting Christian values such as traditional marriage. One wonders if the Left would have been able to force

Brandon Eich out of Mozilla if evangelicals had possessed unity and a social media presence sufficient to counterattack the assault used to destroy him. Without such an evangelical presence, the destruction of a man such as Brandon Eich puts every CEO and other prominent person on notice that they are vulnerable to a similar demise if they display even the least opposition to the gay agenda. Therefore, a similar evangelical presence is essential for effectively engaging in the culture war.

Rallies

The social action center could also be used to organize rallies in various areas of the country, which could provide encouragement and spiritual input to evangelicals as well as a means of evangelistic outreach. Imagine the impact if in even moderate-sized population centers evangelicals could fill stadiums to overflowing with only a modest amount of advertising because of the social action center's coordination of evangelical efforts through social media.

Such rallies could enhance unity and provide a sense of solidarity, consequently energizing participants and attracting others.

Demonstrations

Demonstrations comprise a more dramatic strategy, but one legitimized in some instances by the aggression of the Left, the radical nature of the societal changes they are imposing on our country, and the resulting destruction of our nation.

I believe that if in 1973 when the Supreme Court decided *Roe v. Wade* a massive evangelical demonstration had been organized and launched in our nation's capital, accompanied by a massive public relations campaign designed to educate the United States population on the cruel nature of abortion, the lives of millions of babies could have been spared.

While babies continue to be slaughtered, encouraged by our present administration and funded by our present Congress, can we avoid the responsibility to act aggressively to spare their lives? Shrinking from the use of every means available to us leaves the blood of babies on our hands.

Abortion is not the only cause in our society that demands a more aggressive strategy. Our leadership would need wisdom to determine which battles we should fight, how, and when.

To be effective, demonstrations would need clearly defined objectives, effective plans for reaching those objectives, full participation, and the will to push against resistance and outlast opposition. Carefully chosen and well-executed implementation of this strategy would serve to significantly advance the fight against the Left and reestablish a Christian culture in our nation.

THE FIRST STEP

If the contemporary evangelical church is willing to take the first step, the rest of the strategy outlined above will fall into place resulting in victory. As asserted above, that first step is prayer. The need is not for some special prayer initiative, concerts of prayer, or even prayer meetings, though these are good and helpful. The need is for churches to carve out a significant segment of the primary church service—for example, half an hour—for that purpose. Churches need to shorten other activities, make the service longer, or do whatever else is needed to make this happen.

Willingness to take this first essential step, one within the reach of every church, one that costs no money, will provide the power and momentum for the rest of the strategy and the resulting victory. There is no question whether the evangelical church can take back America. It can. The only question is whether we have the commitment to the Lord, to our children, and to this country to begin the process by a meaningful, biblical commitment to prayer.

CHAPTER 9

HOUR of DECISION

Sinkable

On the tenth day of April, 1912, the *Titanic*, the largest ship afloat, left Southampton, England, on her maiden voyage to New York City. So confident were her builders that she was unsinkable that they included only enough lifeboats to accommodate half of her 2,200 passengers and crew, and those were only intended to pick up passengers of other ships that may have sunk.

When at 11:40 PM on April 14 she hit an iceberg and began to take on water, so confident were the passengers that she was unsinkable that for a while activities on the ship continued as usual and without anxiety. Elizabeth Shutes, a survivor reported being assured that everything was okay and consequently took no action to prepare to abandon the ship. It was not until she overheard an officer state, "We can keep the water out for a while," that she knew danger was serious and imminent.[142]

Sometime within the two hours and 40 minutes between the *Titanic's* collision with the iceberg and its sinking beneath the waters the awful reality of disaster set in. During that time men took their wives and children to lifeboats, knowing that they were seeing them for the last time. Within the next few hours, 1522 passengers and crew perished in the icy waters.

Most Americans convey a belief that our nation is unsinkable. In fact, recently I heard a talk show host after lamenting our societal decline conclude, "There will always be an America," connoting that while our nation may not continue to enjoy its previous heights of freedom and affluence, it will continue on as a society only with diminished levels of these qualities. This same conviction that America is unsinkable reflects itself in both secular and evangelical attitudes and lack of definitive actions. Though in the 1960s we hit an iceberg and are taking on water, we will not sink but only float a little lower in the water.

Adding to the tragedy of the *Titanic* are the high prospects that she could have been saved. Joseph M Greely has written an article explaining various actions that could have been taken that likely would have prevented the *Titanic* from sinking, or at least kept it afloat long enough to rescue all of the passengers.[143] The *Carpathia*, the ship that rescued passengers from her lifeboats, arrived less than two hours after the *Titanic* sank. Greely calculates that appropriate action would have kept the *Titanic* afloat at least that long. He believes that the inactivity of the captain, who seemed to be in shock, ultimately resulted in the sinking of the ship. How tragic if history should record that the demise of the United States resulted from the inactivity of its people, especially evangelical Christians, who have within their grasp the capacity to save it.

Need for Aggressive Action

It is crucial to come to grips with the realities confronting us. The culture being imposed on our society by the Left is engendering selfishness and draining it of agape, shriveling it to a vestige of the nation we once were. The resulting dangers that threaten our way of life and very existence are real and terrible. The judgment God is about to mete out on us is terrifying. Only bold, aggressive, definitive action by the evangelical church will save us. We are not merely dealing with political battles for power or promoting abstract philosophical preferences. The issue confronting us is our very survival. If we do not diametrically reverse the course in which America is traveling, life as we know it will cease to exist.

If you believe that some of the courses of action described above are too aggressive, I would invite you to consider the actions the Left is taking. In an America unquestionably founded with a Christian cultural orientation, they have fought for and won prohibition against prayer and Bible reading in schools, legalized the murder of unborn babies, changed the definition of marriage to include homosexual relationships, and given sexual preference legal priority over religious conviction, just to reiterate a few of their victories.

The point is that the Left has not been timid in its agenda to take over a country that does not belong to them. Instead, they have been on the offensive, imposing their bold and aggressive agenda on us, while we have been on the defensive, weak, and tentative in our response. They have consistently taken the initiative and set the agenda while we have consistently failed to act but instead managed only to react to their initiatives, positioning ourselves so as never to *take* ground but at best not to lose too much. Consequently, the evil internal enemies of this country have relentlessly advanced their agenda.

Unless the American evangelical church gets off the defensive and goes on the offensive, unless it develops an agenda of its own that does more than seek to slow the liberal juggernaut but rather seeks to aggressively take back this country, unless we stop living in fear of the media and other elements of the Left and start acting in courage, we will allow the wicked forces currently dominating this country to drag it to its demise—and us and our children with it.

This country was founded predominantly by Christians and with a Christian cultural orientation. That cultural orientation brought this nation success. Therefore, our position, fighting for and demanding a return to that orientation, represents the rational and rightful realignment of America. The enemies of Christianity are the intruders in this nation, and we are its rightful heirs. We must divest ourselves of the attitude that somehow this is their country and we are outsiders, having to settle for whatever crumbs they are willing to drop from their table. Instead, we must rid this nation of their evil influence, reestablishing the God of the Bible, the Creator referenced in the Declaration of Independence, as the God in whom we trust and the God whose authority we acknowledge.

Though liberals enjoy stipulating rules of engagement for our troops— rules responsible for the maiming and death of many of our courageous soldiers—they themselves observed no rules of engagement in their declaration of war on our nation, willing to lie, cheat, and employ other immoral tactics to gain power and impose their evil agenda on us.

Our only options are to defeat them or to be destroyed by them. As our nation fought for its very existence during World War II, General Douglas MacArthur eloquently framed the realities confronting us in these terms: "From the Far East I send you one single thought, one sole idea—written in red on every beachhead from Australia to Tokyo—There is no substitute for victory!" That same reality confronts the evangelical church today in our war against the internal enemies of America.

Soon it will be too late, but I believe that the door of opportunity is still cracked open sufficiently for God's people in America to achieve victory if we are willing to fight. If we pray that God provides us with the will and courage and wisdom to do so, if we commit ourselves to defeat those who have imposed an ugly, godless, agape-devouring culture on our nation, if instead we restore our life-giving, agape-producing Christian culture to its rightful place, then the future of this nation will be that expressed by Francis Scott Key in the final verse of our National Anthem:

> Then conquer we must, when our cause it is just,
> And this be our motto: "In God is our trust."
> And the star-spangled banner in triumph shall wave
> O'er the land of the free and the home of the brave!

Endnotes

1   [1]http://www.quotationspage.com/quote/35028.html
2   http://www.nationalreview.com/article/374303/   untruthful-and-untrustworthy-government-victor-davis-hanson
3   http://lemonsmile.tumblr.com
4   Olasky, Marvin. *The Tragedy of American Compasssion.* Wheaton, IL: Crossway Books, 1992.
5   http://www.theroadtoemmaus.org/RdLb/21PbAr/Hst/US/Orig13ReligHist.htm
6   http://www.westernjournalism.com/this-day-73-years-agomarked-a-turning-point-in-the-pacific-war/
7   Bloom, Allan. *The Closing of the American Mind*: New York: Simon & Schuster, 1987, p. 58.
8   Mangalwadi, Vishal (2011-05-10). *The Book that Made Your World: How the Bible Created the Soul of Western Civilization.* Nashville: Thomas Nelson [Kindle Edition, p. 58].
9   Rees, D. Vaughn. The 'Jesus Family in Communist China; *Modern Miracle of New Testament Christianity.* London: Paternoster Press, 1959.
10 Obama, Barack (2007-01-09). *Dreams from My Father: A Story of Race and Inheritance.* Crown Publishing Group [Kindle Edition, p. 48].
11 Ibid., p. 50.
12 https://www.youtube.com/embed/YjntXYDPw44
13 Ibib p. 101.
14 https://www.youtube.com/embed/YjntXYDPw44   15   Ibid, Mangalwadi, Vishal.
16 Waite, Linda J. and Maggie Gallagher. *The Case for Marriage: Why Married People Are Happier, Healthier, and Better Off Financially.*
New York: Broadway Books, 2000, p. 203.

17 Wilson, James, Q. *The Marriage Problem: How Our Culture Has Weakened Families*. HarperCollins Publishers, 2002, p. 3.

18 http://www.nydailynews.com/entertainment/tv-movies/americans-spend-34-hours-week-watching-tv-nielsen-numbers-article-1.1162285

19 Postman, Neil. *Amusing Ourselves to Death: Public Discourse in the Age of Show Business*. Penguin Books, 1985, p. 71.

20 Ibid. p. 73.

21 Ibid. p. 73.

22 Ibid. p. 78.

23 Bork, Robert H. *Slouching Towards Gomorrah: Modern Liberalism and American Decline*. New York: Regan Books, 1996, p. 263.

24 Ibid. p. 264.

25 Ibid.

26 Searle, John R. "Rationality and Realism, What is at Stake?" *Daedalius*, Fall 1993, p. 55.

27 Barone, Michael. *Hard America, Soft America: Competition vs. Coddling and the Battle for the Nation's Future*. New York: Crown Forum, 2004, p. 12.

28 Ibid. p. 13.

29 http://www.merriam-webster.com/dictionary/subjectivism

30 Robert C. Solomon (Ed.). *Existentialism*. New York: Modern Library, 1974, p. 329.

31 Norman Mailer. "The White Negro," in *Existentialism*, ed. Robert C. Solomon. New York: Modern Library, 1974, pp. 331-332.

32 Mailer, p. 334.

33 Mailer, p. 335.

34 Whitehead, p. 66-67.

35 Eskridge, Larry (2013-05-31). *God's Forever Family: The Jesus People Movement in America*. Oxford University Press USA [Kindle Edition, p. 30].

36 Whitehead, p. 5.

37 Whitehead, pp. 66-68.

38 Whitehead, p. 33.

39 It has been asserted that Dostoevsky did not say this. The following link, however, makes the case that he did. http://infidels.org/library/modern/andrei_volkov/dostoevsky.html

40 http://www.cnsnews.com/commentary/rachel-sheffield/when-kansas-instituted-work-requirements-get-foodstamps-guess-what

41 Diana West. *The Death of the Grown-Up*. New York: St. Martin's Griffin, 2007, pp. 1-2.

42 Ibid. p. 4.

43 Solomon, p. 335-336.

44 Solomon, p. 335-336

45 William Bennett. "Does Honor Have a Future," *Imprimis*, December 1998, p. 1.

46 https://en.wikipedia.org/wiki/Norman_Mailer

47 http://nypost.com/2014/02/07/   obamacare-freeing-the-job-locked-poets/

48 Rogers, Carl R., *Client-Centered Therapy*. Boston: Houghton Mifflin Company, 1965, p. 159.

49 Ibid.

50 Kilpatrick, William Kirk. *Christianity Today*: "Therapy for the Masses," November 8, 1985, p. 21.

51 Carl R. Rogers. *On Becoming a Person*: Boston: Houghton, Mifflin Company, 1961, p. 163.

52 Ibid. Kilpatrick.

53 http://www.christianpost.com/news/mozilla-ceo-on-gay-marriage-row-i-keep-my-personal-beliefs-out-of-the-office-117217/ 54 Letter from William C. Coulson dated November 25, 1997, 1.

55 William Coulson. "We overcame their traditions, we overcame their faith." *The Latin Mass*. Harrison, NY, Special Edition, 13.

56 Ibid. p. 14.

57 Ibid. p. 17.

58 Ibid. p. 14. 59 Ibid.

60 Ibid. p. 13.

61 Ibid.

62 Ibid.

63 Ibid.

64 Ibid. p. 14.

65 Ibid.

66 Ibid.

67 Ibid.

68 Ibid. pp. 14-15.

69 Ibid. p. 15.

70 Ibid. p. 15.

71 Kugelmann, Robert. "An Encounter between Psychology and Religion: Humanistic Psychology and the Immaculate Heart of Mary." *Journal of the History of the Behavioral Sciences*, vol. 41(4), 347-365, Fall 2005.

72 Coulson, William R., *Groups, Gimmicks, and Instant Gurus.* New York: Harper & Row Publishers, 1972, pp. 116-124.

73 Letter from William C. Coulson dated November 25, 1997, p. 1.

74 Carl R. Rogers (quoted from a speech at the 1981 annual meeting of the Association of Humanistic Psychology). *Association for Humanistic Psychology Newsletter*, Special Edition, Fall 1981.

75 http://en.wikipedia.org/wiki/Polyamory

76 http://knowledgenuts.com/2013/11/03/the-difference-between-psychopaths-and-sociopaths/

77 http://www.psychologytoday.com/blog/wicked-deeds/201401/how-tell-sociopath-psychopath

78 (I)n the mental health field there is some consensus that psychopathy is more of an innate phenomenon whereas sociopathy, which has a similar clinical presentation to psychopathy, is more the result of environmental factors (poverty, exposure to violence, permissive or neglectful parenting, etc.). http://blogs.psychcentral.com/forensic-focus/2010/07/sociopathy-vs-psychopathy/

79 http://www.charismanews.com/opinion/the-flaming-herald/43894-the-great-deception-in-the-american-church 80 Trump, Donald J.; Schwartz, Tony. Trump: The Art of the Deal (Kindle Locations 821-822). Random House Publishing Group. Kindle Edition.

81 Ibid. Kindle Locations 904-906.

82 http://www.charismanews.com/   us/44167-poll-shows-true-bible-believers-at-record-low

83 http://www.foxnews.com/politics/2015/07/09/oregon-allowing-15-year-olds-to-get-state-subsidized-sex-change-operations/

84 http://www.patheos.com/blogs/revangelical/2014/10/01/a-correction-evangelical-churches-are-losing-millennials-not-megachurches.html

85 http://www.gospelherald.com/articles/52128/20140806/

chaldean-christian-leader-isis-systematically-beheading-children-in-iraq.htm

86 http://www.gatestoneinstitute.org/7700/ easter-christians-slaughtered

87 Hart, David Bentley. *Atheist Delusions: The Christian Revolution and Its Fashionable Enemies*. New Haven & London: Yale

University Press, 2009, p. xi.

88 http://nchfp.uga.edu/publications/nchfp/lit_rev/cure_smoke_cure.html

89 http://www.dailymail.co.uk/sciencetech/article-3181290/Howfar-away-candle-Raging-debate-finally-extinguished-thanksstudy-puts-distance-just-1-6-miles.html

90 http://www.gallup.com/poll/159548/identify-christian.aspx

91 http://www.patheos.com/blogs/blackwhiteandgray/2013/03/how-many-americans-are-evangelical-christians-born-again-christians/ 92 Ibid.

93 https://www.barna.org/barna-update/article/13-culture/111-survey-explores-who-qualifies-as-an-evangelical#.VcXmsSb49SE

94 Schaeffer, Francis A. *The Great Evangelical Disaster*. Westchester, Illinois: Crossway Books, 1984, pp. 63-65.

95 Eskridge, Larry. *God's Forever Family: The Jesus People Movement in America*. New York: Oxford University Press, 2013.

96 Ibid. p. 45.

97 Ibid. p. 209.

98 Ibid. p. 206.

99 Steven Furtick, *(Un)Qualified: How God Uses Broken People to Do Big Things*, Colorado Springs, Colorado: Multnomah Books, 2016, p.8.

100 Ibid.

101 Jeremiah, David. *God Loves You: He Always Has—He Always Will*. New York, Boston, Nashville: Faith Words, 2012, p. xii.

102 Ibid. p. 3.

103 Ibid.

104 Yancey, Philip, What's So Amazing About Grace? Grand Rapids: Zondervan Publishing House, 1997, p. 45.

105 Ibid., p. 15.

106 Ibid., p. 70.

107 Thayer, Joseph Henry, *Greek-English Lexicon of the New Testament*, Grand Rapids: Zondervan Publishing House, 1970, p. 549.

108 Jeremiah, p. 21.

109 McDowell, Josh and Bob Hostetler. Wheaton, Illinois: Tyndale House Publishers, 2002, pp. 86-87.

110 http://www.christianitytoday.com/ct/2013/october-web-only/billy-graham-interview-my-hope-easy-believism.html?start=2

111 Dana, H. E. and Julius R. Mantey. *A Manual Grammar of the Greek New Testament*. New York: The Macmillan Company, 1927, p. 105.

112 http://www.radical.net/blog/post/ the-sinners-prayer-and-the-sbc-part-i/ 113 Ibid.

114 Yancey, p. 71.

115 Ibid., p. 72.

116 Keller, Timothy. *The Freedom of Self Forgetfulness*, 10Publishing. Kindle Edition, Chorley, England, 2012, Kindle Locations 294-295..

117 Ibid.

118 Jeremiah, p. 19.

119 Ibid., p. 272.

120 http://www.christianitytoday.com/ct/2013/december-webonly/wolf-of-wall-street.html

121 http://blogs.thegospelcoalition.org/trevinwax/2014/01/06/evangelicals-and-hollywood-muck/

122 http://www.christianitytoday.com/ct/2014/january-web-only/ why-we-review-r-rated-films.html

123 http://blogs.thegospelcoalition.org/trevinwax/2014/01/29/christians-and-movies-are-we-contextualizing-or-compromising/

124 http://www.desiringgod.org/articles/ seven-questions-to-ask-before-you-watch-deadpool

125 http://www.provenmen.org/press-releases/2014-pornography-survey-of-christian-men-shocking-new-national-survey-reveals-high-levels-of-pornography-use-and-rampant-extramaritalaffairs-among-christian-men/

126 http://www.christianpost.com/news/christian-sexperts-exposedangers-of-erotica-as-fifty-shades-tops-100-million-sales-prepares-for-big-screen-115658/

127 http://www.afajournal.org/2012/December/1212heroes.html

128 http://www.booksandculture.com/articles/2005/janfeb/3.8.html?paging=off

129 Tim Stafford, "The Third Coming of George Barna," Christianity Today, August 8, 2002, p. 34.

130 Boom, Corrie Ten; Elizabeth Sherrill; John Sherrill. The Hiding Place (p. 151). Baker Publishing Group. Kindle Edition.

131 Ibid., p. 152.

132 http://www.bpnews.net/44914/ sbc-reports-more-churches-fewer-people

133 Singer, Peter. Peter Singer FAQ, Princeton University, accessed 8 March 2009

134 http://www.evolutionnews.org/2014/10/peter_singer_to090641.html

135 http://digitalcommons.unl.edu/cgi/viewcontent.cgi?article=1053&context=etas

136 Alinsky, Saul. *Rules for Radicals: A Practical Primer for Realistic Radicals*. New York: Vintage Books, 1971, p. 24.

137 Postman, ibid. p. vii-viii.

138 http://www.historyplace.com/worldhistory/genocide/stalin.htm

139 http://billygraham.org/story/ billy-graham-my-heart-aches-for-america/

140 Marshall, Kirk and Hunter Madsen. *After the Ball – How America will conquer its fear and hatred of Gays in the 90s*. New York: Penguin Books, 1989.

141 http://www.massresistance.org/docs/issues/gay_strategies/after_the_ball.html

142 http://www.eyewitnesstohistory.com/titanic.htm

143 http://www.sshsa.org/media/splash/SavingtheTitanic.pdfii

Made in the USA
Monee, IL
28 October 2022

16655371R00174